THE REAL WITCHES'
BOOK OF SPELLS AND R

THE

REAL WITCHES' BOOK OF SPELLS AND RITUALS

KATE WEST

Element
An Imprint of HarperCollins*Publishers*
77–85 Fulham Palace Road,
Hammersmith, London W6 8JB

The website address is:
www.harpercollins.co.uk

and *Element* are trademarks of
HarperCollins*Publishers* Limited

Published by Element 2003

7 9 10 8

A catalogue record for this book
is available from the British Library

ISBN-13 978-0-00-715111-0
ISBN-10 0-00-715111-X

Printed in China

CONTENTS

This book is dedicated to
Steve and Taliesin,
with all my love.

'Now we are together once more, let it always be so.
Blessed Be.'

THANK YOUS

It may only take one author to write a book, but like the swan sailing serenely down the river, you don't see all the work going on out of sight! So once again I tend my grateful thanks to all those who have made it possible:

To Steve and Tali, who are always there to support me with their love and patience. You are ever in my heart, and you are my reason for writing and being.

To Debs and Natz for their ongoing love and support, and for all the practical help, not to mention helping with the childcare! Visit soon and often.

To Rocky and Jane for helping with the move, making it possible for me to get back to the keyboard quickly. Live long and prosper!

To the members of the Hearth of Hecate and the Covenant of Aradia who have supported and encouraged me, and taught me more than they yet know.

To Mike, for his friendship, companionship, advice and sense of humour which have helped turn dark days into light days. Also for the discussion, debate and the new perspectives. Slainthe!

To Merlyn and Epona of the Children of Artemis, who make it possible for the Witches of today to communicate, meet, share and love, all in the name of the Goddess: for organizing Witchfest; for your personal support, love and encouragement; for being there for me, and with me, in mirth and reverence, through everything from computer failure to blind panic! Thanks also to all the members of the Children of Artemis through whom the Craft will continue. May your Gatherings grow ever stronger.

To Helen, Kate, Katherine, Katy, Victoria and especially Vicky, as well as everyone else at HarperCollins who help to turn ideas into reality, even as they confuse me with their names!

Above all, thank you to Gerald Gardner, Doreen Valiente, Alex and Maxine Sanders, and the others of the Craft who have led, and still are, leading the way.

Thank you one and all.

May you achieve your highest ideals and your fondest desires.

Blessed Be

ONE

WITCHCRAFT AND MAGIC

Merry Meet, welcome to *The Real Witches' Book of Spells and Rituals*!

Magic really does work. It's not a myth or imagination. It may not yet be scientifically proven, but it does work. Magic is all around us and is practised by almost everyone, even though they may not realize it! Crossing fingers, touching wood, 'kissing it better', wearing a Saint Christopher for safe travel, making a friendship band, blowing out the candles on a cake or dropping a coin into a well and making a wish are all acts of magic. The practitioner may not really believe in it, and so it may not fully work, but it's still magic. The difference between these magics and the magic of Witchcraft lies in the fact that Witches do it with intent, focus and balance – they believe it will work and it does.

But why does anyone want to use magic? Everyone seeks control of their lives; from the youngest toddler to the oldest wise woman, we all want a say in what happens to us. Magic was more common in times past when we were still close to our native beliefs. It may have been driven underground and turned into superstition for a while, but now it is returning. In a world where just about everything is overlooked or controlled, by laws and people outside our personal influence, we are now remembering and returning to the old ways of taking personal control of our lives and our world, and of making the changes we seek in them. The Craft gives us the ability to do the former and the skills to work the magic to do the latter.

In the Craft we learn:

★ Self-development and understanding.

★ Personal responsibility and control.

★ To live with nature and the elements, in balance and harmony.

★ The cycles of the seasons and how they relate to us today.

★ To comprehend the energies created by the phases of the Moon and the Sun.

★ How the elements relate to us, our lives and our personal balance.

★ To use the energies both within and outside of us.

★ How to personally communicate with the Divine.

★ To live as a part of the real world whilst enhancing our inner lives.

★ To focus our will and direct our intent.

★ When and how to use the above to create magic to change our world and our lives.

★ How to structure our magic through Rites and Rituals to make it work.

In the Craft we use magic and spells to:

★ Understand ourselves and those around us.

★ Make personal change.

★ Understand the world and our place in it.

✸ Bring inner peace and harmony.

✸ Bring about physical, emotional and spiritual healing, for ourselves, our near and dear, and for those who seek it for themselves and others.

✸ Ease communication and aid understanding.

✸ Aid in study, tests and exams.

✸ Find work, do well at it and achieve our potential.

✸ Protect ourselves, our homes and our near and dear.

✸ Find and nurture friendship, romance, love and partnership.

✸ Work towards healing the land and protecting the life that grows from it.

✸ Help us in all aspects of our lives, and the lives of those we care for.

Many people think that magic is a question of saying the right words, in the right way, at a specified time. They've seen it on TV so it must be true! Others think that it is a question of mixing the right ingredients in the right way. But magic isn't cookery and you need to do more! Some think it requires you to step back from real life, to insulate yourself from normal activities such as work, to isolate yourself from normal people by dressing strangely or behaving oddly. But a Witch must live as a part of the real world, not apart from it, to maintain her/his connection with life. A few still believe that magic involves selling your soul to some mythical devil and invoking hypothetical demons to do your bidding! Magic requires none of these, most especially the latter. Magic will only happen by working with, not against, nature to bring about natural change in life and the world. For magic to work it does not require special ingredients and words, but knowledge, effort, energy and understanding.

In finding out how to make your magic work you will have to clear away your personal emotional baggage and come to terms with who you really are and what you can truly be, which is almost certainly more than you think possible now. You will come to understand and harness your personal energies, as well as the energies of the elements. And you will find that you come to know, and be known by, the Goddess and the God.

In this book I have given you not only a series of spells which might be made to work, but also the foundations of the magical practice of Witchcraft, so that you can make your spells work if you are prepared to put the effort in. I know, even as I write this, that there are some readers who will want to go straight into trying the spells, and I cannot stop you. But I do offer the following caution; attempts to practise magic without a good understanding of the basic techniques can result in the magic failing to work, or working in a way that you did not intend. In magic, as in all things, you should be careful what you wish for, as you just might get it!

Most of the magics practised by the non-Witch are done to ward off the bad things in life, rather than to bring on the good. But Witchcraft is not just there to fix that which has gone, or might go, wrong. If you work your spells within the practice of the Craft, you can take control of your life and make positive change. Just remember, magic does not happen 'as if by magic' – you have to work at it!

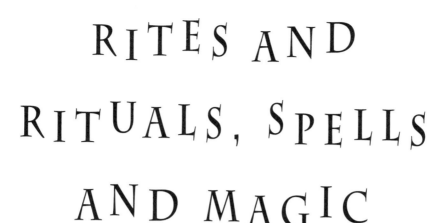

TWO

RITES AND RITUALS, SPELLS AND MAGIC

MAGICAL TERMS

There are many terms associated with the working of magic: spells, incantations, charms, rites, rituals, and so on. Before we look at actually how to create magic, I'd like to examine some of these terms, so that we all know what we are talking about!

RITES AND RITUALS

A Ritual is a series of thoughts, words and actions performed to bring about a specific result. A series of Rites can go to make up a Ritual. Rites and Rituals are not confined to Witchcraft or magical working, although these are the contexts to which we tend to relate these terms. To clarify: your 'Ritual of getting up' could be broken down like this: 'the Rite of waking', then 'the Rite of visiting the bathroom', 'the Rite of making a cup of tea or coffee', and so on. In the Craft we use the term Rites to define pieces of magical working such as creating the Sacred Space, raising power, working a spell, and so on. These Rites can then be placed together to form a Ritual for a specific purpose which could be the working of magic, the celebration of a life event, or maybe a festival.

MAGIC AND SPELLS

Magic is often defined as the ability to create change through the application of will. A spell is defined by the dictionary as a magical formula, but in the Craft we consider it to be more of a process, as magic is not just the doing or saying of things in a certain order. Many Witches do not use the word 'spell' to describe their magical working as it tends to conjure up somewhat simplistic images from fiction and mythology rather than expressing the true process of harnessing and focusing internal and external energies to create change.

INCANTATIONS AND CHANTS

Many people expect a 'spell' to be, or at least to include, a few rhyming lines which are repeated or even chanted to make something happen. This would be an incantation, and some Witches do use them as a part of their magical process. But it is not necessary to have poetic ability to make magic work.

Chants are verses or songs, usually chanted by Witches working in a group. They are most often used in the Craft as a technique for raising power, that is the harnessing and focusing of the energies of the group. Some Solitary Witches also use chants, but often within their heads rather than out loud.

CHARMS, TALISMANS, TOTEMS, ETC

These are objects which are magically charged so that they may be placed where the magic is desired to work or which may be carried on the person. The definitions between them are often blurred but frequently Talismans are paper or parchment with symbols to represent the magical intent, whereas Charms are frequently jewellery, stones or other objects. Totems are usually a group of objects which are kept together,

often in a Totem Bag, which represent a grouping of things or people. A Totem Bag may contain objects to represent each of your family members with the intent of bonding the family together. You may also come across other terms used to describe these kinds of magical artefacts, such as Amulet – usually a charm, which is worn with a protective intent. Sometimes you will have to assess the meaning of a term by the item and the purpose for which it is intended.

'WORDS OF POWER'

From time to time you may hear, or read, about 'words of power', and some people do believe that there are, out there somewhere, special words which if said in a special way will create magical effects. This belief is more appropriate to the realm of the Ritual Magician than that of the Witch. It is true that resonances and vibrations, which are found in many things, can be utilized to help make change. However, their magical 'power' comes from the way in which the practitioner can bring those energies into balance with the elements both within and without.

Having said that, it is worth remembering that all words can have the power to make change, depending on how you say them and who you say them to! How many times have you said something that you later regretted? This is why in the Craft we tend to emphasize the need to think before you speak or, for that matter, act.

HOW MAGIC WORKS

Briefly speaking, magic works when you can harness, balance and focus the five elements of Air, Fire, Water, Earth and Spirit, both within yourself and from outside. This is a complex ability, which comes more easily with practice, so we usually start by using a number of visual links and cues to help bring all these elements together. The elements exist inside us and outside of us and they have many symbolic representations, visual and mental links, which may be used and which are often termed correspondences.

Understanding of the five elements is one of the most important concepts of the Craft, and the foundation of working magic. Together with visualization, which I'll talk about later in this chapter, this is what makes Magic work. All the candles, incense, cords, images and other tools are just that; tools that you use to implement and enhance your understanding of the elements and your ability to visualize.

So what are the elements?

AIR

Air is within us as our thoughts, and as such should be the first element to be brought into use, for thought should always precede anything else! Air represents the thinking and planning stage of any proposed action, magical or otherwise.

Externally, Air is everything from the gentle breeze that ruffles the leaves to the destructive force and power of the hurricane or tornado. Air is all around us and without it we cannot breathe. We take the external air into our being with every breath and, with practice, learn to draw on that external energy to fuel our internal thoughts.

Air also represents and is represented by the direction East, incense or a feather on the Altar, the season of Spring, the morning, and often the colour yellow.

FIRE

Fire is our passions and enthusiasms, it is present when we become enthusiastic and excited by an idea. It is the difference between having an idea and really wanting to put that idea into action, or the difference between needing something to read and wanting to buy that particular new book!

Fire is everything from the spark that falls from a match to the full energy of the Sun, or the inferno of a volcano. Without fire there would be no heat, no light and no life.

Fire is represented by the direction South, a candle or crystal on the Altar, the season of Summer, midday and the afternoon, and usually by the colour red.

WATER

Water is our emotions. It is when we become emotionally involved in an idea or project, when it actually becomes important to us.

Externally, it encompasses the gentlest raindrop, the streams, rivers and oceans, the torrential downpour of a summer storm to the awe-inspiring tidal wave or tsunami. Water is essential to all life; we drink it, bathe in it and use it daily with little thought.

Water is represented by the direction West, a bowl of water or a shell on the Altar, the season of Autumn, the evening, and often by the colour blue.

EARTH

Earth is our physical self, our body. It is the stage in a process when we move from the mental aspects to the physical and 'make it real' in the world.

Externally, it is the land, the soil, rocks, stones and mountains. It is the foundation from which all life springs and to which it ultimately returns for rebirth.

Earth is represented by the direction North (often called the place of power), salt or a stone on the Altar, the season of Winter, the night, and often by the colour green.

SPIRIT

The essential self that makes us who we are, sometimes called the soul, is our Spirit.

Outside of us the Spirit is the Goddess and the God, and that Divine essence permeates all things.

Spirit is represented by the centre of the Circle and by the Circle itself as it is all places at all times. In the Circle we ourselves also represent Spirit, as do the Goddess and God we call upon in our workings. On the Altar, Spirit may be represented by statues or pictures of the Goddess and the God, by a gold and a silver candle, or not at all because it is everywhere. It has no time and no season for it is present in all times and seasons. It is often represented by the colour violet, or by the electric blue of the Circle itself.

When preparing to work Magic we commence by setting the Altar with representations of the elements, so that they are indeed present in actuality. We then invoke the elements in the Quarters (the four compass points) and invite the Goddess and the God to complete the five elements. These steps are part of creating the Sacred Space, which is not just an area, but a key step in making Magic work. In Ritual we call upon the elements externally. But we also need to evoke the elements within, and often this starts before the practical steps of creating the Sacred Space. It begins when we think carefully about the Magic we wish to perform, and continues as we become enthusiastic and emotionally involved in it. The process culminates in the Circle when we put those mental steps into action in the actual creating of the Magic, by whichever means we select, and when we imbue it with the spiritual energy of our inner self.

I have mentioned that we need to have the elements in balance. This is essential; you can easily see the problems that might be caused if your actions are powered by emotion and passion, but lack thought. Magic without any passion will be flat and without energy, magic without emotion will be weak and uninvolved, and so on. Where one element is in greater strength than another you also get imbalance, which is why it is a bad idea to work Magic when ill, very angry or upset. This is one of the reasons why it is so difficult, for even the most experienced Witch, to work magic for those people and things which are closest and most important to them, because their emotional involvement can be overwhelming.

In order to be able to harness, balance and focus the energies of the elements we need to spend some time actually getting to know and understand them. For some people this can be done by spending time simply experiencing them in the natural world, and this is one of the reasons why so many Witches like to work with plants and nature, even if that means just keeping a couple of pot plants. Others may find that they need to spend time using visualization or meditation techniques, such as pathworking. All tend to find that they need to do some mental and spiritual 'house-keeping' from time to time, to ensure that they clear away the 'baggage' caused by daily life and relationships. It used to be common in the Craft to hear the term 'tests of the Elements', and this referred to actual tasks, often set by the High Priestess of the Coven, which had to be completed before the Witch was considered to be accepted for the next level of learning. These 'tests' seem to have died away in modern times, but it is still a good idea to set yourself tasks which will expose you (safely) to experiences of the elements in their natural state. These might include going to a hilltop to experience strong winds, lying down in strong sunlight to meditate (not just to sunbathe!), immersing yourself fully in the sea, or visiting a deep dark cave and turning your torch off for a few minutes. Deliberately seeking to experience the Spirit is somewhat harder to envisage, but often the best way to set about this is to devise a meditation which can be performed in Circle or to perform a Self-Blessing, as on page 39.

VISUALIZATION

After understanding, harnessing and balancing the Elements, the next most important technique in being able to work Magic is that of visualization. Visualization is simply being able to imagine so strongly, that what you imagine seems as 'real' as the 'real world'. It is not just a matter of seeing the 'picture' in your mind, but also of being able to experience the other senses of sound, taste, touch and smell, too. Whilst a lucky few find that this comes naturally, many people find it extremely difficult at first, but it really is just a matter of practice. The secret is not to expect too much too soon. Start by bringing to mind recent, mundane events, such as the last meal you ate, or the experience of watching TV last night. When you can conjure these up in your mind's eye so clearly that you can remember sounds that you may not have been aware of at the time, then it is time to move on to less personal experiences. Many people soon realize that the technique of visualization is something that they practise in an unformed way when they daydream. For them it is more a question of learning to direct their 'daydreaming mode', rather than learning a new technique.

Visualization is important in the practice of magic because the more strongly you can visualize your magic actually working the more effective it will be. In many cases it is best if you actually visualize the whole process which will bring about the desired change, rather than just focussing on the end result. For example, if someone has an infected finger, it can be more effective if you can visualize the white blood cells rushing to the site to destroy the infection, rather than simply focusing on a healed finger. Likewise if you can visualize two warring parties meeting and agreeing to talk things through, then visualize their discussion, with both sides being patient, your chances of bringing about a reconciliation are far greater than if you just hope that they will 'make it up'.

The ability to visualize means that, after much practice, you will be able to perform magic without tools and equipment. There comes a time when you can learn to utilize the elements, create your Sacred Space and work your magic with no Altar, words or actions, other than the visualization within your mind.

PREPARING TO WORK MAGIC

Having talked about how to make Magic work we need to look at the things we need to do before we can actually start doing it. We've already seen why you need to have your 'internal elements' in balance, but there are other things you need to consider before you start waving that 'magic wand'! As I've said before, one of the sayings of the Craft, which seems to have made it into everyday speech, is 'Be Careful What You Wish For'. This is because, first, there can be sometimes quite a large gap between what you ask for and what you really want. 'I want gold' could result in your being given a gold sheet of paper or a gold-coloured flower. Secondly, you need to think carefully through all the potential consequences. 'I want gold' could result in inheriting money through the loss of a loved one. So you need to formulate your magic very carefully. You'll find other cautions later in this chapter, but don't expect these to cover all eventualities. Personal responsibility is one of the key tenets of the Craft and you are personally responsible for all the effects of your magic, whether you foresaw them or not!

In order to prepare your magic it is a good idea carefully to think through not only what you want to happen, but also what might happen, good or bad, as a result. A good many Witches place a spell of protection over their car. Done carefully this can help to avoid accidents (although careful driving is still a prerequisite!), damage and theft. But done without due thought it can also result in a car which seems, from the actions of other road users, to have become less visible, resulting in several 'close calls' on the road!

You also need to consider your environment. You will be less likely to be able to focus if there are distractions, both physical and mental. This is why you should have a clear and tidy working space, should turn off the TV, radio and phone and ensure that you will be free from disturbances from others. If possible lock the door, ensure the children are abed and any pets are settled out of the way. You also need to ensure that you yourself are prepared, that you are neither hungry nor thirsty, nor likely to need the bathroom halfway through. Then you need to be able to clear your mind of all the worries and concerns of daily life. For this we often use the Rite of Banishment of Unwanted Influences *(see page 37)*, which allows us to rid ourselves of outside thoughts. Many Witches find that the best way to personally prepare is to bathe, and then dress in special clothes, which they reserve for Ritual and Magical work. This has the effect of helping you to distance magical work from daily life. For some, the setting of the Altar helps to enhance this process as it is a Rite in itself which focuses the mind on the work to come.

Speaking of setting the Altar, it is essential to ensure that you have everything to hand which you will need. It is very distracting, whether working on your own or in a group, to have to pause to leave the Circle to collect something. For this reason many Witches write a short summary of what they are about to do, together with a list of the tools they will need. For some, this writing of their intent becomes not just part of the preparation but also part of the Magic itself.

When working in a group or Coven it is also important that everyone present is aware of the intention of the Ritual and that they agree with the Magic to be worked. If just one person in a group disagrees with the purpose of the Magic they can have an adverse effect on the outcome. At the least they weaken the Magic, at worst they can prevent it happening at all. Everyone needs to be aware of exactly what is going to happen, and their role in it, as the energy flows more freely when everyone can move smoothly and knowledgeably throughout the Ritual. Hence in Coven working it is usual to find that a copy of the Ritual, with roles assigned, is available to everyone on their arrival at the Covenstead. In addition, the High Priestess will then go through that Ritual with the whole group prior to the start of working, to ensure that everyone understands exactly what is supposed to happen and what is expected of them.

WHAT PREVENTS MAGIC FROM WORKING?

Having looked at what makes magic work we also need to look at the things that can prevent it from working.

Asking for the Wrong Thing

As mentioned above, you must be careful what you wish for, otherwise you may get what you asked for, not what you actually want. Generally speaking, the more time you spend considering what you really want to achieve, and considering all the potential outcomes, the better you will be able to formulate your wishes and direct your intent.

Insufficient Belief

It is not necessary for your subject to believe that magic works for it to happen, this is not a form of faith healing. Although having said that, if your subject, or any participant in the Ritual, actively disbelieves that it will work, that will have a negative effect on the outcome. Think of it this way; you are applying positive thought towards making something happen, and if someone else is applying negative thought then the two thoughts may cancel each other out, or the lesser of the two energies will weaken the stronger.

However, it is essential that *you* believe that your magic will work. If you have doubts about your ability, or the 'rightness' of your actions, then these will weaken or even stop your energy from working.

Too Much Talk

Although I have said that in a Coven everyone must be aware of what is to happen, talk about magical working should not extend beyond those actively taking part. First, for the reason above, the more people who are aware of your magic the more likely someone will hear about it who will have negative thoughts towards the outcome.

Please also remember that however cautious you are about who you tell, and however much they promise to keep it quiet, secrets are only secret when no one knows about them. You must have heard someone say 'can you keep a secret?' just before telling you something they are not supposed to be communicating!

The second reason is because talking about your magic can actually reduce the energy and focus you can put into that magic. Think back to the last time you felt really strongly about something, perhaps an injustice or some gossip – the more you talked this over with your friends and family the less outraged or strongly you felt. This actually shows the way your energy is being dissipated by simple communication.

Need as Against Desire

Many people confuse what they need and what they want; you may 'need a drink', in which case water will suffice, whereas you want, or desire, champagne. Hence in Magic, if you say you 'need a Porsche', the result may cover your need for transport, resulting in a free bus pass, rather than your desire for a fast smart car. I have often been asked if it is possible to change a flat tyre by magic? The answer is yes, but your request is more likely to be granted through the arrival of someone who will help you to change your tyre, rather than by some kind of conjuring trick in which the jack leaps out of the car, the screws undo themselves, and the wheel is replaced by some invisible agency! However carefully you phrase your wishes there are some times when you get what you need rather than what you desire. This is because there is a part of your mind which, rather sensibly, is aware of what is required to solve your 'problem', and will function at that level. This is an integral part of the kind of magic performed by Witches rather than other kinds of less acceptable practices where self is considered to be all.

You are Asking for Something Outside of Nature

This is especially pertinent in the case of money spells. Money does not exist in the natural world. In nature, effort is rewarded in practical terms; you plant then you can reap, the bat flies at dusk and hence can catch his dinner. Hence money magic is likely to either give you what you asked for in an unpleasant way – inheritance, for example, or in a useless way – you crash your car and get paid on the insurance, leaving you financially no better off. If you work for the opportunity to earn money, then you are working within the natural course of things, whereby your effort can be rewarded with payment in the way in which the world works.

It's Not Meant to Be

There are also occasions when magic will not work at all. In short, I believe that this is because the Goddess and the God know best and, once we have taken the step of dedicating ourselves to them, they do in fact watch over us and step in to prevent some of our greater follies. They also have their own plans and purposes and sometimes it is not for the individual to be allowed to interfere with them. The sort of magic which falls into this category tends to be associated with serious illness, and we just have to accept that in some cases that person's time to move on has indeed come. This is not to say that you shouldn't work for the remission of major illness, but that it will not always work. Do also remember that you can also work for the relief of pain, and for the emotional healing and comfort of that person's near and dear.

You are Too Close to the Problem

It is sometimes very hard to work magic for yourself and for those close to you, not because of any natural laws against it, but simply because your focus and concentration will not be all they should be. It is hard enough to remain focused on dressing a bad cut which is bleeding heavily if this is someone you care for deeply, let alone bringing the elements into balance, raising energy and working magic. Similarly, if you have pressing physical or emotional concerns in your own life, you will find it almost impossible to become mentally and physically prepared for any kind of magic unless you can put them aside. If those very concerns are to be the focus of your magic then you will find it nigh on impossible to put them aside as well as focus on them at the same time! In these circumstances you need to find someone else, who you trust implicitly, to work magic for you.

Love Magic

This is an area where magic can go wrong even if it works perfectly! If you work magic to make someone love you, sooner or later you will be wondering whether it is you they love or the spell which is working. If you work this kind of magic for someone else you will then be perceived as being responsible for their relationship, a bit like being the instigator of an arranged marriage where one partner is not aware that it has been arranged. At the least you will find yourself drawn into every hiccup in the relationship, at the worst you may find yourself being blamed for every argument or problem, or even the fact that person B did not turn out to be exactly what person A had hoped for some ten years down the road! If you must get involved in relationship magic then stay with some of the less direct options, such as increased confidence, the opportunity to meet a person with whom you can be happy, and so on.

You Fail to Pay for What You Have Received

Magic should be seen as an exchange of energies. Whilst you put some of the energy into the spell, much of it comes from outside of you, from the elements, the Goddess and the God. This energy should be repaid. This is not to say that you are going to give them money, but rather that you should do something to repay the energy. This should be something which expresses your thanks, whereby you put your energy back into the land, or into honouring the Goddess and the God. Tending growing things, be they plants, pets or children, is one way. Creating something in honour of the Divine is another. But whether you choose to trim your hedge, clear litter from a local park, take your child to the swings, or paint a picture, it should be done with the intent of giving thanks to the Goddess and the God and to the elements. Every act of magic should be repaid in some way, and as soon as possible, it is a part of making the magic work. It is not a question of a bargain where you will pay for it if it works; it is more a question of giving thanks for being able to access the energies and for the attention of the elements, the Goddess and the God. Should you fail to repay the energies, your magic will decline over time and, in due course, fail.

Having looked at the ways in which magic does and doesn't work, let's move on to some of the Rituals into which we put our spells and magics.

THREE

CASTING THE CIRCLE, AND OTHER FREQUENT RITES

As I said in the last chapter a Ritual is usually constructed out of several separate pieces called Rites. Many of these are performed in the same way and to avoid repetition later in the book I have put these basic Rites into this chapter, so that you can refer to them whenever you need to.

Basically, there are two kinds of Ritual; Esbats or working Rituals where magic is performed, and those which are celebratory, for instance Sabbats and Rites of Passage. In the former, energy or power is raised to fuel an act or acts of magic, and therefore a Circle should be cast. As the latter are celebratory it is not necessary to raise power and therefore to actually cast a Circle. This division between Esbats and Sabbats is not fixed as it is possible to work magic at the Sabbats (so long as it fits with the theme of that Sabbat), in which case you will need a Circle. Also, you can work magic at other phases of the Moon, and these Rituals will also need a Circle. Similarly, you may choose to hold a celebration, perhaps a Wiccaning or Handfasting, at an Esbat, in which case you will not need a Circle. Initiation Rituals, whilst celebratory, are also magical workings and will need a Circle and the raising of energy, even though you are not working any spells as such.

There is also a difference between working on your own as a Solitary and working in a group or Coven. In the former you have only yourself to prepare, in the latter you have others to consider and communicate with. In the former you can work largely in

your head, silently and perhaps sitting on the floor. In the latter you will need to speak out loud and probably move around one another. You will also find that it is helpful to have more tools and visible objects when working with others, as these visual keys help to ensure that everyone is focused on the same thing at the same time. When starting out as a Solitary you may find that these same visual keys help you to retain focus, as you will have much to remember as well as keeping your intent clear.

THE WORKING SPACE

This is the room or area you intend to work in. Witches do not need purpose-built temples or even a special room in the house as they can create their Sacred Space wherever they wish to. The area in which you are going to create that space is your working space. It should be spacious enough for you, whether you are one or many, to move freely in, and indoors this may mean moving some of your furniture. Again, if it is indoors it should be clean, tidy and free from too many distractions, as you not only need to focus but you are also inviting the Goddess and the God, so try to make it somewhere you feel they would come to! If outdoors you need to ensure that you are neither trespassing nor are likely to be disturbed. If you are Solitary, or few in number, then you should be doubly careful that you are not going to be accosted by passers-by wondering what you are up to. You also need to ensure that it is safe, with no hidden cliffs, rabbit holes, broken glass or rusting metal to be discovered by the unwary. The working space is generally considered to be circular, although you may need to compromise somewhat if you are short of space or have a non-circular area to work in.

Whilst it would be nice to be able to align your working space with the points of the compass, so that your North really is in the direction of North, it is not always possible. In this case try to align as closely as you can, whilst still being able to use the space in a reasonable manner.

THE ALTAR AND WORKING TOOLS

Here I am going to give a fairly basic Altar layout with a selection of the tools most commonly placed on it. There are other ways of setting the Altar and a great many other tools which may be placed on it. Some Witches like to have all their working tools to hand, others prefer to have only those which they are going to use. Whichever course you choose it is as well to check the tools against your Ritual notes to ensure that you have everything which you are going to use, before you Create your Sacred Space.

Working tools do not have to be expensive or bought from specialist suppliers, you can select ordinary everyday objects for many of them, or make your own. It is, however, preferable if your working tools can be kept separate from other household items and their use reserved for Ritual and magic as, with use, they will build up their own reservoir of magical energy.

ALTAR

The Altar is simply the surface on which you place everything you will need to work with. If you are on your own and intend to work sitting on the floor, then it could be as simple as a small cloth placed in front of you, although do ensure that if you are using candles you can keep them safe. However, most Witches prefer to use some kind of table or other surface of adequate size at a convenient height. When working outside you may like to use a convenient rock or tree stump, or to take a box with you for the purpose.

The Altar can be placed in one of a number of parts of the Circle:

✷ *The Centre*, to allow you maximum use of the circumference. This is especially useful when working indoors with limited space and a large number of people. This is less convenient if you intend to Circle dance, or to have any other central feature such as a cauldron or fire.

✮ *The East*, which is the starting point of the Circle, as it represents Air and thought. This does mean that when it comes to actually Casting the Circle you will have to move around nearly the whole circle (as you always move Deosil in Circle) before commencing to actually Cast it at the North-East.

✮ *The North-East*, or point of entry. This is fine unless and until you wish to have someone come in at the point of entry, as in Initiations for example.

✮ *The North*, or point of power. This is where I prefer to have the Altar.

Whichever you choose, it is important that you and everyone else in the Circle know at which point the Altar is set. Generally speaking it is best to choose your Altar point and then keep that for all your Rituals in order to avoid subsequent confusion!

ALTAR CLOTH

It is usual to cover the Altar with some kind of cloth, kept especially for the purpose. This not only protects the surface from any spills but also helps to mark the change of use from daily to Ritual. An Altar cloth does not need to be particularly fancy, or bought from a specialist supplier, but it does need to be kept clean and unrumpled. You may choose to have different cloths for each of the Sabbats and others for different kinds of magical working, or you may simply have the one for all Craft purposes. Whichever you choose is up to you, there is no right or wrong choice.

REPRESENTATIONS OF THE ELEMENTS

✮ *Earth*. Earth is usually represented by salt in a small container. Some consider that it should be rock salt rather than sea salt, but again it is what feels right to you that is most appropriate. However, you could also use soil, a small rock or pebble.

✴ *Air*. Air is generally represented by incense, which may be of a scent to complement your magic or the festival. Incense comes in sticks, cones and loose, but whichever you select you will need to ensure that you have a fireproof stand or container to place it in or on. Please ensure that this container does not itself become so hot that it could set fire to the underlying surface. If using loose incense you will also need 'self-igniting charcoal' on which to burn it, and probably some kind of tongs to hold that charcoal whilst setting it alight. Loose incense is usually burned in a container called a Thurible *(see Appendix 2, Terms and Definitions)*. Please consider the effects of burning incense on any smoke detector you may have fitted! You will also need matches. If you cannot burn incense you could substitute essential oil in an oil burner, or even a feather to represent air.

✴ *Fire*. Fire is usually represented by a candle, in which case you will need a safe candleholder. You may also like to have a snuffer with which to extinguish the flame later on. If you cannot have a naked flame then a small faceted crystal is a good alternative.

✴ *Water*. Water is generally represented by a small bowl or dish of water. Some purists like to collect rainwater for this purpose, rather than using the chemically treated stuff that comes from the tap. As a substitute you can have a seashell or other object which represents water.

THE GODDESS AND THE GOD

It is usual to have something to represent the Goddess and the God, and hence the Spirit. This could be statues of your chosen Deities, candles – one for each or one for both, or other objects which you feel encapsulate their Spirit on the Altar.

ALTAR PENTACLE

There are many fine Pentacles available today, but you can just as easily create your own in salt (if you have a steady drawing hand) or paint one onto a flat stone or circular board. If you were to look closely at mine you might notice a distinct similarity to a circular breadboard! In addition to the Pentagram (*see Terms and Definitions, page 274*), other symbols of the Craft may also decorate the Pentacle.

ATHAME

This is the Witches' blade. Strictly speaking, you do not need an Athame, as anything you cannot invoke with a finger you will not be able to invoke with the knife! Many consider that the Athame should be placed on the Altar, however these days many Witches will wear theirs in a special holder or scabbard which hangs from a cord at the waist. Certainly, if you are working in a group it is easier to have your Athame at your belt than it is to have 10 to 20 placed on the Altar.

WINE AND CAKES

Most, if not all, Rituals will contain the Rite of Wine and Cakes, so you will need a Chalice with wine in it (or fruit juice if you cannot or should not drink alcohol). If there are many of you, you may need to have the bottle on hand for topping up. Red wine is usual, although on some festivals and other occasions you might feel something else is more appropriate. Also, you should have a plate with enough biscuits for everyone in Circle plus one (for the offering). These can be specially made, or you can buy ordinary small biscuits. An alternative is pieces of fruit.

NOTES OR SCRIPT

This can be a short note to remind yourself of the purpose and steps of your Ritual, or it could be a whole 'script' in a special book, supported in a book holder, which everyone in Circle can access if the need arises. This latter option is more often used in complex Rituals which are performed infrequently, such as Handfasting.

AND ALSO

There are many other tools which can be placed on, or by, the Altar for specific purposes:

★ *Boline*, the white-handled knife used for cutting and carving, etc.

★ *Sword*, sometimes used for casting the Circle.

★ *Cauldron*, for containing fire to burn things, or water for scrying.

★ *Besom*, or broom for sweeping the Circle and for use in Handfasting.

★ *Wand*, sometimes used for invoking Air and Water.

★ *Scourge*, representing the sorrows of life and used in some Covens to maintain and enforce discipline.

★ *Cords*, representing self-control and discipline and used in cord magics.

There are other objects, such as parchment, crystals, etc, into which the magic can be placed in specific spells, and these form charms, talismans, and so on. You may also wish to add to your Altar pictures of your 'clients', flowers to decorate, gifts for Coven members, and so on. There is more on these in Chapter 6, Magical Resources.

What you should not place on the Altar are things unconnected with the Craft and the Ritual: tea and coffee cups (although a glass of water might be placed there if you feel the need to sip during Ritual), ashtrays, cigarettes, and any other bits and pieces from daily life.

CREATING THE SACRED SPACE

Having tidied and cleaned your working space, set your Altar and checked that you have everything you need, you are now ready to create your Sacred Space. In a Coven, whilst one or two people will prepare the Altar, the others will be checking that they understand the Ritual and, where these are used, changing into their Ritual clothes.

The steps are as follows:

☆ Centring.

☆ Blessing the Elements on the Altar.

☆ Invoking each of the Elements – Air, Fire, Water, and lastly, Earth.

☆ Inviting the Goddess and the God.

☆ Casting the Circle.

If you are working in a group then you can have different people taking different roles and they can stand at the appropriate points of the Circle to do so, either staying in place or moving (Deosil) into place to perform their parts. Depending on numbers you may have enough individuals to cover all the parts or some may have to double up on roles. In group working it is important that everyone is focused on each action every time. So when one person is invoking Air, they will say the words and perform the actions whilst visualizing the element, and everyone else will turn to face the East and will also visualize that element. When working on your own you can remain in one place and either remain facing the Altar or turn to face the different directions.

CIRCLE ETIQUETTE

Before I move onto the actual method of Creating the Sacred Space, there are some rules which really must be followed in Circle:

★ Move Deosil, clockwise, at all times. Walking Widdershins, anticlockwise, undoes things and is reserved for a very few occasions. If this means you have to walk the whole circumference to get to where you should be, that's fine.

★ Take your time. There is no hurry in Circle, so try to move sedately and carefully. Also give other people the time to return to their place or get to where they should be.

★ Repeat the Blessed Be's. Every time someone says 'Blessed Be', it should be echoed by everyone in Circle, preferably in unison, although that takes some practice.

★ Remain focused. Even when it is not your turn, or someone seems to be unnecessarily long-winded, remain focused on what is happening and on the purpose of the Ritual. There should be no whispered comments, witty asides or small talk.

★ Never, ever, touch another Witch's Athame. The Athame is personal to each Witch, far more so than, say, a toothbrush. To touch another Witch's Athame, unless they have specifically asked you to, is the height of bad manners.

HOLDING THE ATHAME

Your Athame is held in your strong hand (right if you are right-handed or vice versa), with your forefinger pointing along the flat edge of the blade towards the tip. You should hold it firmly, so that when moving around it is not likely to fly out of your hand and injure someone.

CENTRING

Everyone gathers and stands in a Circle facing inwards. In our Coven people will usually stand so that they are in place for whichever part of Creating the Sacred Space they will be performing. We also try to ensure that men and women alternate around the Circle to balance the energies. The High Priestess stands in front of the Altar with her High Priest on her right-hand side, and she goes through the outline of the Ritual to ensure everyone knows what they will be doing. Everyone holds hands. The High Priest then says:

'Let us centre ourselves. Feel the earth beneath your feet that is as our flesh. Feel the air which passes in and out of your lungs, which is as our thoughts. Feel the fire that is around us and which is our passions. Feel the water which flows in our veins and is our emotions. Blessed Be.'

In my Coven and its Daughter Covens we then together recite *The Witches' Rune*, **originally written by Doreen Valiente:**

Darksome night and shining moon
East then south then west and north
Hearken to the Witches' Rune
Here we come to call ye forth.

Earth and water, air and fire
Wand and pentacle and sword
Work ye unto our desire
Hearken ye unto our word

Cords and censer, scourge and knife
Powers of the Witches' blade
Waken all ye unto life
Come ye as the charm is made

Queen of Heaven, Queen of Hel
Horned Hunter of the Night
Lend your power unto our spell
Work our will by magic rite

By all the power of land and sea
By all the might of Moon and Sun
As we do will so mote it be
Chant the spell and be it done.

There are other versions of the Rune which differ somewhat, but this is the version we use.

BLESSING THE ELEMENTS ON THE ALTAR

Until you have Blessed the Elements they are still objects in the mundane world rather than representations of the Elemental energies. Note that Air, Fire and Water are Blessed and Consecrated, whereas Earth is simply Blessed. This is because salt is deemed to be pure in itself. It is usual for one person to do the whole of Blessing the Elements, otherwise you are going to have a crush at the Altar.

Firstly, light the Altar candle(s) and the incense.

Take a pinch of salt and place it on the Altar Pentacle. Inscribe an invoking Pentagram *(see Appendix 2, Terms and Definitions)* over it with your Athame and say,

'I do bless thee O creature of Earth to make thee fit for these our Rites.'

Kiss your forefinger and say, *'Blessed Be'.*

In a group everyone will echo this and every other *'Blessed Be'.*

With your Athame, draw an invoking Pentagram in the smoke of the incense and say,

'I do bless and consecrate thee O creature of Air to make thee pure and fit for these our Rites.'

Kiss your forefinger and say, *'Blessed Be'.*

With your Athame, draw an invoking Pentagram in the flame of the candle and say,

'I do bless and consecrate thee, O creature of Fire to make thee pure and fit for these our Rites.'

Kiss your forefinger and say, *'Blessed Be'.*

With your Athame, draw an invoking Pentagram in the water and say,

'I do bless and consecrate thee, O creature of Water to make thee pure and fit for these our Rites.'

Kiss your forefinger and say, *'Blessed Be'.* Then say,

I call on Earth to bind my spell,
Air to speed its passage well,
Bright as Fire shall it glow,
And deep as ocean's tides shall flow.
Count the elements fourfold,
For in the Fifth the Spell shall hold.
Blessed Be.

This latter verse, derived from Alex Sanders, is used in our group of Covens and not necessarily by other Covens.

INVOKING THE ELEMENTS

This is also referred to as Calling the Quarters. Some groups will have Quarter lights denoting the places in the Circle. These are candles either on tall candleholders, or on convenient pieces of furniture, and are generally yellow for Air, red for Fire, blue for Water and green for Earth. Some groups will use different colour correspondences, such as blue for Air, green for Water and yellow (or brown) for Earth, although Fire tends to continue to be red. Quarter lights are frequently employed outdoors where the edge of the Circle may be less well defined and then these candles may be placed in glass jars to prevent them damaging the environment, or being extinguished by the wind or the movement of group members. Other groups may place different indicators at these points, perhaps a Thurible for Air, the Sword for Fire, the Cauldron for Water, and Besom for Earth.

Where possible it is helpful to have one person assigned to invoke each element, and that person will then banish the same element at the end of the Ritual. If for any reason it is not possible for the same person to banish that which they invoked it is the responsibility of the High Priestess to ensure that the banishing is carried out.

The person invoking each element will stand at the appropriate point of the Circle and one at a time will turn outwards and, drawing the invoking Pentagram of that element with their Athame, will say,

'I do summon, stir and call ye O element of Air (Fire/Water/Earth). Raphael (Michael/Gabriel/Uriel), guardian of the gateway of the East (South/West/North), attend with us, guard us, guide us and protect us in these our Rites. Hail and welcome.'

They kiss their forefinger and say *'Blessed Be'.* **They then turn back to the rest of the group ready to face the next direction as the next element is invoked.**

While the person invoking an element is saying their words, everyone else will turn to face that direction and they, and the rest of the group, will visualize that element, either in its natural form of wind, flame, water or land, or in the form of the elemental Guardians Raphael, Michael, Gabriel, and Uriel. Raphael would be a young man dressed in the colours of Spring, and so on. Note that not all Covens will employ the Guardians when calling the Quarters.

INVITING THE GODDESS AND THE GOD

The Goddess and the God are not invoked, they are invited. This can be done by one person inviting each or, more usually, with one person inviting both. You can invite them by name (the following text gives the names we use in our Circle) or more simply as the Goddess and the God.

The designated person turns to face the Altar and raises their arms in a gentle curve to each side of their head and, visualizing the Goddess and the God, says,

'I call upon the Old Gods, upon Hecate and Herne, upon Ceridwyn and Cernunnos, to be with us. To watch over us, to guard us, guide us and protect us during these our Rites.'

When they feel sure that the Goddess and the God are present, they lower their arms and cross them over their chest and say, *'Blessed Be'.*

During this everyone will face the Altar and will support the visualization; this is why it is important that everyone in the group needs to know which Goddess and God forms are being used. In time everyone will easily be able to visualize the same thing.

CASTING THE CIRCLE

Some Covens will use the Coven Sword for this, but an Athame or the forefinger of your strong hand is just as good. If the 'caster' is short then it may be preferable for the rest of the group to move inwards to allow the 'caster' to walk around them, rather than having everyone ducking to avoid the point of the Sword or Athame!

The Circle is Cast starting in the North-East and moving Deosil around the Circle with a good overlap at the starting point. The caster walks around the Circle and, raising their hand high, directs an electric blue light over the heads of the group towards the outer circumference of the area. This should be visualized by all present. As it is created it should be thought of as merging to form a complete sphere, which encompasses the space above the group as well as that beneath them, so that it can be visualized as extending above the ceiling and beneath the floor. As they progress around the Circle they say,

'I conjure this Circle as a place between the worlds, as a time out of time, a place of containment and protection.'

When they have completed the circuit they kiss their forefinger and say, *'Blessed Be'.*

THE RITES AND MAGIC

The Sacred Space is now complete and ready for whatever Rites, magic, and/or celebration is intended to take place. Everyone should now be facing the centre of the Circle unless and until they need to perform or support another action. At this point anyone needing to leave the Circle should cut a doorway in the Circle to leave, and close it after themselves. Anyone needing to enter will have to have a doorway cut for them by someone within the Circle, who will also seal it after their entry. However, it is preferable that this should not be necessary as continually opening and closing doorways in the Circle is disruptive to the group and the Ritual, as well as ultimately weakening the Circle itself. To cut a doorway, take your Athame or forefinger and draw an opening which starts and ends at the floor, and which is large enough for a person to pass through. As you cut you visualize the creation of a doorway in the sphere. To close the doorway reverse the process and visualize the sphere being made whole again.

At this point in your Ritual you will insert whichever Rites, magic and spells you intend to perform. As this is to be the subject of the rest of this book, here I will move straight on to Removing of the Sacred Space so that you have both ends of the Ritual conveniently together.

REMOVING THE SACRED SPACE

These steps should be performed by the same individuals who performed the invoking actions to create the Sacred Space. They will be standing in the same portions of the Circle and, as in the creation, the rest of the group will support their visualizations.

THE ELEMENTS ARE BANISHED

The person banishing each element will stand at the appropriate point of the Circle and one at a time will turn outwards and, drawing the banishing Pentagram of that element with their Athame, will say,

'*I do banish thee O element of Air (Fire/Water/Earth). Raphael (Michael/Gabriel/Uriel), guardian of the gateway of the East (South/West/North), depart from this place with our thanks for guarding, guiding and protecting us in these our Rites. Hail and Farewell.*'

They kiss their forefinger and say, '*Blessed Be*'.

THE GODDESS AND THE GOD ARE THANKED

Again the Goddess and the God are thanked rather than banished or dismissed. This is because we treat the Divine with respect. Similarly, the person or people who invited them should be the one(s) to thank them.

The designated person turns to face the Altar and raises their arms in a gentle curve to each side of their head and, visualizing the Goddess and the God, says,

'I give thanks to the Old Gods, to Hecate and Herne, to Ceridwyn and Cernunnos, for being with us. For watching over, guarding, guiding and protecting us during these our Rites. Depart in peace, Hail and Farewell.'

They visualize the Goddess and the God leaving and then they lower their arms and, crossing them over their chest, say, *'Blessed Be'*.

THE CIRCLE IS REMOVED

Where a Circle has been cast it should also be removed, and by the same person who put it in place.

Once more they start in the North-East and move Deosil around the Circle, using Athame, sword or forefinger as before. As they move they say,

'I do banish this Circle and return this space to this time and this place.'

Kissing their forefinger they say, *'Blessed Be'*.

TO COMPLETE

Everyone faces the centre of the Circle and joins hands. The High Priestess will say,

'Our Circle is ended but our fellowship remains unbroken. And so we say (at which point everyone joins in to say in unison), *Merry Meet, Merry Part and Merry Meet Again.'*

If there is to be a feast then the High Priestess will add, *'Let the feasting begin!'*

Contrary to popular belief this is not a signal to race the High Priestess to the last of the Altar wine, but rather to indicate that it is time to retrieve feasting foods, drink, plates, etc. from wherever they have been placed. Even if a feast is not held there should be some kind of food and drink, perhaps tea and biscuits, taken after working Ritual or magic as this helps to return you to the here and now, and to replenish the energy you have spent. This is often referred to as 'grounding'.

In our Coven this is usually the point at which we extinguish any candles which have been lit for anything other than an actual spell, i.e. the Altar candles and quarter lights. Candles that have been lit for a magical purpose are stood in a safe place so that they may continue to burn.

SOLITARY CREATION AND REMOVAL OF THE SACRED SPACE

If you are working on your own then it is not necessary to speak your words out loud, nor is it necessary for you to have so large a working space. You may also find that, with practice, it is possible for you to visualize the invoking and banishing Pentagrams, the elements, the Goddess and the God, as well as the Circle without arm movements, or indeed moving from one part of the Circle to another. But the basic steps still remain as those above. Similarly, you may not feel the need for so formal an Altar, or for so many tools, etc. These things all come with practice and only you will be able to tell when you are ready to do most of your work as visualization. Until that time comes it is better to use a more formal system as this leaves you free to focus your visualization skills on the actual magic.

OTHER RITES FREQUENTLY FOUND
WITHIN RITUAL

There are several Rites which take place in many Rituals. To avoid repeating them elsewhere in the book I have placed them here so that when they are referred to you can look back and find the complete text in this chapter. Some of them, such as the Rite of Banishing Unwanted Influences and the Rite of Self-Blessing, can be practised as the sole content of your Ritual. The latter is especially good if you feel you need to practise your Craft and want something simple but meaningful to centre your Ritual around.

THE RITE OF BANISHING UNWANTED INFLUENCES

This Rite is often performed just after creating the Sacred Space. It is designed to help to remove outside thoughts, feelings and other mental distractions, which might otherwise interfere with your focus and balance. It is especially useful when you need to perform Ritual or Magic after a stressful day, or when going through an emotional period in your life.

On the Altar you will also need a small dish and a small cloth or towel.

After the Sacred Space has been created one person should step up to the Altar, take some of the consecrated and blessed water and place it into the small dish. They then add a little of the blessed Salt, and inscribing an invoking Pentagram say,

'I call upon the Old Gods to bless and consecrate this water that it may banish all that is not needful to us. May it take away all outside influences, distractions and negativity. May it leave us pure and free to work our Rites and magic.'

They kiss their forefinger and say, *'Blessed Be'*.

That person then places the cloth over their forearm and holding the bowl with both hands takes it to each person in the Circle, moving Deosil at all times. As the bowl carrier steps in front of a person, that person will place the tips of all their fingers into the water and visualize all their negativities draining down through their arms and fingers and into the water. When they have finished they remove their fingers and, using the cloth on the carrier's arm, dry their fingers. They say *'Blessed Be'*, which is echoed by everyone. The carrier then moves on to the next person. Once everyone has finished, the carrier passes the bowl to the last person, who holds it so that the carrier can also perform this Rite. Lastly, the bowl is placed to the rear of the Altar. Later it should be carefully disposed of either down the drain or on a patch of land where you are not trying to grow anything, as the negative influences contained in the water can and do interfere with the growth of plants.

In our Coven we tend to reserve a special bowl for this so that any residual negativities cannot contaminate future workings. Alternatively, you can cleanse the vessel by placing it overnight in the light of the Moon or by placing it under running water for 10 minutes whilst visualizing all negativities being washed away.

THE RITE OF SELF-BLESSING

As mentioned above this is a good Rite to perform if you wish to practise working Ritual. It is also beneficial if you are feeling down, or if you feel the need to become closer to the Goddess, perhaps prior to meditation or divination.

To perform this Rite you will need something with which to anoint yourself. This can be a perfumed oil, some wine, or even salt and water prepared as in the above Rite of Banishment of Unwanted Influences. Place some of your chosen anointing liquid into a small dish, draw an invoking Pentagram over it and say,

'I call upon the Goddess to bless and consecrate this oil (water/wine etc.), to make it pure and fit for this my Rite. Blessed Be.'

Then, kneeling before the Altar, take a few deep breaths to centre yourself and visualize the Goddess standing before you. Take your time to picture her in as much detail as you can, imagine her smiling lovingly at you. Then say,

'Bless me Mother for I am your child.'

For each of the following steps dip your finger in the oil and anoint the mentioned part with just a smear. Anoint your eyes (on the eyebrow to avoid getting oil into your eyes) and say,

'Blessed Be my eyes that I may see thy path.'

Anoint your nose and say,

'Blessed Be my nose that I may breathe your essence.'

Anoint your mouth (just above the lips) and say,

'Blessed Be my mouth that I might speak of thee.'

Anoint your heart (the centre of your chest) and say,

'Blessed Be my breast that I may be faithful to thee.'

Anoint just above your pubic bone and say,

'Blessed Be my womb (for a woman or *phallus* if a man), *that bringest forth life, as thou bringest life eternal.'*

Anoint your knees and say,

'Blessed Be my knees that shall kneel at the Sacred Altar.'

Anoint your feet and say,

'Blessed Be my feet that I may walk in thy ways.'

Lastly, wrap your arms about yourself and visualize the Goddess holding you, as a mother holds her child, and say,

'Bless me Mother for I am thy child.'

Remain where you are for a few moments feeling the love of the Mother Goddess surrounding and enfolding you. Then rise and return Deosil to your place in the Circle so that the next person can take their place at the Altar.

THE FIVE-FOLD KISS

This is similar in many ways to the Rite of Self-Blessing, however the Five-Fold Kiss is given by one person to another. It may be performed to welcome a new Initiate, or to confer blessing upon individuals within the group. The Five-Fold Kiss can be performed within gender or, as is more usual, between genders. Here, to avoid confusion with lots of he/she's etc., I have denoted the recipient as Priestess and the giver (or kisser) as Priest, but you can adjust the gender to suit your circumstances.

The Priestess (receiver) stands, feet slightly parted (for balance) with her arms to her sides. She should look straight ahead and focus on the Goddess and the God, rather than watching the Priest's movements. The Priest kneels in front of her and says,

'Blessed Be your feet, which have brought thee in these ways,'

and kisses first her right then her left foot. He says,

'Blessed Be thy knees, which shall kneel at the Sacred Altar,'

and kisses her right then left knee. He says,

'Blessed be thy womb, which bringeth forth the life of man,'

and kisses her on the lower belly. (Where a Priestess is giving the Five-Fold Kiss to a Priest she kisses him in the same place but would say 'phallus' rather than 'womb'.) He then rises to his feet and says,

'Blessed Be thy breast, formed in strength and beauty,'

and kisses her right then left breasts. He kisses her on the lips and says,

'Blessed Be thy lips, that shall utter the Sacred Names.'

Finally he says, *'Blessed Be,'* **and everyone echoes him.**

DRAWING DOWN THE MOON AND THE CHARGE OF THE GODDESS

Some groups will perform this Rite at every Ritual, others will use it as a method of power raising at Esbats and still others will only perform it at the Major Sabbats. In Drawing Down the Moon, the Goddess is invoked into the Priestess (usually the High Priestess) by the Priest (usually the High Priest), and the words she then speaks (The Charge) are the words of the Goddess. The Charge may be derived from Valiente's Charge of the Goddess, it may be written by the High Priestess, or the Priestess may speak the words which come to her at the time. In a previous work I attributed the Charge to Gerald Gardner, however, it has since become almost universally believed that his High Priestess Doreen Valiente wrote the original. She wrote several versions and these have been altered and added to by other Witches over the years; the one below is just one of many versions now to be found in the modern Craft. I usually recommend to Priestesses that they should memorize the Charge, even though when the time arrives they may find that other words will come to them.

The Priestess stands with her back to the Altar, preferably facing towards the Moon. The Priest commences by giving her the Five-Fold Kiss (see above).

The Priestess now allows her hands to move slightly away from her sides until they are at the 5 and 7 points of the clock with her palms facing forward. Whilst he continues she should look over his head and focus on allowing the spirit of the Goddess to enter her.

With the forefinger of his strong hand the Priest then touches the Priestess in the sigil of the First Degree: right breast, left breast, womb and right breast, whilst saying,

'I invoke thee and call upon thee Mighty Mother of us all, bringer of all fruitfulness, by seed and root, by stem and bud, by flower and fruit do I invoke thee to descend upon this the body of thy servant and Priestess.'

He then kneels and, spreading his arms outwards and downwards, says,

'Hail Aradia, from the Amalthean Horn. Pour forth thy store of love. I lowly bend before thee, I adore thee to the end. With loving sacrifice thy shrine adorn. Thy foot is to my lip.'

He kisses her feet and continues,

'My prayer upborn upon the rising incense. Then spend thine ancient love O Mighty One, descend to aid me who without thee am forlorn.'

The Priest then rises and faces the group and says,

'Listen to the words of the Great Mother, she who, of old, was also called among men Artemis, Astarte, Dione, Melusine, Aphrodite, Ceridwen, Dana, Arianrhod, Isis, Bride and by many other names.'

He then steps to the side and the Priestess, facing the group, raises her arms and delivers the Charge.

THE CHARGE OF THE GODDESS

'Whenever ye have need of any thing, once in the month and better it be when the Moon is full, then shall ye assemble in some secret place and worship the spirit of me who are Queen of all Witcheries. There shall ye assemble, ye who are fain to learn all sorcery, and yet have not won its deepest secrets. To these I shall teach things that are as yet unknown. And ye shall be free from slavery, and as a sign that ye be really free, ye shall be naked in your Rites. And ye shall dance, sing, feast, make music, and love, all in my name. For mine is the ecstasy of the spirit, and mine is also joy on Earth, for my law is love unto all things. Keep pure your highest ideal, strive ever towards it, let naught stop you, nor turn you aside. For mine is the secret door which opens on to the land of youth, and mine is the cup of the wine of life, and the Cauldron of Ceridwyn, which is the Holy Grail of immortality. For I am the gracious Goddess who giveth the gift of the joy of life unto the heart of man, upon Earth I give knowledge of the spirit eternal, and beyond death I give peace and freedom and reunion with those who have gone before. Nor do I demand sacrifice, for behold I am the gracious Mother of all living, and my love is poured out upon the earth. And thou who thinkest to seek for me, know that thy seeking and yearning shall avail thee not, unless thou knowest the mystery, that if that which thou seekest thou findest not within thee, then thou shalt never find it without thee. For behold, I have been with thee from the beginning and I am that which is attained at the end of all desire.'

After the Charge has been delivered the Priestess lowers her arms and crosses them over her breast. She then says, *'Blessed Be'*, which is echoed by the rest of the group.

It is then usual for that Priestess to lead the group in the Raising of Power for the magic which is to be worked. Where Drawing Down the Moon is performed simply for celebration, at one of the Sabbats, it takes place towards the end of the Ritual and is followed by the Rite of Wine and Cakes and the Sabbat Blessing.

At first it may seem that Drawing Down the Moon is something which can only be done within a group, or at the least a partnership; however, this is not the case. The

Solitary Witch can also Draw Down the Moon on her or his own. It is best done at the Full Moon and with the Moon in clear sight. After the usual preparation, stand facing the Moon with your arms raised to each side of your head, as in the above Rite. Look directly at the Moon, although if it is very bright you may need to focus just above the Moon to save straining your eyes. As you gaze, visualize the Goddess in all her beauty and strength. In your mind call to her and ask her to join with you, to become part of you. When you feel certain that you can feel her power within you, lower your arms and cross them over your chest. Recite the Charge, either aloud or in your head, and then move on to the remainder of your Ritual. Be sure to remember to ground yourself after your Ritual. Many Witches find that this is a very powerful and energizing Rite and gives them a physical and emotional boost which lasts several days, as well as empowering them to carry out their magic.

RAISING POWER

Whilst raising power is not a Rite in itself, it is an essential part of any Ritual where magic is to be performed. A group will work together to combine their energies in a way whereby the High Priestess can direct that power towards the desired outcome. A Solitary Witch also raises power, and then focuses and directs her or his own energy. Whilst Drawing Down the Moon does raise energy which is then focused in the High Priestess, it is usual to then move on to supplement this power with energy derived from the group as well. There are many ways to raise energy, the most common of which are dance, chant and drumming. Frequently two, or even all three, of these techniques will be used together.

There are other methods such as binding, scourging, astral projection and trance, but these are all techniques which need to be taught on a one-to-one basis.

✵ *Dance.* Sometimes called Circle Dance. The actual dance can be as simple or intricate as the group wishes, and may involve snaking around the Circle, or weaving in and out of each other. At its simplest, members of the group, holding hands, dance Deosil around the Circle. They are led by the High Priestess who determines the pace of the dance and the time at which she perceives sufficient energy has been raised. At that point she will raise her arms to indicate that it is time to stop. Some High Priestesses will join in the dance, in which case raising her arms causes everyone else to follow suit. Others will stand in the centre of the dancers. In either case, at the point where she raises her arms, she is directing the energy towards the group's intent. There is then a pause whilst the energy is directed, and whilst everyone gets their breath back.

★ *Chanting.* There are a huge number of chants used in the Craft today. Some are universal, others may be written within the Coven. Most chants have their own tune, or may be known by different tunes, but the simple repetition of words to a beat will suffice if you are not musical. It can be helpful, where there are newcomers to a group, to set aside a period of time for chant practice as it is important that everyone can chant together.

★ *Drumming.* Drumming can supplement the energy of either dance or chant, or indeed both. However, it is important that your drummers do have rhythm, as anyone who cannot hold a beat and remain in time will detract from the energy rather than increase it! You also need to ensure that drumming does not drown out chanting, or irritate any neighbours. Where you have too many people for safe dancing, or some who cannot dance, then drumming is a way of ensuring that everyone participates in raising power. However, I have found that there are some people who feel self-conscious dancing and therefore prefer to drum rather than dance, and you need to decide whether you are going to let them 'off the hook' in this way!

Solitary Witches can raise power by any of the above three methods, or indeed by doing two or even all three at once, if they are very well co-ordinated. As with many things in the Craft you will probably need to try different options to see which works best for you.

Whilst energy is not raised for magical working at most celebrations, chanting, dancing and drumming still take place in order to raise energy within the group, and because they are such an integral part of celebrating the Craft today.

CLEANSING AN OBJECT

Anything you purchase will have been handled by other people and will have traces of their energies on it. This particularly applies to anything second-hand where it may have been used for a number of purposes before you receive it. Obviously, anything you intend to use magically or in a spell will need these energies removed before you use it. There are several ways to cleanse an item and you will need to select the most suitable, as some techniques are definitely wrong for some things – for example, you wouldn't run a book under water for 10 minutes!

✯ *Moonlight.* An item can be placed in the light of the Full Moon overnight and the Moon will not only cleanse it but will empower it too. It is best to do this on a windowsill, especially for small items, as just placing it outside can result in it being moved or you forgetting where you put it. An indoor windowsill is also better as your item is less likely to be knocked off by a curious bird, or blown off in a high wind.

✯ *Running water.* Many things can be placed under running water for 10 minutes whilst you visualize all negativity being washed away. Obviously this is no use for anything that will spoil through getting wet.

✯ *Through the elements.* You can cleanse an item by passing it through the elements in the same way as you consecrate it (see below). But do be aware that this means taking an uncleansed item into the Circle.

CONSECRATING AN OBJECT

When you first get any of your magical tools, especially your Athame, they should be consecrated. Likewise, in many spells and magics you may decide to use an object to focus the magic onto, and this too should be consecrated. It could be a candle which burns down to release the energy, a talisman which is carried by someone who was not present at the Ritual, or any one of a number of other items. In many cases, where someone comes to you seeking magic it can be helpful to get them to provide anything like this as not only does it link them to the magic, but keeps down the costs. The object in question should be cleansed (see above), and should be placed on the Altar prior to the start of the Ritual.

At the appropriate point in the Ritual the High Priestess takes the item from the Altar. First she consecrates it with the elements. She passes it through the incense smoke and says,

'I do consecrate this ... (name of item) with Air, that it may ... (name the purpose it is being consecrated for).'

She repeats this with Fire (being careful not to set light to it), Water (by sprinkling a few drops on it) and Earth (sprinkling a few grains of salt onto it).

At this point it may be necessary to do something to the object. Perhaps carve a name on a candle, anoint an object, or some other part of the spell.

She then holds it up over the Altar and says,

'I call upon the Goddess and the God (she may name the aspects or Godforms appropriate) to bring ... (whatever the attributes of the spell might be) to ... (name of the person for whom the magic is being worked).'

She pauses a moment whilst visualizing the Goddess and the God also blessing the candle, then says, *'Blessed Be'.*

NAMING AN OBJECT

This is very similar to the above in actions and words, but is performed to bring about a different intent. Here the object represents a person, not an action or event. Naming an object is often useful when your magic is intended to affect two people, perhaps in a reconciliation. It can be used where you have no picture, physical or mental, of a person, or to strengthen the energy of a picture. It is frequently used in fertility magic or where an image of the person is created.

In this case as the object is passed through each of the elements it is named. For example, as the High Priestess passes it through the incense smoke she says,

'I do name this … (name of item) … (name of person), that it may be … (name of person) … in this our Ritual.'

And she repeats this with each element. She then holds it up over the Altar and says,

'I call upon the Goddess and the God, to know that this is … (name of person), and to lend their energy in his/her good.'

She pauses a moment whilst visualizing the Goddess and the God acknowledging the person, then says, *'Blessed Be'*.

THE RITE OF WINE AND CAKES

The Rite of Wine and Cakes is performed at the end of all Rituals, prior to removing the Sacred Space. It has the two-fold purpose of sharing the Blessing of the Goddess and the God, as well as being a preliminary step in the grounding necessary after working any kind of Ritual or magic.

To perform this you will need on your Altar wine in a chalice and 'cakes' on a plate. The wine used is generally red in colour, although you may prefer to use a sweet wine or mead for some of the festivals. Some groups prefer to use port or another fortified wine for this Rite. If you do not wish alcohol in your Ritual then grape or another fruit juice is just as acceptable. The cakes can be anything from home-made, moon-shaped biscuits, to commercially available crackers, or slices of apple. Whichever you prefer, try not to have them too large as you will have a long pause whilst everyone chomps their way to the end! Most groups will have one more 'cake' than they have participants so that one remains to go with a little of the wine as an offering of thanks. The offering is usually taken outside after the Ritual and scattered on the Earth. Members of our group often bring their dogs with them to Rituals, as they come from the same sire (or, with the addition of a new generation, grandsire!). As a result we frequently have additional cakes which are then shared with any of our dogs who might also be attending.

The High Priestess and High Priest stand in front of the Altar, facing the group, with the High Priest on the High Priestess's right-hand side. The High Priest takes the chalice and, holding it up to the whole group, says,

'Behold the Chalice, the cauldron of Ceridwyn, the fount of all knowledge and life.'

He then turns towards the High Priestess and kneels to face her. The High Priestess takes her Athame, holding it in both hands with the blade pointing upwards, and displays it to the group, saying,

'Behold the Athame, symbol of the Horned God.'

She turns it so that the blade points downwards and lowers it into the wine saying,

'As the cup is to the female so the Athame is to the male.'

Both High Priestess and High Priest should look into one another's eyes and continue together, saying,

'And co-joined together, they bring forth life eternal.'

The High Priestess then raises the Athame out of the wine and says, *'Blessed Be'*.

The High Priest then rises to his feet and, holding the chalice in both hands, offers it to the High Priestess, who also places her hands on the chalice. The High Priest then kisses her on the right then left cheek saying,

'In perfect love and perfect trust. Blessed Be.'

She echoes his *'Blessed Be'* and then kisses him in the same manner, using the same words. After he has echoed her *'Blessed Be'*, he releases the chalice and she takes a sip. The High Priestess then turns to her left and offers the chalice in exactly the same way to the person standing there.

It is often at this point in Ritual where some (usually men who have chosen to stand next to each other) realize that they would prefer to have alternated male and female!

Thus the chalice passes Deosil around the Circle until the High Priest has drunk from it and replaced it on the Altar.

The High Priest then takes the plate of 'cakes' and again kneels before the High Priestess. She takes her Athame and, drawing an invoking Pentagram over the 'cakes', says,

'I bless and consecrate these cakes, symbol of the bounty of the Great Goddess. As they feed our bodies let Her love sustain us in heart, mind and spirit. Blessed Be.'

The High Priest then offers the cakes to the High Priestess in exactly the same way as he did with the wine, and she accepts in the same way, taking a biscuit. However, she does not bite into it until after she has passed the plate in the same way as before, to the person on her left, saying,

'In Perfect Love and Perfect Trust.'

The plate thus passes Deosil around the Circle with everyone taking a 'cake' and only biting into it after they have passed the plate to their neighbour.

The reason for not eating before you pass the plate on is to avoid pebble-dashing your neighbour with biscuit crumbs whilst trying to kiss them and speak.

If you have less than about six people in Circle it is a good idea to let the wine return to the Altar before starting the cakes, to avoid a bottleneck. However, in a larger group, the cakes can be started after the High Priestess has passed on the wine. You need to wait until everyone has finished chewing before moving on with the next part of your Ritual.

The Rite of Wine and Cakes is sometimes confused with the Great Rite. Where the Great Rite is celebrated symbolically (as is most usual), wine is consecrated in much the same way as it is for the Rite of Wine and Cakes, but with a different focus and intent, and without the consecration of cakes. The Great Rite celebrates the physical union of the Goddess and the God, the Priest and Priestess who perform it actually become the Goddess and the God during the Ritual. In the Rite of Wine and Cakes they remain High Priestess and High Priest and invoke the blessing of the Goddess and the God.

Witches on their own can still perform the Rite of Wine and Cakes, although they will have to say (either aloud or in their head) both parts of the text and, obviously, hold both Chalice and Athame, with one hand each. The cakes can remain on the Altar when you consecrate them. It is also helpful to ensure that your Athame is on your Altar and not kept at your belt, otherwise you can run out of hands in the middle of your Rite. Instead of kissing a neighbour when saying, '*In Perfect Love and Perfect Trust*', you can raise your glass to the Goddess and the God.

THE SABBAT, OR OTHER, BLESSING

In celebratory Rituals, Sabbats, Rites of Passage and so on, it is usual for the High Priestess, or one of the more experienced group members, to give a Blessing. This takes place after the Rite of Wine and Cakes. The Blessing should reflect the nature of the Ritual, and in the case of a Sabbat should relate that festival to the Wheel of the Year (*see Appendix 2, Terms and Definitions*) as a whole, in order to put it into context.

PUTTING RITES INTO RITUALS

As mentioned above there are two basic kinds of Ritual; working and celebratory. And as you will have gathered the above Rites can be incorporated into both kinds in different ways. But the following gives an idea of how these Rites are incorporated.

WORKING RITUALS – USUALLY ESBATS

DEFINE THE PURPOSE AND COMMUNICATE IT*

PREPARE THE AREA*

SET THE ALTAR*

CREATE THE SACRED SPACE*

BANISH UNWANTED INFLUENCES AND/OR SELF-BLESSING

PREPARE THE MAGIC OR SPELLS*

DRAWING DOWN THE MOON

RAISING POWER*

THE MAGIC OR SPELLS*

THE RITE OF WINE AND CAKES*

REMOVING THE SACRED SPACE*

GROUNDING*

TIDY AWAY*

CELEBRATORY RITUALS – USUALLY SABBATS

DEFINE THE PURPOSE AND COMMUNICATE IT*

PREPARE THE AREA*

SET THE ALTAR*

CREATE THE SACRED SPACE*

INTRODUCE THE FESTIVAL*

CHANTING AND DANCING, TO RAISE ENERGY FOR CELEBRATION RATHER THAN
FOR WORKING MAGIC*

BANISH UNWANTED INFLUENCES AND/OR SELF-BLESSING

CELEBRATE THE FESTIVAL*

DRAWING DOWN THE MOON (OCCASIONALLY)

THE RITE OF WINE AND CAKES*

THE SABBAT OR OTHER BLESSING*

REMOVING THE SACRED SPACE*

FEASTING

TIDY AWAY*

Not every celebration or working will require all the above steps but those items marked * really should be performed. Although I have not marked Feasting as essential for celebrations, it would be hard to imagine a festival with no feast! Sometimes some steps will occur in a slightly different order, perhaps because you prepare the Altar before everyone arrives, or at the same time when the tidying away, grounding and writing up are done by different people.

There is more on constructing Rituals, and on assigning roles within Ritual, in Chapter 10. But now let us move on to some Rituals and Spells in the next chapters.

FOUR

MOON

WORKINGS

Witches work magic in accordance with the phases of the Moon, of which the Full Moon is often considered to be the best time. It is sometimes said that magic should only be worked at the Full Moon, or Esbat. This is when the Moon is at its strongest. For many magics this is the case. However, not all magic can wait for the next Full Moon; you may only have two days before a job interview or your friend may have been admitted to hospital as an emergency. It is important to appreciate all the aspects of the Moon, the kind of magic which each is most beneficial for, and the different ways that each problem can be approached. To do this we need to understand the cycle of the Moon.

THE CYCLE OF THE MOON

The Moon orbits the Earth once every 28 and a bit days, and the Sun orbits the Earth once every 365 and a bit days. The orbits of the Earth and Moon mean that differing amounts of sunlight reflect off the Moon, making the illuminated part change shape from our perspective. It is that illuminated part which reflects the aspects of the Goddess and which we use in timing our magic. These phases remain constant whether the sky is overcast or not.

From the perspective of the Witch the phases of the Moon are thus:

✦ *New Moon*, when a thin sliver of Moon (a reverse C) appears in the sky. The New Moon is considered to last for three days, the first day being its first appearance in the sky. This is the time for magic which involves new things, fresh starts, new beginnings. The Rites of Naming, and Wiccaning, are often held at the New Moon.

✦ *Waxing Moon*, when the Moon is increasing. This is the period from the end of the New Moon to the start of the Full Moon. It is the time of growth, and for magic which involves growth and increase.

✦ *Full Moon*, when the Moon appears as a sphere in the sky. The Full Moon is a traditional time for Witches to meet to work magic and these meetings are called Esbats. The period of the Full Moon is generally considered to be three days, being the day before, the day of, and the day after, the actual Full Moon. This is the traditional time for magic and a particularly good time for magic and spells connected with healing, protection and fertility. The Full Moon is also associated with all kinds of divination. Handfasting and Rites of coming of age are often held at the Full Moon.

✦ *Waning Moon*, when the Moon is decreasing in size. A time for sending things away; old habits, unwanted feelings. The late Waning Moon, a day or so prior to the Dark Moon, is often a time for holding the Rite of Withdrawal, not to banish our feelings but to say goodbye. Rites of Croning are also sometimes held at this phase.

✦ *Dark of Moon*, the three days when there is no Moon visible in the sky. It is better not to work Magic or spells at the time when the Moon is hiding her face, as the energies at this time can be confusing and it is easier for things to misfire. Many High Priestesses actually forbid their Covenors from working Magic at this time.

The New Moon represents the Goddess in her Maiden aspect, the Full represents the Mother, and the Dark Moon represents the Crone, or Wise One. The Maiden continues through the waxing period until she can be seen to be becoming the Mother, much as a pregnancy develops. The Mother aspect continues into the waning period until she can be seen to be becoming the Crone. It is important to remember that the phases are not isolated, that the energies grow and blend with each other to form a smooth changeover from one phase to the next.

Looking at the above, many Witches feel that new relationships or work should be worked for at the New Moon, healing should be performed at the Full, and giving up bad habits at the Waning Moon. Where the magic can wait, this is fine. But there are often alternative ways of looking at things. For example, if your friend is sick you can work to banish illness at the Waning Moon, work for new strength at the New. If you are seeking a new job you can work for opportunity at the New, confidence at the Full and driving away negative thoughts at the Waning, and so on. In the chapter on spells and magics I shall try to suggest a Moon phase for each working, but, if matters are urgent, do try to look at an alternative. Having said that, do also try to be honest about the urgency. You may feel that you cannot wait two weeks before meeting the person of your dreams, but I doubt that anything bad will happen if you wait! On the other hand a sick child or a job interview could well be urgent. Cleansing your new house should be done as soon as it becomes yours. Also remember that, where possible, you should plan and work in advance, after all, it's no use remembering your exams the night before, for revision or for magic!

But let us move on to some example Rituals timed to the phases of the Moon. Remember that many of the steps and Rites which go into the Ritual can be found in Chapter 3 – these are marked *. Alternative spells and magics can be found in Chapter 5.

NEW MOON RITUAL

The purpose of this Ritual is to bring the 'right' person into the life of John, who finished an unhappy relationship several months ago and who seeks a partner. When John approached us, he described the character attributes he was seeking and wrote them all down. He agreed that a good relationship was more important than how someone looks and so refrained from adding anything about physical appearance.

In addition to the usual tools you will need:

THE BOLINE

JOHN'S PAPER DESCRIBING WHAT HE SEEKS IN A PERSON

A LENGTH OF PINK THREAD (APPROX. 2 FEET LONG)

A PINK CANDLE AND A SEPARATE HOLDER

SOME ROSE-SCENTED ANOINTING OIL

Prepare the working space.*

Communicate the purpose of the Ritual.*

Set the Altar.*

Create the Sacred Space.*

Rite of Banishing Unwanted Influences.* Everyone in Circle should be reminded that, in addition to any 'personal baggage', they are also to banish any preconceptions about the 'right' kind of person for John.

The High Priestess reminds them of the purpose of the Ritual and reads the attributes from John's paper.

The group raises energy by dance and chant.* Whilst they do this they visualize John and the type of person he is interested in. The most effective chant for this would be one where the attributes on John's paper are repeated over and over again. When the High Priestess considers that enough energy has been raised she signals for the dancing to stop.

The chanting continues gently whilst the High Priestess takes the candle and inscribes the sigil of John's sun sign onto it near the top. Beneath that she inscribes the sigil of Venus and a heart. She then anoints the candle with oil, starting from the middle of its length and moving out towards the ends. As she does so she visualizes John meeting the right person. She passes the candle to the person on her left and they too massage the oil into the candle. It passes all the way around the Circle until it returns to the High Priestess. The chanting stops.

The High Priestess now consecrates* the candle, asking that it may bring a suitable person to John. When she presents it to the Goddess and the God she calls upon the Maiden and the Hunter and will ask for friendship, love and happiness for John. She places the candle in its holder in the centre of the Altar and lights it from the Altar candle saying,

'As this burns, so it sends a beacon of light that John may find the person he is seeking. Blessed Be.'

The High Priestess takes John's paper and likewise consecrates it.* Once it has been passed through the elements she folds it carefully and ties it with the pink thread. Holding it up to the Goddess and the God she says,

'I call upon the Maiden and the Hunter to bless this token, that it might draw friendship, love and happiness to John. Blessed Be.'

She places the token on the floor in the centre of the Circle.

Once again the group raise energy by dance and chant.* This time when the High Priestess considers that sufficient has been done she directs the energy both up and out of the Circle towards John and down into the token on the floor. The token is now placed onto the Altar, to be given to John later.

The Rite of Wine and Cakes.*
Removing the Sacred Space.*
Grounding.*
Tidy Away.*

After the Ritual, preferably within three days, the token is given to John so that he can carry it with him at all times. He is reminded that although magic works it is not necessarily instant, and he should not expect the next person he meets to necessarily be 'the one'! He is also told that, once the magic has worked, he can dispose of the token by burning it (carefully) or by burying it in the earth.

NOTE ON CANDLE MAGIC

Whilst any candle used for magic should be allowed to burn all the way down it should never be left unattended. If you cannot supervise the candle until its end you can either burn it over three successive nights, or pass it to your 'client' to do so themselves.

 ## FULL MOON (ESBAT) RITUAL

Sue is approaching her final nursing exams and has asked for help. She knows she has worked hard and has the knowledge, but she tends to get anxious and flustered during tests. She has been asked to provide a small flat piece of agate. The day before the Ritual the agate was washed in rainwater and placed on a windowsill (inside) overnight in the light of the Full Moon, to cleanse it.

In addition, you need on your Altar:

> SUE'S AGATE
>
> SOME ROSEMARY OIL
>
> A VERY FINE PAINTBRUSH (AN EYELINER BRUSH WORKS REALLY WELL FOR THIS KIND OF DELICATE WORK)

Prepare the working space.*
Communicate the purpose of the Ritual.*
Set the Altar.*
Create the Sacred Space.*

Rite of Banishing Unwanted Influences.*
Drawing Down the Moon.*

After the Charge the High Priestess reminds everyone why they are present. She takes the agate and consecrates it through the elements for Sue.*

Then, taking the oil and brush she paints a caduceus (two serpents entwined around a staff, a universal symbol of healers) onto it with the oil before asking the blessing of the Goddess as Mother, and God as All-Father.*

The High Priestess then takes the agate and passes it to the person on her left. They hold it in their hand and speak aloud an aspect of the spell for Sue. This could be, 'to remember knowledge', 'to be free from nerves', 'to achieve her potential as a healer', and so on. The agate is passed around until everyone has placed a thought into it. When it reaches the High Priestess again, she should add any aspect(s) she feels the others may have missed before placing it back onto the Altar.

Everyone will dance and chant to raise power,* which the High Priestess will direct into the stone, to be given to Sue to carry with her up to and through her exam period.

The Rite of Wine and Cakes is performed.*
The Sacred Space is removed.*
Grounding.*
Tidy Away.*

 WAXING MOON RITUAL

Jane has been ill for some time and her doctor is sending her for tests in two days. You feel the need to take action now as working before a disease has been formally diagnosed often results in a minor and easily cured problem, rather than a major one, being identified. You have never met Jane and know nothing of her other than a brief physical description and her date of birth.

Before the Ritual you get your best artist to draw a picture of a woman of Jane's description. On it is marked the area of her illness and over her head is placed her date of birth. (Note that date of birth is more accurate than the sigil of her birth sign, although the latter can be used where there is little space.)

Define the purpose and communicate it.*
Prepare the area.*
Set the Altar,* including the picture of Jane and a fireproof dish.
Create the Sacred Space.*

The picture of Jane is named,* and then placed in the centre of the Circle, where the High Priestess kneels and places her hands, one to each side of Jane, on to it.

The rest of the Coven raise power* and direct it towards the High Priestess who focuses on drawing the energy from them and passing it into Jane through her strong hand, and on drawing the illness from Jane through her other hand. As they do this they all chant, '*In with health and healing energy. Out with sickness and illness,*' **over and over again. When the High Priestess feels that all illness has been replaced with health, or when she feels she can withdraw no more illness from Jane, she takes the picture to the Altar and sets it alight from the Altar candle, placing it in the fireproof dish for safety. The High Priestess says,**

'*As this flame is bright may it fill Jane with healing energy, as it burns let it take all illness from her. Blessed Be.*'

The chanting continues until the picture has burnt away.
Banish Unwanted Influences.* This is done to remove all the illness that has been taken from Jane, so it is helpful if someone other than the High Priestess consecrates the water in the bowl and takes it around.

The Rite of Wine and Cakes.*
Removing the Sacred Space.*
Grounding.*
Tidy Away.*

Anyone who is feeling unwell him- or herself should not really attempt this Ritual as you are drawing illness out of someone into yourself before banishing it. Where the Ritual is worked by a Solitary, they will need to prepare the Banishing bowl before commencing the magic.

As you can see from the above, Working Rituals all follow a like pattern; there may be some steps which change and others which are moved, but the basic outline is similar. This is the structure into which you place your magic, and which goes toward making it work. You may find that you perform very similar Rituals every month, sometimes with only one thing to work for, and at other times with many requests for help to carry out.

FIVE

SpElls And

mAgics

Whilst magic does not have to take place within an elaborate Circle, you still need to invoke the elements, invite the Goddess and the God, and Cast a Circle to contain the energy you raise and raise that energy to make your magic work. For this reason you do need to understand these concepts and actions before you can simplify them.

In this chapter I shall be looking at the magic worked within the Sacred Space, whether it be formal or created mentally. As detailed in Chapter 3, the following are the steps involved in a working Ritual, those marked # are essential, the others are added when needed. 'The Magic or Spells' is the step we will be looking at in this chapter; it presupposes that you have looked at and mastered the other steps and that you understand their purpose.

DEFINE THE PURPOSE, AND WHERE YOU ARE WORKING IN A GROUP
    COMMUNICATE IT#
PREPARE THE AREA#
SET THE ALTAR#
CREATE THE SACRED SPACE#
BANISH UNWANTED INFLUENCES
SELF-BLESSING
PREPARE THE MAGIC OR SPELLS
DRAWING DOWN THE MOON
RAISING POWER#
THE MAGIC OR SPELLS#

THE RITE OF WINE AND CAKES
REMOVING THE SACRED SPACE#
GROUNDING#
TIDY AWAY#

Magic can be used to help in every sphere of life, but it would not be possible to cover every eventuality in anything short of an encyclopaedia! However, I have tried to cover those problems I am most frequently asked about and in Chapter 10 I will look at ways of devising your own spells. In each of the following spells you will find a list of the things you need on your Altar in addition to the usual tools, and a note of the best time to work your magic, together with any preparation you may need to do. Everywhere you see an asterisk (*) look back to Chapter 3 for details.

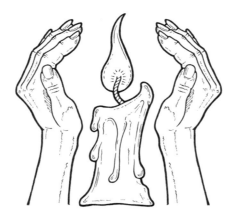

RELATIONSHIPS

Relationship magic is an area which is always fraught with difficulty. If you work magic to attract an individual, how will you know whether they really like you or whether it is just the magic? If you work a similar spell for someone else, will they blame you every time they argue, or when they become just plain bored with their partner's devotion? However, if you phrase your wishes carefully, and mean them, then you will be able to work effective and successful magic to enhance relationships.

TO FIND A PARTNER

Prior to your working you will need to give some thought to the characteristics you seek in a future partner. It is a good idea to write these down so that you can check you are not trying to describe a specific individual and so that you do not miss something important.

On a Friday at the New Moon, or in the first five days after, take:

> 1 WHITE CANDLE
>
> 1 NEW PIN

Whilst raising power, focus on the attributes you are interested in; you can even chant them aloud or in your head. Now consecrate the candle through the elements.* Next, heat the tip of the pin carefully in your Altar candle and insert it through the white candle at the centre. Light the white candle from the Altar candle and, visualizing the Goddess and the God, say,

'I call upon Venus and Aphrodite, upon Eros and Adonis, bring to me a man/woman who I can care for and who will care for me. Let him/her be … (read the list you have prepared). Let us be friends and companions and, if it be right, true partners in life. As this flame burns let him/her come to me, as the pin drops let him/her be drawn to me. As is my will, so mote it be. Blessed Be.'

Stay and meditate a few minutes on the characteristics you seek. The candle should be allowed to burn all the way down, but remember, as you should never leave a burning candle unattended you need to have planned for this time in advance.

TO APPEAR ATTRACTIVE TO OTHERS

This is not to say you are not attractive in your own right, but we can all do with a little extra help from time to time. I have written extensively about this in *The Real Witches' Kitchen*, but here's a short spell to be going on with.

In advance of your Ritual:

> TAKE ONE TABLESPOONFUL FRESH ROSEMARY AND STEEP FOR ½ HOUR IN ½ PINT (300ML) HOT WATER. STRAIN, BOTTLE AND LABEL.
>
> TAKE A PIECE OF GOLD (IT CAN BE JEWELLERY) AND STEEP IN RAINWATER FOR 3 NIGHTS OVER THE FULL MOON. STRAIN, RETURN THE JEWELLERY TO WHENCE IT CAME, BOTTLE AND LABEL THE WATER.

You will also need:

> ¼ PINT (150ML) ROSE WATER (OBTAINABLE FROM MOST CHEMISTS)
> I SMALL PIECE OF CITRINE
> I SMALL PIECE OF AMBER

The Ritual should be performed on a Friday close to, or at, the Full Moon.

Place the rosemary water, rose water, 'gold' water, and gemstones on your Altar. Whilst raising power, focus on your 'best points' increasing, and visualize your 'bad points' diminishing and fading away. Consecrate the waters and gemstones through the elements* in the usual way but additionally asking each element the following:

'May this Rosemary water purify me and drive out all imperfections. May this Rose water bring me confidence in myself. May this gold water make me appear as gold to those around me. May this Amber make me appear fair of face. May this Citrine make me fair of self.'

Once all have been consecrated, put them away safely until the time comes when you need them.

On the day(s) when you feel most in need of a boost to your appearance add some of the Rosemary and Gold waters and the gemstones to a cool bath, bathe for at least 15 minutes whilst visualizing the Rosemary driving away imperfections, the Gold making you appear attractive, the Amber making you fair of face and the Citrine, fair of self. Carefully retrieve the gemstones before you pull the plug! After your bath, perform a Self-Blessing* anointing yourself with the Rose water. Carry the gemstones in your purse or pocket.

Of course if you are in a real hurry to use this then you may need to time it so that your gold is steeped for three nights preceding the Full Moon in order that all is in readiness for working on the Full Moon. Alternatively, you can prepare and consecrate the 'ingredients' in advance, although the Rosemary water will only keep for one month in a cool place.

MEETING AND MAKING FRIENDS

You will need:

A PIECE OF PAPER, YOUR BEST OR FAVOURITE KIND

A PEN OR PENCIL, PREFERABLY ONE GIVEN TO YOU BY A FRIEND OR YOUR
   FAVOURITE ONE

A SHALLOW FIREPROOF DISH; AN OLD SAUCER IS FINE

This Ritual is best performed a day or so just before the Full Moon, preferably on a Friday.

In the Preparing Magic* part of your Ritual, take the piece of paper and divide it into two columns. On the left-hand side write a list of the personal attributes you can bring to a friendship: kind, witty, caring, etc. On the right-hand side write a list of the things you like to do: walking, dancing, watching videos, etc. Ensure that you include 'meeting and making friends'. On the reverse draw a sketch of yourself surrounded by people of both genders, having fun. If you're no good at art, draw stick men and women but make sure they all have smiling faces.

In the Working Magic* part of your Ritual, consecrate your paper through the elements.* Then, holding it up over the Altar to the North, say,

'I call upon the Old Gods to aid me. As the Goddess and the God walk together hand in hand they are not alone. I ask that you bring companions and friends into my life that, likewise, I am not alone. Blessed Be.'

Then take the paper and set light to it in the Altar candle, place it safely in your fireproof dish and watch it burn. As it does so say,

'May the winds of Air carry my request. May the flames of Fire give it life. May the fluids of Water spread it even as the rains fall. May the Earth receive it and give it flesh. Blessed Be.'

Wait until the paper has completely turned to ash before moving on to the next step in your Ritual.

After you have tidied away, take the ashes outside and scatter them in the winds. Your magic will start to work at the next rainfall. Be aware, however, that it will not work as quickly or as well if you remain secluded in your home as it will if you make a point of being out and about!

RECONCILING DIFFERENCES

You will need:

1 STONE FOR EACH PERSON YOU SEEK TO RECONCILE. MAKE THEM OF EASILY
RECOGNIZABLE SHAPES, SIZES OR COLOURS. YOU CAN USE GEMSTONES
RELATED TO PEOPLE'S CHARACTER OR BIRTH SIGN, OR YOU CAN JUST USE
PEBBLES FOUND ON THE GROUND.

3 SMALL STICKS (USED MATCHES WORK FINE) TO BE PLACED BETWEEN EACH
OF THE PARTIES. IF THERE ARE 3 STONES YOU WILL NEED 9 STICKS.

This should be performed on the night of the Full Moon.

**Name* each of the stones for one of the people concerned. Also Name* the sticks
(as a bunch, not individually) as 'obstacles to reconciling differences'. At the point
where you Name the sticks, say to the Goddess and God,**

*'I call upon the Goddess and the God to know that these are the obstacles which stand between …
and … (names of the parties) I ask them to lend their power that these obstructions to clear
thought, communication and understanding might be removed even as these tokens are removed.
I ask them to lend their aid to bring … and … (names of parties) together for the good of all.
Blessed Be.'*

**Place the stones in a pattern with the sticks between them, somewhere where they
will be undisturbed by others, for three days and nights. Complete your Ritual as
usual.**

**On each of the three nights following your Ritual remove one of the sticks from
between each pair of stones, and move the stones closer to each other. Say,**

*'With the energy and love of the Goddess and the God, I remove this obstacle to bring … and …
(names of parties) closer together. Blessed Be.'*

You do not need to perform a Ritual on these nights, simply perform the above action. Once all the sticks have been removed the stones should be touching; either keep them like this or tie them in a cloth and keep for one full Lunar cycle. The sticks should be burned in a fire or buried in the ground.

Do not expect miracles from this spell – if two parties have been warring for some time, it may take equally long for them to reconcile their differences. Similarly, do not expect this to reunite a divorced couple, but you should be able to expect them to be able to communicate in a friendlier manner. If you are one of the parties you are working for, make sure that you are also prepared to make the first overtures towards repairing the relationship. There is little point in working magic to make others more reasonable if you are not prepared to put something of yourself into the mix!

 STAYING IN TOUCH

Sometimes life separates us from those we care for, for example, work or family may cause them to move away, temporarily or long term. This is an adaptation of spell which, from ancient times, has been used to ensure the safe return of husbands sent off to war. I have altered it so that it can be used at any time when someone you care for has to be away.

You will need:

> 2 GEMSTONES; FOR A PARTNER OR LOVER USE AQUAMARINE OR MOSS AGATE,
> FOR A FAMILY MEMBER USE HAEMATITE OR SMOKY QUARTZ, FOR A FRIEND
> USE ROSE QUARTZ.
> A CLOTH OF A COLOUR YOU BOTH LIKE, OR A GREENY-BLUE ONE
> SOME VIOLET THREAD

Again, this should be performed on a Friday during the Waxing Moon.

Name* one of your stones for yourself and the other for the person you wish to stay in contact with. Place the stones together in the cloth and tie it tightly with the thread. Hold it up to the Goddess and the God and say,

'I call upon the Goddess and the God. As these stones which are myself and … (name of the other) are bound together, let the bonds of our friendship know no distance. Blessed Be.'

Then pass the bundle through Air and say, *'Let Air speed our thoughts and messages'*, **pass it briefly through the candle flame and say,** *'Let Fire keep us in each others' hearts,'* **sprinkle it with water and say,** *'Let no river or ocean stand in the way of our love,'* **and sprinkle with salt, saying,** *'Let the Earth itself be no barrier between us. Blessed Be.'*

Close your Ritual as usual.

After your Ritual, place the stones in their cloth in a safe place, and don't forget your side of staying in touch: phone or write regularly!

MAKING A CLEAN BREAK

It would be nice to think that you only need to work magic to bring people closer, but sometimes you may also want someone out of your life. This is a spell for making parting a swifter and less painful process. Do be aware that the spell does work, so if you have any doubt or have only just had an argument, it would be better to wait a while until your feelings cool and you are sure that you are not doing something you may later regret. I usually counsel waiting a full lunar cycle or more before using this spell.

In advance of the Ritual devise a sigil for the person you wish to part from. This could be a combination of their initials entwined with the sigil of their sun sign, or something more complex of your own devising. Whatever it is it should represent that person as honestly as you feel you can be, so try not to do it with a head full of anger! Draw this sigil in rough as you will need to copy it during your Ritual.

On your Altar you will need:

> THE DRAWING OF THE SIGIL
>
> A PIECE OF THIN TISSUE PAPER
>
> A PEN WHICH WILL WRITE ON TISSUE WITHOUT TEARING IT
>
> A SMALL PEBBLE
>
> SOME BLACK THREAD

This Ritual is best performed on a Saturday during the Waning Moon, at least five days after the Full Moon, but not at the Dark of Moon.

While you are Preparing to work Magic* draw the sigil onto the tissue, and place it in the centre of the Altar. Whilst raising power focus on the person and on the reasons you wish them out of your life.

In working Magic,* Name* the tissue through the elements, being careful not to set it alight! When naming it before the Goddess and the God say,

'I call upon the Goddess and the God to know that this is … (name). Our friendship is over, what was shared is separate, what were bonds need to be severed. I seek no harm to him/her but rather that he/she should turn and prosper elsewhere. Blessed Be.'

Wrap the tissue around the stone and tie it with the thread saying,

'As I wrap this stone with … (name) my heart is heavy with sorrow. As I tie these knots I stand firm in my belief. When I cast these from me I sever all bonds and set him/her free. As I do will, so mote it be. Blessed Be.'

Set the bundle to one side and conclude your Ritual in the usual way.

Within three days of completing your Ritual take the stone to a stream, river or the sea and throw it as far as you can into the waters saying,

'I cast thee from me, as tissue melts and threads unravel, so may you be gone from my life. May both you and I find happiness elsewhere. Blessed Be.'

Once the tissue has dissolved and the threads worked loose, the person will move out of your life. Note that the threads need to be tight enough to hold the tissue around the stone until it enters the waters, but not so tight that they will never come undone.

FAMILY

There are many difficulties associated with family life; here I have covered but a few. However, there are many things which can create tension and disorder within the household, which are related to other spells in this chapter. If family tension is caused by ill health look at the healing spells; where it is caused by a shortage of money look in the section on study, work and career, and so on. Also be very careful that you do not fall into the trap of deciding what is best for your near and dear, regardless of what they wish. For example, it is easy from the perspective of a parent to want your youngster to go to college, to get a highly paid job and so on, but they may be happier doing a vocational course and having a poorly paid career which they find satisfying.

Equally, it can be tempting to work magic to bring two people back together when they have decided to split up. Whilst you can work to increase communication, or even for the resolution of problems, to actively work to bring them back together, regardless of the feelings of one or both, would be to interfere with their personal freedom and may well make matters worse for both of them.

GETTING PREGNANT

Think very carefully about performing this spell; this is a new life you are attempting to bring into the world, one for which you are, to an extent, morally responsible even if you performed the magic for another. Secondly, especially when working for someone else, you must ensure that you are totally focused. Otherwise, should the spell backfire you could be left literally carrying the baby! Additionally, try never to work this unless you are sure that *both* parties to the pregnancy really want a child.

You will need:

> SOME QUICK DRYING MODELLING CLAY (THE KIND FOUND IN TOY STORES IS IDEAL)
>
> A BOLINE OR OTHER TOOL FOR INSCRIBING IN THE CLAY
>
> A BOARD OR PLATE ONTO WHICH YOUR IMAGE CAN BE PLACED UNTIL IT IS FULLY DRIED
>
> A CLOTH OF A COLOUR WHICH REMINDS YOU OF PREGNANCY: IT COULD BE RED FOR THE MOTHER, BUT BLUE IS ALSO A FREQUENT CHOICE

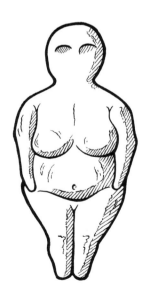

This Ritual should be performed at the Full Moon. When calling upon the Goddess ensure that you invoke her as Mother and invoke the God as All Father.

Prior to working this spell you should perform the Rite of Banishing Unwanted Influences* so that your mind is as focused as it can be.

In Preparing the Magic* you need to make an image of an overtly and heavily pregnant woman. She needs to have exaggerated breasts, belly and hips. If you can make her in the likeness of the woman you are working for that is excellent, you can even glue a photograph of her face onto the head of your image, but otherwise focus on the pregnant aspects. Ancient images such as this have been found in several lands and many periods throughout history; in the Craft they are often called fith-faths.

Whilst Raising Power* focus on pregnancy, on the sperm entering the egg, the growth of the foetus, the swelling of the woman's body, and any other positive aspects of pregnancy you can envisage.

Once energy has been raised take your Boline and inscribe the initials of the woman into the back of the image, then Name* the image in the usual way.

Take the image and place it carefully on your board or plate. Once it is fully dry, usually a couple of days, wrap it in the cloth and put it in a safe place, or give it to the woman to keep safely.

This spell is invariably successful, but just occasionally, however strong your magic, it does not happen quickly or at all. In these cases you can try a second time, but if that is not successful it may be better to leave things in the hands of the Goddess as she may have her reasons.

SAFE PREGNANCY

Magic alone will not guarantee a safe pregnancy. The mother-to-be needs to take care of herself, to eat, rest, sleep, exercise sensibly; this is personal responsibility in action. However, as Witches we can aid this process.

You will need:

> THE FITH-FATH YOU MADE FOR THE ABOVE SPELL, BUT ONLY IF THIS IS FOR THE SAME PERSON, OR THE TOOLS TO MAKE ONE AS DETAILED ABOVE
>
> A CLOTH AS ABOVE
>
> ALSO YOU WILL NEED 3 LENGTHS OF RED THREAD, ABOUT 3 FEET IN LENGTH. IF YOUR IMAGE IS OVER 6 INCHES IN LENGTH YOU MAY NEED LONGER THREADS

Again this should be performed at the Full Moon.

When preparing your magic*; knot the three threads at one end, and secure it so that you can plait the threads. Whilst plaiting, visualize the threads becoming a mental chain of strength and security designed to protect the unborn child and its mother. Once you have plaited them knot the other end of the threads.

Where you have worked the above spell for getting pregnant you, or she, will already have a fith-fath, otherwise you need to make one in a similar way to the above spell.

Raise energy focusing on the growth of the pregnancy, omitting conception. Name* the image through the elements and inscribe the initials on its back as before. Next hold it up over the Altar and visualize the Mother Goddess fully pregnant, and say,

'Oh great Mother of us all, bringer of all life and fruitfulness, I beseech thee to bring strength to … (name of woman) and her womb. May her child grow safe, strong and healthy within her, may she bring forth life, even as you bring forth life eternal. I call upon you, intercede with the God your Consort and mate, to cast his strong arms around her and her unborn child, to keep them safe until the time is right for her child to join the world. Bless her that she too may experience the joys of motherhood. Blessed Be.'

Now take your plaited threads and tie them around the fith-fath thus: place the centre of the plait at the back of the neck, bring it over the shoulders and cross it between the breasts. Take it around the back, cross over and return to the front, under the pregnant bulge, and knot it three times. As you tie it say,

'I tie this thread to secure this child in love and safety, to ward all ills from mother and child. It is a barrier of protection, created by the love of the Mother Goddess and the All Father God. May its strength hold until the time is right. Blessed Be.'

This can be done on a fith-fath which is not yet dry, in which case you need to set the image aside until it is dry before wrapping it.

For this spell you should retain the image until the time is right, unless you can be sure that the mother will have it to hand when the time comes. Furthermore, try to ensure that you will be told when she goes into labour. It is important that when labour commences, or should the birth become overdue, you cut and remove the thread to prevent it impeding birth. Do not worry if there is some confusion over 'dates', cutting the thread will not actually induce labour.

☀ CHILDBIRTH ☀

Magic to ensure safe childbirth should ideally take place about a month before the child is due. Don't worry if nature then expedites things, it is not your magic which has caused it!

You will need:

A SMALL PIECE OF AMBER, GROUND IN A PESTLE AND MORTAR AND ADDED TO
  YOUR INCENSE, OR AMBER-SCENTED INCENSE
A PIECE OF AMBER WHICH IS ROUNDED, WITHOUT ROUGH EDGES
A GOLD OR ORANGE PIECE OF CLOTH
WHERE YOU HAVE A FITH-FATH FOR THIS PERSON IT SHOULD BE PLACED ON
  THE ALTAR

This Ritual should be performed in the three days immediately after the Full Moon.

Mix the ground Amber well into a little of your incense, and burn as usual. Invite the Goddess as Mother and the God as All Father. Consecrate,* but do not name, the piece of Amber through the Elements, asking that it be a talisman for the safe birth of the child. Next raise energy* whilst holding the piece of Amber. Instead of directing it out towards your intent, focus on pouring the energy you raise into the Amber. Next hold it up towards the Goddess and the God and say,

'I call upon the Mother Goddess and the All Father God to add their strength to this token, that she who it is made for might be delivered safely of a healthy child.'

Visualize the Goddess and the God reaching out to touch the Amber and adding their power. When you feel sure that this has happened, say,

'May the might of the Old Ones protect and strengthen both. May the love of the Goddess and the God be with them in the time to come. May they be safe and whole and brought swiftly to health and strength, home and family. Blessed Be.'

Wrap the Amber in the cloth, to be given to the mother-to-be.

Ideally the Amber would be worn or held by the mother during the birth. However, these days most births take place in hospital and the medical staff tend to remove jewellery and to discourage the 'patient' from holding or carrying anything. In this case, the Amber can be held by a 'birthing partner', who can keep it near to the mother-to-be, or it can be placed in the 'hospital bag' with all the other things considered necessary.

If the woman who you are working for cannot for any reason be given the Amber then either place it on the fith-fath or keep it safe for her.

Obviously, where you performed the spell for safe pregnancy, you will also need to cut the thread on the fith-fath at the time the baby is due or when labour starts. This does not need to be done as part of a Ritual, or in Circle, but should be done with the intent in mind. Interestingly, the morning I started labour the first thing I noticed was that the thread had fallen off my image of its own volition.

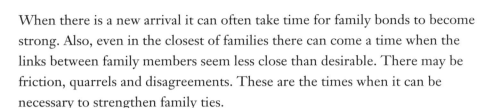

TO STRENGTHEN BONDS
WITH BABIES AND CHILDREN

When there is a new arrival it can often take time for family bonds to become strong. Also, even in the closest of families there can come a time when the links between family members seem less close than desirable. There may be friction, quarrels and disagreements. These are the times when it can be necessary to strengthen family ties.

This is a 'kitchen Ritual' so you will not be creating your Sacred Space in the same way as usual. Instead you should mentally invoke the elements and invite the Goddess and the God, perhaps in a short meditation which you perform before you start.

At, or just after, the New Moon you will need to make a cake or something similar which can be divided to share amongst the family. Select a recipe which will be enjoyed by everyone, although very small babies will not, of course, be actually eating it. Into this, in addition to the usual ingredients, you will need to add a pinch of saffron, 3 drops of rose water and a silver or gold ring which has been carefully washed and rinsed under running water (don't worry, you get this back later!). If you are concerned that someone may bite or even swallow the ring then place it at the bottom of your cake tin so that it can be removed after cooking but before eating.

Whilst making the cake you should think about each of the family members in turn and focus on them relating to one another with tolerance, love and happiness. As you blend the ingredients be sure to only stir, beat or whisk, in a clockwise direction. Once the recipe is complete add the pinch of saffron saying,

'This is the golden Sun of the fields which brings strength and fertility to the land. May it bring warmth of feeling to us all, even as the Sun God brings his love to us. Blessed Be.'

Then add the 3 drops of Rose water, saying,

'These drops are as the rain which falls on the land for the growth and fertility of all life. May they refresh our love, bring tolerance and enhance wisdom for each of us, even as the aspects of the Triple Goddess give their love to us. Blessed Be.'

Stir your cake three more times clockwise, saying,

'Even as the ingredients in this dish become bonded together may the bonds in this family be strengthened. As we eat of it may it sustain our love each for the others. Blessed Be.'

Just before placing the mixture in the tin put the ring into the centre of it, saying,

'This ring is as the Circle of our family. It is placed at the bottom, for it is as the base from which we spring, and in the middle, for it is as the centre of our hearts where we care for one another. Blessed Be.'

The cake should then be cooked according to its recipe, and then the ring removed if you prefer not to leave it until the cake has been eaten.

Where possible, gather the whole family together to eat the cake. As you cut it say (I would suggest in your head unless everyone is aware of why you are doing this!),

'I call upon the Goddess and the God to strengthen our bonds and our love for each other. May all who share this be united. Blessed Be.'

Then eat and enjoy!

Very small babies cannot, of course, eat cake, so take a little and wrap it in a tissue and place it under the baby's mattress, where he or she cannot get at it, and leave it overnight. Remember to remove it in the morning!

FOR INCREASED PATIENCE!

As a mother, and also as a daughter and sister, I am only too aware that patience is one of those essentials for a happy family which can often be in short supply. Our lives are busy and often we bring home attitudes which, whilst fine in the workplace to get the job done, treat our near and dear with less consideration than we would hope for. It is one thing to expect a fellow worker to only need telling once, it is quite another thing to expect your toddler to spring into action when they feel that playing is far more important and interesting than cleaning their teeth! Similarly, a fascinating event on your favourite TV programme can make you less than enthusiastic about doing the washing in order that everyone has a clean shirt.

The following Ritual is in two parts; one where you are working for 'now' and the second so that you can tap into the spell whenever you need to. If you are going through a particularly trying time, you might want to refresh the magic every month by repeating the whole Ritual.

In advance of your magic you will need to collect some rainwater and leave it on your windowsill in the light of the Full Moon for one night.

You will also need:

> 1 WHITE CANDLE
>
> SOME YLANG-YLANG OIL
>
> 1 LENGTH OF WHITE THREAD, ABOUT 1 FOOT (30 CM) LONG
>
> SCISSORS
>
> 1 CLEAR CRYSTAL ON A THREAD – THE KIND SOLD AS WINDOW CRYSTALS OR
>   RAINBOW MAKERS ARE EXCELLENT. THOROUGHLY CLEANSE* BEFORE USE
>
> THE PREPARED RAINWATER
>
> TWO BOWLS OR DISHES

This Ritual should be performed at, or just after, the New Moon for preference, but you can do it at any phase of the Moon except the last quarter.

Once your Sacred Space* is created, use some of the rainwater and perform the Rite of Banishing Unwanted Influences* and focus on your impatience draining away into the bowl.

Next, using a separate dish of the rainwater, do a Self-Blessing.*
Now consecrate* your candle and anoint it with one or two drops of the oil, saying,

'I call upon the Goddess and the God to bring me strength of purpose. Let me have patience with those I love, send me a listening ear and time to hear with it, give me a sympathetic mind and a tolerant heart. Above all let me see more clearly the good things I have, the kindness and love of those around me. Blessed Be.'

Take the white thread and tie it once around the candle about one third of the way down from the wick. Knot the thread three times saying with each knot,

'This first is my ears, let them hear clearly. This second is my eyes, let them see clearly. This last is my heart, may it ever be open to those I love.'

Cut the thread close to the knots, leaving only a single thread tied around the candle, and say, *'Blessed Be.'*

Next, light the candle from your Altar candle and say,

'As this flame burns let it cleanse and purify. May it bring light to illuminate and warmth to heal. Blessed Be.'

Place the candle in a safe place and be sure to keep a careful eye on it to ensure that the thread burns through safely.

Now consecrate* the crystal through the elements and hold it up to the Goddess and the God, saying,

'I call upon the Goddess and the God to lend me their aid. Let this shine as a symbol of my love for my family, may it remove all obstacles to our happiness, and may it give me the strength to be patient and understanding. Blessed Be.'

After the Ritual hang the crystal in one of the family rooms of the house, preferably in a south-facing window so that it will catch the light. Whenever you feel yourself becoming impatient go to your crystal and (in your head) ask the Goddess and the God to bring you calm and to strengthen your control. Please remember to polish the crystal regularly to keep it shining brightly.

PROBLEMS OF COMMUNICATION I

As with the above spell, even in the best of families there are times when communication goes wrong, or ceases to happen at all! It can sometimes be helpful to remember that when talking to strangers we are careful to be clear and concise about what we say, but within the family we often talk in a kind of 'domestic shorthand' which can lead to misunderstandings. Also, within the family we often let our manners slip and 'forget our Ps and Qs'. Whilst you don't want to be overly formal in family life, you might sometimes want to consider whether you would treat a stranger as badly as you sometimes do your near and dear!

This is another spell in two parts; the first is to work for yourself and the second to work on the rest of the family.

You will need:

> 5 BEADS WITH REASONABLY LARGE HOLES, ONE IN EACH OF THE FOLLOWING COLOURS: YELLOW, RED, BLUE, GREEN AND PURPLE
> SEVERAL LENGTHS OF THREAD ABOUT 3 FEET (1 M) IN LENGTH; ONE FOR EACH PERSON IN YOUR FAMILY, IN COLOURS WHICH REMIND YOU OF THE INDIVIDUALS. PLAIT OR TWIST THE THREADS TO MAKE A SINGLE STRAND
> A SMALL PURSE, POUCH OR OTHER 'CONTAINER' WHICH YOU CAN CARRY AT ALL TIMES
> SEVERAL FEATHERS, THE SAME NUMBER AS THE NUMBER OF FAMILY MEMBERS

Consecrate the beads as follows:

Take the yellow one and pass it through the incense smoke and say,

'I do consecrate thee with Air, that my thoughts and words be clear. Blessed Be.'

Thread it onto your combined strand (you may find that dipping the end into some melted wax and rolling it between your finger and thumb makes it easier to pass through the beads).

Pass the red one through the candle flame and say,

'I do consecrate thee with Fire, that my passions not rule my mind and tongue. Blessed Be.'

Add to the thread. Dip the blue in the water and say,

'I do consecrate thee with Water, that my emotions be clearly expressed. Blessed Be.'

Add to the thread. Sprinkle the green with salt and say,

'I do consecrate thee with Earth, that I might remain grounded in reality. Blessed Be.'

Add to the thread. Hold the purple up to the Goddess and the God and say,

'I ask the blessing of the Goddess and the God that their Spirit might be with me and bring me balance. Blessed Be.'

Add this last to the thread and then knot it into a circle.

Hold the whole ring of beads up to the Goddess and the God and say,

'These threads are as us, linked together by the elements, which unite all. As Earth and Air, Fire and Water are in balance, so are they awakened by the Spirit. Let the Goddess and the God awaken the Spirit in each of us to bring us closer in unity and understanding. Blessed Be.'

Place it into your pouch and carry it with you at all times.

Now take the feathers, consecrate* them in the usual way, asking that, as representations of air and thought, they might improve communication.

After your Ritual place one feather in the bedroom of each person. When placing objects of this kind I find that the best place is either over the doorway, so that the effects will be reinforced every time someone passes under it, or close to the head of a person's bed so that it can work during sleep.

Whenever you feel that there are problems in communication take hold of your circlet of beads and, by running your fingers over the beads, invoke the elements whilst focusing on the people represented by the threads.

COMMUNICATION II

A second way to address problems of communication is rather more direct, but no less 'Witchy' for that. If you and another have an issue which you feel needs to be addressed, then you need to get together to talk about it. One of the better ways to do this is to arrange a meeting between you. Ask them when would be a suitable time for a chat, a time when both of you can expect to be undisturbed and when neither will be in a hurry to be somewhere else. Give them some idea of why you wish to talk, after all, you've had time to prepare your thoughts. Ensure that you are prepared, give thought to what you feel the problem is and how you would like it resolved. Make sure that you use 'I' statements rather than 'you' ones; for example, *'I feel sad when you talk to me like that,'* rather than, *'You make me upset when …'*.

To aid you in your discussions make up a magical oil to aid communication:

    3 DROPS LAVENDER, FOR HEALING

    2 DROPS NEROLI, FOR A TRANQUIL ATMOSPHERE

    2 DROPS SANDALWOOD, FOR EXPRESSION

    2 DROPS YLANG-YLANG, FOR CONFIDENCE

Blend these together and then, in a Sacred Space, consecrate* them as an aid to communication. The oil can be used in an oil burner, if you are sure both parties will find that acceptable, or you can wear it.

STUDY, WORK AND CAREER

As has been said many times before; you should be careful what you wish for and it is never a good idea to work magic for money. Money is not a concept found in nature and therefore not one on which natural magic will readily work. If you work magic for money you could find that you inherit it from a loved one, or that you obtain it through insurance and need it to replace the damaged object. Similarly, it can be risky to work magic for success in an exam or a job interview, for there is no use in a qualification you cannot support with knowledge or in a job which subsequently turns out to be one you are unhappy in. However, there are other ways of addressing these areas:

 STUDY

This is not just limited to exams at school and college. As we go through life there are many times we may need to understand and learn new subjects. It could be related to work, perhaps towards a promotion, or home life; setting up a new computer or even programming an unfamiliar heating system. It could even be understanding a new area of the Craft. At any time when you need to be able to dismiss distractions, focus with a clear mind, understand new concepts and retain information, use the following which can be prepared in advance.

You will need to collect some rainwater, about ¼ pint (150 ml), and then place this in a clear, spotlessly clean jar overnight in the light of the Full Moon. Add a handful of clean, crushed Rosemary leaves, fresh is best. Label and store in a cool dark place. If you are using fresh Rosemary then you can use the stems from which the leaves came to make an Asperger *(see Appendix 2, Terms and Definitions)*.

For your Ritual you will need:

> THE ROSEMARY WATER
>
> THE ASPERGER
>
> A SPRIG OF FRESH ROSEMARY

Your Ritual should take place at, or within the week following, the New Moon, preferably on a Wednesday. If possible, perform the Ritual in the area in which you would normally study.

First, perform the Rite of Banishing Unwanted Influences.* If you have not already done so consecrate* your Asperger. Then consecrate* through the elements both your Rosemary water and sprig of Rosemary, focusing on driving out distractions, bringing a clear mind, and on having a strong memory. (Not for nothing is the saying 'Rosemary for remembrance'.) Note that when consecrating liquids it is perfectly acceptable to keep them within their container! Next, hold each up to the Goddess and the God and say,

'I call upon the Goddess and the God to aid me in my study of … (name the subject/s). Bring me a fresh and focused mind, aid my understanding and my memory. Blessed Be.'

This can be made in advance and stored, in a cool dark place, for up to three months in which case you might prefer to ask the Goddess and God to aid you in all studies rather than naming a specific subject.

If you have been able to create your Sacred Space in your study area then use the Asperger to lightly sprinkle some of the Rosemary water around the outer edges of the area before removing your Sacred Space, being careful to move Deosil at all times. Whilst Aspersing, say,

'I cleanse this area from all distractions that it might be a place of focus and concentration, a place of understanding and of knowledge. Blessed Be.'

Be very careful not to sprinkle any electric outlets or equipment! If you cannot perform your magic in your study area then complete the Ritual in the usual way and then Asperge your study area. Alternatively you can Asperge books, writing implements, etc. which you take to study elsewhere. Repeat the Asperging each time you are about to commence learning, or once a day, whichever is less. Each time you start studying, place the consecrated sprig of Rosemary on your desk, wear it or carry it about your person.

Remember, magic can never replace real work in the real world, it can only enhance the effort you are prepared to put in.

EXAMS AND TESTS, PRESENTATIONS AND PUBLIC SPEAKING

Just like study, exams and tests go on into our adult lives. Even if you never take up a formal area of study after school you may find there are other times when you know your knowledge is going to be tested, perhaps in Rites of Initiation to the Craft! There may also be occasions when you are called upon to display your knowledge and, however accustomed or well prepared you may be, you may feel the need to ensure that your knowledge and confidence are boosted.

For this Ritual you will need:

> A SMALL POUCH OR BAG TIED WITH, OR MADE OF A MATERIAL CONTAINING,
>   GOLD THREADS
> A SMALL SPRIG OF ROSEMARY (IF YOU PERFORMED THE ABOVE SPELL THEN YOU
>   CAN USE THE SAME SPRIG)
> A SPRIG OF BASIL, OR A FEW LEAVES
> A SUNSTONE

This Ritual should be performed at, or just before, the Full Moon, and preferably on a Sunday.

SpELLS AND MAGICS

When Creating the Sacred Space,* invite the Goddess in all her aspects as Maiden, Mother and Crone, invite the God as the Sun King. Whilst raising energy* ensure that you focus only on success, do not allow even the tiniest thought of failure to enter your mind. Consecrate* the herbs, stone and pouch through the elements, then place the herbs and stone within the pouch and secure. Now hold the pouch up to the Goddess and the God saying,

'I call upon the Triple Goddess, I call upon the Sun King, bring clarity to my mind, let me recall all that is needful to succeed in … (name the test/event or whatever). May my work be as a testament to my love for them and their support of me. Blessed Be.'

Keep the pouch in a safe place until you need it, then take it with you. Whenever you feel you need help, touch it and recall the Ritual you performed.

Just before any test or examination perform a Self-Blessing.* If you do not have the time or space to do this in full, simply close your eyes and visualize yourself performing the Rite.

 FINDING A JOB

Bearing in mind what I said at the start of this section you really shouldn't work magic for a specific job, but rather for one in which you will be happy and in which you can succeed. I can say this with some authority as I did once do just that and found myself doing work I hated under circumstances which made me seriously unhappy and at times quite ill! So, the first thing to do is to rid yourself of any preconceived ideas about which job you want and focus instead on which things you enjoy in your working life.

Prior to your Ritual take a sheet of paper and make two lists, one of the things you like or want in your working life, the other of the things you want to avoid. Try to remember the peripheral things which can make or break; colleagues you can get on with, ease of travel, meeting people, shift patterns, overtime, etc. Take your time over this, perhaps doing it over several days. Once it is completed, write it out neatly onto a single sheet with two columns: likes and dislikes. It's not essential, but I always find it helpful to place something like this under my pillow for a night as it can often help to prompt the mind.

In the week preceding your Ritual collect two or three 'Situations Vacant' pages from the magazines or papers which cover your general field of interest.

You will need:

> YOUR SHEET OF LIKES AND DISLIKES
>
> THE 'SITUATIONS VACANT' PAGES YOU COLLECTED
>
> A SHORT LENGTH OF THREAD
>
> A PURPLE CORD ABOUT 3 FEET IN LENGTH
>
> SOME ANOINTING OIL

This Ritual is best performed on a Thursday during the Waxing Moon.

After creating the Sacred Space* take the cord and, starting at one end, place a series of single knots in it saying,

For the first knot: *'With this knot I will hear of the work I seek. Blessed Be.'*
For the second knot: *'With this knot I will make a good application. Blessed Be.'*
For the third knot: *'With this knot my application will bring an interview. Blessed Be.'*
For the fourth knot: *'With this knot my interview will bring an offer. Blessed Be.'*
For the fifth knot: *'With this knot the offer will be acceptable. Blessed Be.'*
For the sixth knot: *'With this knot the job will be mine. Blessed Be.'*
For the seventh knot: *'With this knot the work will be all I hope for. Blessed Be.'*

As you make each knot take a moment to visualize that step actually taking place. The knots do not need to be evenly spaced, indeed you should be left with a long unknotted 'tail' so that you can identify which end is which.

Take your sheet of likes and dislikes and the 'Situations Vacant' pages, roll them into a tube and secure with the thread. Wrap the cord around the papers, do not knot it again.

Now consecrate* the whole in the usual way. Place it in the centre of the Circle and raise power* whilst, once again, visualizing each of the steps taking place. When you feel that enough energy has been raised, hold the papers with the cord wrapped around them up to the Goddess and the God and say,

'I call upon the Goddess and the God to bring me success in my enterprise, may they grant me work in which I can be happy and successful, as well as rewards from that work which will meet my needs. As is my will so mote it be. Blessed Be.'

After your Ritual put this in a safe place. As each of the steps come to pass, take it out and untie the knot which relates to it, starting at the end without a long tail. When you actually start work, you can take the papers and cord and dispose of them by burning or burying.

 INTERVIEWS

Whilst the above spell contains a step relating to interview you still might like
to reinforce your magic at this time.

You will need:

A SUNSTONE

A PIECE OF AMBER

3 YELLOW CANDLES AND HOLDERS

SOME BASE OIL, ALMOND OR SIMILAR

ESSENTIAL OILS OF SANDALWOOD, FRANKINCENSE, ROSEMARY AND JASMINE

A SMALL BOTTLE (TO PLACE YOUR BLENDED OILS INTO)

This Ritual is ideally performed at the Waxing or Full Moon, but you may find
that you don't always get enough advance notice for this to be possible. In this
case perform the Ritual anyway but when you Cast the Circle* visualize the Full
Moon as strongly as you can. If the Waxing or Full Moon occur after the
interview but before you find out how you did, repeat the Ritual at that time.
The first part of the Ritual needs to be performed in the bathroom, the second
part can be done anywhere (within a Sacred Space), but you may as well do
both in the bathroom. This is a Ritual bath, not one where you need to wash or
perform other acts of personal hygiene or physical maintenance!

Having secured undisturbed use of the bathroom, gather your Altar equipment, tools and the above 'ingredients', and create your Sacred Space* as usual. Run a moderately warm bath, add 3 drops of each of the oils, the Sunstone and the Amber. Light the three candles and place them as best you can around the bath. Draw an invoking Pentagram *(see Appendix 2, Terms and Definitions)* over the water and say,

'I call upon the Goddess and the God to bless and consecrate these waters that they bring me confidence and allow me to give of my best. Blessed Be.'

Undress and get into the water, immerse yourself completely (head under the water too) three times, saying,

'May the Goddess and the God watch over me, may they guard, guide and protect me in the ordeal to come. Blessed Be.'

Now spend a little longer in the water and meditate on the forthcoming event, visualize yourself entering the room, meeting the interviewer(s), answering and asking questions, and making a good impression. When you feel that you have fully rehearsed a successful interview get out of the water, dry yourself and move on to the next step.

NB: remember to remove the stones before pulling the plug to stop them disappearing down the drain!

Into the small bottle place 2 drops Sandalwood, 2 drops Frankincense, 2 drops Rosemary, and 1 drop Jasmine oils. Add approx. 20 ml of the base oil. Seal the bottle and shake well to mix. Consecrate* the oil and put to one side.

On the morning of your interview perform a Self-Blessing* using the oil you consecrated in the above step. Use only a few drops otherwise you will smell too strongly! If you are, or may be pregnant do not apply this oil to the skin, place a drop on a tissue and keep it in your pocket.

 PROMOTION

Before you set out to try to achieve a promotion give careful thought to whether you really do want the added responsibility and associated grief, as well as the extra money and recognition of your ability! Also give serious thought to whether you really are doing as well as you would like to think. Sometimes it can be easy to let your desire for something cloud your judgement as to whether it really is your due. If, however, you honestly feel that you have been overlooked, or that the time is overdue, then use the following.

In advance of your Ritual list all the qualities required for the position you seek; try to put yourself in the shoes of the person in charge of giving the promotion. Write these out neatly on some gold paper or card. Review the list to see which skills, abilities and attributes you possess, and which you need to work on. Make a separate note of the things you need to work on and place it where you can read it *every* morning. Don't just put it there, make a point of reading it every morning, and of trying, during the day, to achieve the things you have written!

You will also need to make your own incense from:

2 PARTS FRANKINCENSE

I PART BASIL

I PART CINNAMON

I PART NUTMEG

A PINCH OF SAFFRON

Grind these together in a pestle and mortar and place into a jar with a piece of real gold (a ring or other piece of jewellery is fine). Leave on a windowsill day and night for a full Lunar cycle (29 days), then remove the gold and store it in a cool dark place until you need it.

Your Ritual should take place on a Sunday during the second quarter of the Moon, that is, in the week before the Full Moon.

You will need:

> THE LIST OF REQUIRED ATTRIBUTES ON GOLD PAPER
>
> 1 GOLD CANDLE
>
> 1 GOLD COIN (TAKE A 'COPPER' ONE AND SHINE IT UNTIL IT GLEAMS LIKE GOLD)
>
> YOUR INCENSE (SEE ABOVE), SELF-IGNITING CHARCOAL AND A THURIBLE
>
> A FIREPROOF DISH

During your Ritual use the incense you have made, ensuring that it is burning from beginning to end of your working. Once your Sacred Space has been created, take the paper and consecrate* it through the elements, then hold it up to the Goddess and the God and say,

'I call upon the Goddess and the God to bring about these skills, attributes and this knowledge in me. May they strengthen and enhance all that is needful. Blessed Be.'

Consecrate* the candle in the usual way and light it, saying,

'Gold is the colour of the Sun. May this candle draw the strength and fire of the Sun to me. May the Sun God who brings life and warmth to the land shine his light upon me that my skills might likewise shine and be seen. Blessed Be.'

Now take the paper and light it with the candle. Place it in the fireproof dish to burn away completely. Keep the ashes.

Next, take the coin, consecrate* it through the elements using both the Altar candle and the Gold candle when you get to Fire. Hold it up to the Goddess and the God and say,

'I call upon the Goddess and the God to bless this coin, a token of success. If I am ready, may the Goddess and the God lend their power to draw success to me, to bring me closer to that which is rightfully mine. Blessed Be.'

Remember to allow the Gold candle to burn all the way down, but keep the stub.

After your Ritual carry the coin with you until the Full Moon. On the night of the Full Moon take the candle stub and bury it in the ground, saying,

'From Fire to Earth do I return thee. As is my will so mote it be. Blessed Be.'

Take the coin and cast it into running water (a river, stream or the sea), saying,

'From Earth to Water do I return thee. As is my will so mote it be. Blessed Be.'

Take the ashes from your burnt paper and throw them into the wind over the water and say,

'From Earth through Fire to Air and Water I send thee. As is my will so mote it be. Blessed Be.'

DIFFICULTIES WITH EMPLOYERS

Aside from feeling overdue for promotion there are other difficulties you can experience with your employers, particularly individual supervisors or managers. These may be due to your actions and/or behaviour, in which case the solution lies in personal honesty, responsibility and change. However, some problems are not solely down to the individual, but rather other factors. These might include ingrained prejudice, previous bad experience, pressure from above, problems at home, and so forth. In most cases the root of the problem lies in the manager not seeing the worker clearly, and indeed vice versa.

You will need:

> A SMALL MIRROR WITH A HANDLE
>
> A BLACK CANDLE
>
> A CLOTH OR DUSTER THAT YOU WILL NOT NEED TO USE AGAIN

This Ritual is best performed on a Waning Moon before the Dark of the Moon.

Place the black candle in the centre of the Altar and light it, saying,

'Black is the colour which covers all. Black is the dark which obscures. Black is darkness in which nothing can be seen clearly.'

Take the mirror and hold it over the candle in such a way that soot from the flame forms on the glass; keep doing this until the mirror glass is covered. Try to avoid burning your fingers! Name* the mirror describing it as the unclear vision that both parties have of each other.

Take the cloth and, whilst visualizing grey gauzy veils dropping from sight, clean the mirror with the cloth. Start at the centre and, using a Deosil circular rubbing action, work towards the outer edges. Whilst you are cleaning chant over and again,

'Away with shadows. Bring clear sight.'

Once you are sure that the mirror is thoroughly clean, name* it again, this time calling it the clear sight of both to see one another truly.

If it is possible, take the mirror to work with you and place it at your work station. If that is not acceptable then keep it at home near the door so that you can touch it every day as you leave for work.

GOSSIP AND RUMOUR

Sometimes it is not so much a question of not knowing enough about someone, but of being told too much. The workplace is often a place where rumour and gossip abound and it can be difficult to sort the truth from the information. The first step towards this involves giving it some really serious thought; are you reacting to what is, or to what you have been told? For example, if John says he dislikes the way you speak to him, then that is most probably the way he feels, but if Annie told you that's what John feels you have no way of knowing whether that is the way she perceives how he feels or whether he really does feel it. Put it another way; when the car doesn't start you might say, 'Oh I hate this car,' when you really mean, 'I wish the wretched thing would start'! Someone reporting your comment might well place the emphasis on what you said, rather than on what you meant. Many problems between individuals are caused by another 'helpful soul' adding their two-pennyworth! As it is often difficult to work out exactly who is the root cause of this sort of problem, you are better off working to stop the gossip rather than trying to influence an individual.

You will need a piece of polished Haematite. As you will be taking this to your workplace you might like to find one in a piece of jewellery, on a key ring, or in some other form convenient to carry.

This Ritual takes the form of a meditation within the Sacred Space and should take place at the Full Moon.

After creating your Sacred Space* perform the Rite of Banishing Unwanted Influences,* visualizing all difficulties draining into the water. Then perform a Self-Blessing.*

Consecrate* the Haematite in the usual way. Sitting in the centre of your Circle take the Haematite in your weak hand and place your strong hand over it. Close your eyes and visualize your workplace with everyone in it. It can help if you pick a recent day and run through the events in your mind. Now add to the scene by visualizing thoughts and words as small grey shadows flitting around the room. Next add yourself holding the stone to the scene, and picture the stone working as a magnet in reverse, driving the shadows away from you towards a window or door. Visualize this as strongly as you can, and hold the image for a couple of minutes. Now picture the people behaving well towards you, smiling and being friendly. Concentrate on this image for a few minutes. When you feel sure that the magic has taken effect, place the stone on the Altar and complete your Ritual.

Remember to take the Haematite into work with you every day. As magic rarely works instantly, you will need to be careful not to react to, or in any way encourage by paying attention to, any further instances of gossip or rumour.

PROTECTION AND DEFENCE

Contrary to the view of some people, we do not live in a world full of hidden demons, psychic attacks and vengeful black magicians bent on making life uncomfortable. If you are silly enough to have really upset a fellow Witch they are more likely to simply ignore you, or give you piece of their mind, rather than set out on a course of revenge. They too will follow the Rede and be aware of the Law of Threefold Return! However, some things do leave residual traces of negativity which can affect you and your magic. For example, extreme passions, violent tempers, and so on. In addition, life itself can be fairly hazardous and there is certainly no harm in taking the time and energy to give yourself a bit of magical protection against potential harm.

HOUSE (AREA) CLEANSING

Whenever you move into a new home it is a good idea to thoroughly cleanse it of all energies. You can never be sure of the lives of previous occupants and the energies they may have left behind them. If you can, perform this Ritual before you move your possessions in, as it makes it easier to cover all the ground. Otherwise, perform it as soon as you can. You may also like to use this Ritual to cleanse your home, or a room, if something highly emotional, like a serious argument, has taken place.

In advance of your Ritual collect about a pint of natural water: rain-, river- or seawater. Place this in the light of the Full Moon for three nights.

You will need:

YOUR NATURAL WATER
AN ASPERGER
SOME SALT (UNLESS YOU COLLECTED SEAWATER)
A BESOM OR NEW HOUSEHOLD BROOM

This Ritual can be performed at any phase of the Moon.

Create the Sacred Space* in the usual way but do not cast a Circle. First, take your broom and from the centre of the house sweep outwards, moving Deosil. As you sweep, visualize the broom sweeping not just dirt and dust, but also old thoughts and feelings and any energies left behind.

Next, mix a teaspoon of salt into the natural water (unless it is seawater). Take the Asperger and sprinkle the salted water around the house, again starting at the centre and moving Deosil outwards. Try to lightly sprinkle the whole floor area, but without soaking any carpets! As you go keep repeating,

'Pure salt and pure water, drive all negativity away. Pure salt and pure water, purify this home today.'

After you have done all the floors, take the Asperger and sprinkle a few drops on each windowsill and the doorsteps of any external doors. Any leftover water should be poured away just outside the main entrance to your home or, if you are in a flat, the main entrance to the building.

You might like to combine this Ritual with the next, for household protection.

HOUSE PROTECTION

The purpose of this Ritual is to protect your home, everyone and everything in it, from harm and also from the intrusion of external influences, such as other people's negative thoughts.

You will need:

> SOME IRON FILINGS (IF YOU CANNOT GET THESE THEN USE ROCK SALT
>   CRYSTALS)

This Ritual is best performed at the Full Moon.

If you are performing this immediately after the above Protection spell then the next step is to Cast your Circle.* If you are doing this on its own then Create your Sacred Space* as usual.

Once the Circle is Cast, stand in the centre and visualize the Circle expanding and growing until it envelops your whole property: home, garden and any other external areas. Mentally anchor the Circle at the edges of your property. Now take the iron filings (or rock salt crystals) and, walking Deosil, sprinkle them around the edge of your property. If you live in a home adjoining another, then you will have to use the internal walls for some of your boundary. Where you have to go back on yourself to pass through a doorway, do not sprinkle until you resume the external boundary. Oh, and don't climb through the windows, you'll only look foolish!

When you Take down your Circle,* visualize part of the Circle detaching itself and remaining on the boundary. Every Full Moon spend a few minutes, not as part of any other Ritual, mentally strengthening the Circle on your boundary, by visualizing yourself walking it and sprinkling the iron filings (or rock salt).

TRANSPORT (CARS, BIKES, ETC)

An extension of our homes which cannot easily be included in the above is our personal transport, whether it be car, bike or motorcycle. A fairly common mistake is to perform a general spell of protection, but unfortunately this can result in a kind of invisibility which means that other road users simply do not see you as well as they should! If you find yourself wanting to scream, 'What's wrong with you? Can't you see me?' at other road users, then you should make a point of cleansing your vehicle with salt and water as in the House Cleansing spell. It may be that you, a previous owner, or even a kindly disposed friend has wrought the wrong kind of spell by mistake.

You will need:

> A CIRCLE OF VIOLET CLOTH
>
> A VIOLET CORD
>
> 1 ½ TSP ROSEMARY LEAVES
>
> 1 TSP JUNIPER BERRIES
>
> 1 TSP BASIL LEAVES
>
> ½ TSP FENNEL SEEDS
>
> ½ TSP ROCK SALT CRYSTALS
>
> 2 DROPS OF PEPPERMINT OIL

This spell should be worked at the Full Moon.

Take all the herbs and salt and place in the centre of the violet cloth, then add the oil. Gather the edges up and tie the bundle with the cord. Consecrate* this in the usual way, asking that it bring security and safety to all who travel in (or on, in the case of motorcycles and bikes) your vehicle. Also ask that it might bring security and mechanical health to your vehicle.

Place the bundle in your vehicle or, if on two wheels, carry it on your person whenever you travel.

 TRAVEL AND RETURN

Since mankind began to move from one place to another, Witches and their counterparts have been creating Talismans for protection. Even the Christian church, which claims to eschew magic, has its Saint Christopher! And it's not just protection – there are many quaint customs performed to ensure the safe return of loved ones from their travels; from the stones kept by the wives of sailors, to pieces of a loved one's hair worn in a locket.

You will need:

> A DARK PURPLE OR INDIGO CLOTH
>
> A WHITE CORD
>
> ½ TSP BASIL LEAVES
>
> ½ TSP FENNEL SEEDS
>
> ½ TSP ROSEMARY LEAVES
>
> ½ TSP MUSTARD SEEDS
>
> I LARGE PINCH COARSE SALT
>
> I SMALL CLEAR QUARTZ CRYSTAL

Make this Talisman up in the same way as the above Ritual, and carry on your travels or give to your loved one. To ensure their safe return to you, add a lock of your hair to the bag.

To ensure someone's safe return home, place a lock of their hair (this need not be cut but can be taken from their hairbrush) under the doormat. Say as you do so,

'I call upon the Goddess and the God to bring … (person's name) safely home to this place. Blessed Be.'

☀ INDIVIDUALS ☀

Regrettably, we live in a time when it is not always safe to walk the streets. Now magic is no substitute for common sense, so don't forget to take sensible precautions, or advise your near and dear to do so, in addition to the following.

You will need:

> A PIECE OF JEWELLERY BELONGING TO, OR TO BE GIVEN TO, THE PERSON YOU ARE WORKING FOR. IT SHOULD BE SOMETHING THAT THE RECIPIENT WILL WEAR OFTEN. YOU COULD EVEN USE A SAINT CHRISTOPHER!
> ESSENTIAL OILS OF BLACK PEPPER, JASMINE AND FRANKINCENSE

This is best performed at the Full Moon.

Consecrate* the jewellery as a token of protection, then anoint it with the oils and hold it up to the Goddess and the God, saying,

'I call upon the Goddess and the God to bless this Talisman of protection. May it keep … (name) safe and well in all they do. May the Goddess and the God watch over them, guard them, guide them and keep them from all trials and dangers. Blessed Be.'

UNDER 'ATTACK'/NEGATIVE INFLUENCES

As I said above a person is extremely unlikely to be under any kind of 'psychic attack', although it does seem to be an increasing perception, probably because of the availability of dubious information on the subject. However, negative influences can have a very real effect on our lives: at its simplest, if someone tells you repeatedly that you are clumsy you will drop things in their presence, even if you otherwise wouldn't. Less obviously, if you sense that someone dislikes you, or perhaps is envious, this negativity can have an effect; even if you are not overtly aware of their feelings your subconscious mind may pick up on it.

It is worth mentioning that, as a practising Witch, you may be approached to perform this sort of magic for another. Please be very wary, as feelings of being under attack can sometimes indicate mental or physical imbalance and you do not want to aggravate someone's condition. If you are at all in doubt, gently refuse on the grounds that you do not work this kind of spell, and as tactfully as possible suggest that they see their doctor as there are many physical conditions which can give rise to a feeling of being overlooked.

Here are two spells which can be performed; the first for general negativity, the second where you know who is thinking negatively about you. Please remember in the latter case to make sure that you address any problems between you. If this is, say, because of a boundary dispute, then whilst the magic may mitigate the effects of negativity, the feelings will still remain until the dispute is resolved.

TO COUNTER GENERAL NEGATIVITY

You will need:

A NUMBER OF SMALL MIRRORS, SUFFICIENT TO HAVE ONE FACING EACH
DIRECTION THAT THE WINDOWS OR DOORS OF YOUR HOUSE FACE

This Ritual can be performed at any phase of the Moon, but will work best at
the Full or Waning Moon.

**First, perform the Rite of Banishing Unwanted Influences.* Next consecrate* the
mirrors through the elements asking that they might reflect all negativity. Then
hold them up to the Goddess and the God, saying,**

*'I call upon the Goddess and the God to bless these, that they might deflect and reflect all
negativity. I also ask that the Goddess and the God might make me aware of any way in which I
might have attracted this negativity, and that I might be able to set right any wrongs. Blessed Be.'*

After your Ritual place each mirror, facing outwards, in a window facing each direction.
For most houses this will be a maximum of four.

WHERE YOU SUSPECT A PARTICULAR PERSON

You will need:

A PICTURE OF THAT PERSON (DRAW ONE IF YOU DO NOT HAVE A PHOTO)
TWO MIRRORS OF EQUAL SIZE
A BLACK CLOTH, LARGE ENOUGH TO WRAP BOTH MIRRORS
A BLACK CORD, LONG ENOUGH TO TIE AROUND THE BUNDLE

This Ritual should be performed at the Waning Moon, preferably just before the Dark of the Moon, and on a Saturday.

Perform the Rite of Banishing Unwanted Influences.* Consecrate* the mirrors that they might deflect all negative thoughts. Name* the picture for the person you feel is thinking negatively of you. Place the picture between the mirrors with their reflecting surfaces facing inwards. Wrap the mirrors and picture in the black cloth, making sure there are no gaps, and tie in both directions with the cord. Hold the whole up to the Goddess and the God, saying,

'I call upon the Goddess and the God to bind all negativity generated by … (name). I ask them to ensure that … (name) cannot harm my family, friends, or me, in thought or word or deed. Blessed Be.'

After your Ritual put the wrapped mirrors safely away and keep them until you feel sure that the person no longer harbours any ill will towards you.

HEALING

Healing forms the major part of the work of the Witch. Barely a day goes by without my being asked to heal someone or something. At most of our Esbats we will have a list of two or three people to work healing for, and occasionally the whole of the international Witch community will work synchronously for healing. Healing can be done generally, but is far better done with as much information as possible, so that you can determine exactly how to direct your magic.

In physical healing, if you know the nature of the illness then you can work directly on the causes and to enhance the body's natural healing processes. In emotional healing, perhaps after a bereavement, then understanding the stages of recovery will enable you to work on these. Each of the following spells says 'visualize the healing process'. If you have done your 'homework' you will be able to actually think through and see each step required. If you cannot do this, then focus on making the patient whole, rather than removing the illness.

Note that it is not a good idea to work to remove all pain. Pain is nature's way of indicating that there is a problem, so if you remove it further damage could be caused. Also magic is not a substitute for more conventional medicine, so you or the person who comes to you should also seek medical advice. Having said that, it can sometimes be better to work healing magic before a condition is diagnosed, e.g. when awaiting the results of tests, as the magic can often have the effect of meaning that a less serious cause is identified than that which was feared. Because of this it is best to work your magic as soon as a problem is identified rather than waiting for a particular Lunar phase, hence I have not put suggested times of working.

PHYSICAL HEALING FOR YOURSELF

One of the dilemmas of the Witch is that whilst you can and should work magic for yourself, you shouldn't work when you are really unwell. This is because it is hard enough to bring your elements into balance when well, it is far harder when ill. It is also because raising energy when you are under the weather is counterproductive, as the more energy you raise the weaker, and hence more likely to feel ill, you become. So you need to judge very carefully whether working this simple spell is likely to make you feel worse or better. As a rule of thumb, anything systemic or which gives you a raised temperature is probably best passed to a trusted fellow Witch. However, physical injuries or localized problems can usually be tackled on your own behalf.

You will need:

> 3 LILAC CANDLES AND SECURE HOLDERS
> LAVENDER ESSENTIAL OIL

This Ritual takes place in the bathroom. As you will already be feeling poorly it is better to Create the Sacred Space* by visualization rather than setting up an Altar and going through the more formal steps.

Run a comfortably warm bath and add 10 drops of the lavender oil. Place the three candles around the bath and light them. Create the Sacred Space* in your head before you undress and get into the water. If you can, immerse your whole body briefly three times; if a part of you cannot go under the water (perhaps because of a wound or bandages) then immerse as much as you can. Whilst in the water ask the Goddess and the God to take away your ill health and visualize your symptoms draining away into the water. Then ask them to bring you healing and good health, strength and energy. When you have finished be sure to dry yourself and wrap up well before you remove the Sacred Space,* again in your head.

You can repeat this daily until you feel you have recovered. If you do so then you can reuse the candles, otherwise you will need to place them safely until they have burned all the way down.

PHYSICAL HEALING FOR LOVED ONES

If you feel that you can persuade your near and dear to take part in the above, all is well and good, and they will bathe whilst you perform the Ritual. However, when someone is feeling poorly is probably not the best time to announce that, not only do you practise Witchcraft, but that you want to practise it on them! In this case the following is somewhat more tactful.

You will need:

  I LAVENDER CANDLE

  A BOLINE, OR OTHER TOOL FOR ENGRAVING THE CANDLE

  LAVENDER OIL

  I AMETHYST STONE (IF YOU STUDY GEMSTONES OR HAVE A REFERENCE BOOK
    YOU MAY BE ABLE TO FIND OUT WHICH GEMSTONE IS MOST APPROPRIATE
    FOR THE ILLNESS IN QUESTION, OTHERWISE AMETHYST IS A GOOD ALL-
    PURPOSE HEALING STONE)

Before your Ritual create your own sigil to represent the person you are working for, perhaps their entwined initials or the initial of their forename coupled with something which brings them to mind (I have a friend who I could represent with a cat sitting on top of a J) and look up the sigil of their sun sign.

Once you have Created your Sacred Space,* consecrate* the candle and the stone in the usual way. Carve both the sigils into it, together with the caduceus (this international symbol of healing consists of a staff with two snakes twined about it in the form of a DNA spiral). Next take the oil and anoint the candle, starting in the centre and working out towards the ends. Now hold the candle up to the Goddess and the God and say,

'I call upon the Goddess and the God, upon the healers of all. As this candle burns bring health and strength to … (name). Blessed Be.'

Light the candle and, whilst looking at the flame, visualize the person and visualize the healing process taking place. When you feel sure that your magic has started, take the stone and anoint it with a drop of the oil. Hold this up to the Goddess and the God and say,

'I call upon the Goddess and the God, upon the healers of all. Lend your strength to this token to bring health and healing to … (name). As she/he carries it may she/he grow daily in health and strength. Blessed Be.'

Put the stone safely to one side.

After your Ritual make sure you give the stone to your loved one as soon as possible. If they are not prepared to carry it, then place by the side of their bed.

PHYSICAL HEALING FOR OTHER PEOPLE

Sometimes you may be asked for healing for someone who you hardly know, or who is too far away for you to give them a stone or any other token.

In this case, perform the candle spell above but with the addition of a pin placed halfway down. After the candle has completely burned and the pin is cool, take the pin outside and bury it in the garden. Whilst burying it, say,

'I call upon the Goddess and the God to take the illness from … (name), to bring them health and healing and strength. Blessed Be.'

PHYSICAL HEALING FOR ANIMALS AND PETS

Our pets are just as much a part of our families as people, and sometimes you may also feel moved to work magic for other animals, perhaps something you have heard about on the news or something you yourself have rescued. Additionally, many Witches have favoured forms of wildlife, often endangered, for which they will work magic.

You will need:

> I BROWN CANDLE
>
> A BOLINE OR OTHER INSTRUMENT FOR CARVING THE CANDLE
>
> SOME LAVENDER OIL
>
> IF WORKING FOR A PET, SOME OF ITS FUR (BRUSHED OR STROKED OUT, NOT CUT!)
>
> IF WORKING FOR ANOTHER ANIMAL, A PICTURE

Consecrate the candle as in the above spell for Healing Loved Ones, carve into it the name of your pet or a rough picture of the animal you are working for. Anoint it with the oil and present it and then light it as before.

Take the hair or picture and hold it up to the Goddess and the God, saying,

'I call upon the Goddess and the God to bring healing to … (name). As Mother and Father of all nature and all living things I ask that they bring health and strength to … (name). Blessed Be.'

After your Ritual take the hair or picture outside and bury it as you did the pin in the preceding spell.

EMOTIONAL HEALING

The most common cause of the need for emotional healing is bereavement. The loss of a loved one is extremely traumatic and can be very hard to get over. Whilst we cannot and should not stop the processes of grief we can work to alleviate the emotional pain. It is worth mentioning that in addition to working magic there are many other things we can do to help in these circumstances; practical things like making meals, helping with the housework, etc. Most importantly we can give time, company and a listening ear. One of the worst parts of bereavement can be the fact that no one knows what to say so they avoid the sufferer, who can end up feeling isolated and unloved. Grieving relatives and friends often need to talk about the one they have lost, they do not need to be made to feel a nuisance or social leper!

You will need:

A PINK CANDLE

BOLINE OR OTHER CARVING TOOL

ESSENTIAL OILS OF NEROLI, FRANKINCENSE AND ROSE

A SMALL BOTTLE OF UNSCENTED BUBBLE BATH (OR SHOWER GEL IF THE
     PERSON SHOWERS MORE OFTEN THAN THEY BATHE)

AN ATTRACTIVE BOTTLE WITH A SECURE STOPPER, CAPABLE OF HOLDING AT
     LEAST 25ML

In your Sacred Space consecrate,* carve, anoint, present and light the candle as you did in the physical healing for loved ones spell above.

Still in Circle, place 3 drops of each of the oils into the empty bottle and top up with bubble bath. Replace the stopper tightly. Consecrate the blend through the elements in the usual way, then hold it up to the Goddess and the God and say,

'I call upon the Goddess and the God, from whom all life proceeds and to whom all life returns … (Name of deceased) has moved from this world and walks now in the Summerlands. But behind is left … (name of bereaved) whose sorrow is great. Grant them healing and peace. Give to them the joy of life once more. Blessed Be.'

As soon as you can, give the blended oil and bubble bath to the bereaved as a small gift.

Remember that the grieving process has many natural stages, which need to be allowed to take place before healing can be complete. As Witches we are seeking to lessen the pain and ease the process, not to prevent it happening. So please do not expect the person to suddenly feel 'over it' and revert to 'normal' after your magic. If the person is of the Craft, or sympathetic to it, you might like to suggest they take part in a Rite of Withdrawal *(see page 219)*, but do be tactful about this. Give them plenty of time to get over the worst of their grief first; the Rite of Withdrawal is better performed later rather than too soon.

Remember also that we do not choose who or what we grieve over, it might be a family member or a close friend, but it could just as easily be a pet, a work colleague, the sudden loss of a pregnancy, or even the end of a woman's fertility.

HEALING THE SPIRIT

When someone is feeling sad, low or depressed without a definable 'cause', then the magic we work is for healing the spirit. As with physical healing it is important not to neglect conventional treatment, especially if the feeling interferes with daily life, causes physical neglect or is prolonged. But where we are talking about a general or low level lack of lustre then the following may be enough on its own.

You will need:

    1 ROSE QUARTZ GEMSTONE

    1 CITRINE GEMSTONE

    1 PINK CANDLE

    ESSENTIAL OILS OF ROSE, LAVENDER AND CLARY SAGE

Consecrate* the candle through the elements in the usual way. Anoint it with the oils and present it to the Goddess and the God, saying,

'I call upon the Great Mother and the Lord of the Forest to aid me … (Name) is feeling down. Assist me to raise their spirits, to bring them energy, and help them to see the good that is all around and is within them. Blessed Be.'

Light the candle. Now take the stones and consecrate them, anoint them with the oils and present them, saying,

'I call upon the Goddess and the God to empower these stones that they may take away all negativity. May they lift the spirits and bring the joy of life. Blessed Be.'

Place to one side.

After your Ritual, give the stones to your subject. They may carry them or simply keep them about their home.

There are also several more practical things you can do to lift your spirit. For example, take a walk somewhere you can observe and appreciate the seasons. Any kind of exercise releases endorphins which make you feel better. Seek out light-hearted company and entertainment, and stay away from doom and gloom for a couple of days. Treat yourself to a couple of hours off, and that includes the domestic chores, and do something which you know will bring you pleasure.

ENVIRONMENTAL HEALING

As Witches we are concerned about the environment, we hear news of the latest oil spill, the decimation of the forests, or of species threatened by the destruction of their habitats. Whilst we may feel that there is little we can individually do to affect these issues, every bit of magical help directed at them does go towards improving them. Perhaps if enough people add their energy we can make a real difference.

It is important that you are specific in the way you ask for help: to simply seek 'to heal the planet' is not only too broad a statement but could result in nature deciding that the best way to heal the Earth would be to remove all the people! It is also important that everyone in a Circle focuses on the same problem, so this can only be performed for one issue in one Ritual.

This Ritual takes the form of a meditation in Circle and is best performed at the Full Moon. If you are working in a group then get one person to read the visualization whilst everyone else follows it in their mind.

Create your Sacred Space* and perform a Self-Blessing.*

When you are ready sit, or lie down comfortably, close your eyes, breathe deeply and evenly and visualize the following:

Picture the Earth, a small blue-green plant, revolving in space. See the land and the waters, see the clouds across its surface. See it sparkling like a jewel in the depths of space. Let your mind see below the surface of the planet a great blue-green dragon coiled around the Earth, its nose and tail touching. Take time to visualize it clearly, see its wings and scales. See its noble head. See how the dragon sleeps, see it breathing low and slow. Now reach forward with your mind, touch the dragon, gently wake it from its slumber. See it stir, call out to it. As it wakes see the dragon turn to look at you. See its great golden eyes gaze at you, full of under-standing and compassion for the land. Tell it of the problem you are working on, see the tears glisten in its eyes as it nods in comprehension. Now with your mind call to the dragon, ask it to rise, to take wing to put its energy into resolving the problem. See it rise from the land and take flight, see it circle the Earth three times, moving Deosil. Now with your mind direct it to the part of the Earth where the problem is. See it swoop down to touch the Earth with its great claws, see it move through the surface of the Earth and coil up tightly at the spot you have indicated. When you are certain that the dragon has settled firmly, bid it farewell and withdraw your mind from contact. Once again, visualize the planet as seen from space. Now return to the here and now, remember where you are. Open your eyes.

After this, or any other, meditation it is important to make sure that you are grounded before going on to do anything in the mundane world. So at the end of the Ritual you should make a point of having something to eat and drink.

All magic should be paid for, not in money but in returning something to the natural world, and nowhere is this more appropriate than in environmental healing. You could take part in a tree planting programme, clear litter from a local natural area, make a point of shopping in a more environmentally friendly way – perhaps by buying your vegetables loose rather than pre-packed, or by recycling, and so forth.

DIVINATION

Divination is the art of finding out that which would otherwise be hidden. It is one of the key skills of the Witch, and one we are frequently asked for. There are many techniques which can be used, like Tarot, Runes, Crystal Ball, tea leaves, Pendulums, and so on. It's not possible to describe all the techniques and skills involved here, but I have given a few examples. Divination does not have to take place in a Sacred Space, nor as part of a Ritual, but when it does it is that much easier to perform and tends to be more accurate. Be aware, however, that it is almost impossible to divine accurately for yourself. Most of us have far too many inner feelings and desires to make accurate predictions for our own lives.

Generally speaking, divination is usually more accurate during the Waning Moon, when the Crone, the Wise One, presides. It is also traditionally practised in the dark part of the year, mostly from Samhain to Yule. Having said that, divination can be performed at almost any time, although the time around Litha is usually avoided as it is the time of the trickster Gods and results can be somewhat misleading.

Try to avoid 'testing' your tools of divination, or asking spurious questions. Whatever technique you use will 'know' and you may find that it will affect your results when you really need to know.

Any kind of divination can be aided by the use of *Divination Oil*. Make your own from 2 drops Frankincense, 2 drops Lemongrass, 2 drops Nutmeg, 2 drops Clary Sage, 1 drop Bay and 1 drop Rose oils. This can be worn, applied to your tools of divination or burned in an oil burner. Do not use this oil if you are, or may be, pregnant.

FINDING THINGS

The most common use for this is, obviously, when something has been lost. However, this technique can also be used where you are trying to locate an object or a place. Perhaps you are looking for an outdoor working site, or the best town to look for a certain kind of shop.

You will need:

> A MAP OR PLAN. IF YOU HAVE LOST AN OBJECT IN THE HOUSE, THEN SKETCH OUT THE WHOLE HOUSE LAYOUT AND SEPARATE ROOM LAYOUTS TOO. WHEN LOOKING FOR A LOCATION YOU NEED BOTH A BROAD-SCALE MAP AND THEN ONE OR MORE SHOWING GREATER DETAIL
>
> A PENDULUM (YOU CAN USE DIVINING RODS IF YOU HAVE MASTERED THEM)
>
> A PENCIL AND PAPER, SO THAT YOU CAN MAKE A NOTE ON YOUR PLAN(S) OR ON THE PAPER

Perform the Rite of Banishing Unwanted Influences.* Consecrate* the Pendulum or divining rods whilst focusing on what you seek.

Now you need to 'set' your Pendulum: take it in your strong hand and holding it steady over your other hand, focus as hard as you can on the word 'yes'. Wait a few moments then note the movement of the Pendulum. Repeat this, focusing on the word 'no', and again note the movement. If the two movements are the same, you will need to start over, including the consecration.

Spread the maps or plans out in your Circle, starting with the large-scale one.

Hold your Pendulum in your strong hand over each area in turn, focusing on the object and the question *'Is it here?'* Where it indicates yes on the large-scale plan or map then you can move on to a small-scale one. Use the pencil and paper to note your results as you will need to complete your Ritual and remove your Sacred Space before setting off to find that which you seek.

At the end of your Ritual, cleanse* the pendulum so that it is clean in readiness for next time.

Note that a pendulum should be 'set' every time you use it, and that it will only answer yes/no questions.

DETERMINING THE GENDER
OF AN UNBORN CHILD

This is another technique which uses the Pendulum, and in the same way as above, i.e. by asking a yes/no question. The reason I have given it a separate sub-heading is that many people make the mistake of assuming you can ask is it a boy or a girl. Also it is important to note that this technique is not reliable before about the fourth month of pregnancy as the gender of a child is not fully determined until about that time. It is also not a technique which should be performed by either parent of the unborn child, as most people have some kind of preference, however minimal, which can influence the results. It's also quite a good idea to ask the mother to relax and think of something different so that she cannot subliminally influence the outcome!

ASCERTAINING DATES/DURATIONS

This technique can be used to determine when something will happen, or the duration of something. For example, you can ask 'When will my promotion come?' or 'How long do I have to wait before my promotion comes?' Make sure that you phrase your question clearly as you can get two different answers to what is essentially the same question.

You will need:

A PACK OF PLAYING CARDS. ORDINARY ONES CAN BE USED, BUT IF YOU PREFER TO USE THE TAROT REMOVE THE MAJOR ARCANA

Perform the Rite of Banishing Unwanted Influences.* As you will be laying the cards down in three piles you need to decide whether your answer is likely to be in terms of days, months, years, or in other segments of time. Take the cards and shuffle them whilst focusing on the question. If you are doing this for someone else you will need to focus on them also.

Start laying the first pile of cards down face upwards. Keep going until you reach an ace or you have dealt 31 cards (as there are a maximum of 31 days in the month), at which point you take up the remaining cards, re-shuffle them and start the second pile. Stop when you reach an ace or 12 cards (for the 12 months of the year). Finally, repeat for the third pile, stopping at an ace or 5 cards (it is unreasonable to expect results more than 5 years ahead).

Were you to be working with hours, days and weeks, you would be looking at piles with up to 24, 7, and 10 cards respectively.

You now need to interpret your results:

Say your first pile has an ace as the sixth card, your second has an ace as the eleventh card and your third has an ace as the second card. This would indicate that you can expect your result in 2 years, 11 months and 6 days.

FUTURE – GENERAL

There are books and books written about determining the future, some from the Craft perspective, others treating 'fortune telling' as a kind of party game. If you treat divination lightly then the results you get will be at best very general. If, however, you treat it seriously, and apply your Craft to it, then you can get detailed and accurate results. As with all the Craft the tools you make yourself are the ones with the strongest energy.

In advance of this you will need to make your own set of Witches' Runes.

You will need:

8 PEBBLES OR STONES. THEY SHOULD BE OF SIMILAR SIZE AND OF A SHAPE
WHICH HAS TWO CLEARLY DEFINED SIDES. ENSURE THAT THEY ARE CLEAN
AND DRY, AND IF PURCHASED OR GIVEN BY ANOTHER, CLEANSE THEM

A FINE PAINTBRUSH

PERMANENT PAINTS IN RED, WHITE, YELLOW, BLUE, BLACK, GOLD AND SILVER.
YOU CAN BUY THE OTHER COLOURS MENTIONED BELOW BUT YOU CAN JUST
AS EASILY BLEND THEM WITH THE ONES MENTIONED HERE

A BAG OR POUCH OF NATURAL FABRIC (NOT MAN-MADE FABRIC) BIG ENOUGH
TO CONTAIN THE STONES

The following gives the symbols you should paint onto one side of each stone, and some of their meanings for later interpretation:

THE SUN — GOLD. THE GOD, SUN, MALE PRINCIPAL, HONOUR, GLORY

THE MOON — SILVER. THE GODDESS, MOON, FEMALE PRINCIPAL, DREAMS

TWO CROSSED SPEARS — RED. FIRE, MARS, CONFLICT, ATTACK

A BRANCH WITH LEAVES — GREEN. EARTH, FERTILITY, GROWTH, MONEY

A SNAKE — BLUE. WATER, JUPITER, LUST, AMBITION, CAREER

THREE BIRDS — WHITE. AIR, MERCURY, FLIGHT, TRAVEL, COMMUNICATION,
    KNOWLEDGE

TWO LINKED RINGS — PINK. VENUS, UNITY, PARTNERSHIP, FRIENDS, LOVE,
    ROMANCE

PAINT ONE STONE BLACK AND WHEN IT IS DRIED, ADD A WHITE **#**. SATURN,
    FATE, ENIGMA, UNKNOWN FACTORS AND INFLUENCES

As you paint each stone, focus on the meanings above and any other associations which come to your mind. You might like to note these down as you go, for later reference. Once painted, the stones should be set aside to dry and then placed in the light of the Moon for three nights before the Full Moon. From the night of the Full Moon you should place them in a bag under your pillow for three nights. After this, do not allow anyone else to handle them. The Ritual then takes place at the start of the Waning Moon, the time of divination.

You will need:

YOUR WITCHES' RUNES AND THEIR POUCH
DIVINATION OIL

Create your Sacred Space.* Take the Witches' Runes from their pouch and conse-crate* them. Anoint them with the oil and hold them up to the Goddess and the God, saying,

'I call upon the Goddess and the God to guide my divinations. May they bless these stones that I might see clearly and truly. May they guide my understanding and give me the wisdom to use them well. Blessed Be.'

Your Runes are now ready for their first use. (If you are not going to use them immediately, put them away safely in their pouch.)

Still in Circle take your Runes in both hands and shake them gently. If you have a question or topic in mind, focus on it, otherwise focus on the question,

'What is to happen?'

Cast your stones gently in front of you. Put to one side any which are face down, these do not come into the reading. Then clear your mind and look at the stones.

Those nearest to you are the ones with the most immediate influence. Those near to each other influence one another, with those nearer to you having the stronger influence. Any on top of another (even if only partly) will cancel out the lower one. You can ask further questions, but only up to a maximum of three in any one session.

The Witches' Runes can be used to answer many different questions. Once you have made your own you can experiment to see how they work for you.

COMPATIBILITY

Another one of the more frequently asked questions is, 'Are we compatible?' Whilst this is a question which can be answered, it is not, as some hope, the ultimate indicator that a relationship will last. This is because there are many outside factors which can influence a relationship. Having said that, it is probably the best question to seek to answer, as anything more definitive may result in either one party taking things for granted, or in them abandoning a perfectly good relationship because the 'omens' say it will not last forever!

Prior to your Ritual you will need to first determine the true names of the two parties. A true name is not necessarily the one they were given at birth, nor even the one they are commonly known by, it is the name of who they are, their chosen name. For example, someone may have been called Joanna Sarah Smith by her parents, her friends call her Joss (because of her initials), but to herself she is Jo Smith. So the latter is the name you need to use because it reflects the way she sees herself, and that is the personality she will put into a relationship.

Having done this for both parties you then need to work out the numerological number for each. This means applying numbers to each letter to work out a number for each name. In numerology A=1, B=2, and so on, until Z=26. The letters in each person's true name are thus calculated and added together. They are then reduced to a single digit number. Hence Jo Smith would be 10+15+19+13+9+20+8 = 94, 9+4 = 13, 1+3 = 4, so Jo's number is 4. You also work this out for the other person.

You can get a rough and quick idea of how compatible they are, from the numbers themselves. Where both numbers are the same, these people are alike, but may clash. If both numbers add up (bear in mind you still need to reduce to a single digit) to 1, 3, or 6, these people are very compatible. Where both numbers are odd, or both are even, these people are somewhat compatible, but they must be prepared to work at any relationship. However, this is only the first step.

You will need:

YOUR WITCHES' RUNES

THE NUMBERS OF THE TWO PEOPLE

A SHEET OF PAPER DIVIDED INTO 9 BOXES: 3 ROWS AND 3 COLUMNS

PENCIL FOR MAKING NOTES

This Ritual is best performed during the Waning Moon.

Create the Sacred Space* as usual. Take your Runes in your strong hand and focus on the first person. Cast them (in much the same way as you would throw or roll dice) onto the paper the same number of times as the person's number, so for Jo Smith you would read the fourth cast. As before, discard the face down stones, and also any that have landed off the paper. Mark the positions and signs of the remaining stones on the nine-square chart, identifying them as belonging to Jo Smith.

Repeat this for the other person, ensuring that you can tell which stones belong to which person.

You should now have notes on your paper indicating the positions of the stones of both parties. This is what you base your reading on.

As before, those nearest to you are the ones with the most immediate influence. Those near to each other influence one another, with those nearer to you having the stronger influence. Any on top of another (even if only partly) will cancel out the lower one.

Stones in the centre column indicate general personality traits, those in the right-hand column indicate attitudes to home and family, those in the left are attitudes to work, business and the outside world. If both parties have the same stone in the same box it indicates a high level of compatibility in that area. Where both have the same stone in the same column it indicates a similar approach or outlook. In the same row, they both place a similar emphasis on that subject, even though they may have differing opinions. Where one person's stone covers that of the other, it indicates that, although they share the same views, the stone which overlays belongs to the person who will dominate in that area. This is not necessarily bad; my partner and I have similar thoughts about things technical, but he dominates (it's also his job). We also have similar thoughts about things decorative and artistic, but I dominate because of my skills. By the way, if all the stones from both parties end up in the same box it indicates you did not cast them properly!

By careful study of the Runes you should be able to build up a picture of each person and how they will relate to one another, and from there you can determine how compatible they really are.

Once you have completed your divination and interpretation replace the stones in their bag and destroy the paper. Do not keep it for reference outside of the Circle as subsequent viewings will not be assisted by the magic of the Circle.

FOR HELP IN THE CRAFT

It's a constant source of amazement to me that most Witches forget to use magic to aid them in their Craft work. I am frequently asked how to find a Coven, yet whenever I say 'Have you asked the Goddess?' the answer is invariably 'No'. Yet this should be the most obvious area of life to apply magic to.

FINDING A COVEN AND/OR MENTOR

As mentioned above, I get a lot of requests from people seeking either a Coven to work in or an experienced Witch to act as mentor to guide them in their Craft work.

You will need:

> A LARGE (NOT ENORMOUS) WHITE CANDLE, THE KIND SOLD AS 'CHURCH CANDLES' ARE FINE
>
> A PLATE OR OTHER FIREPROOF DISH TO STAND THE CANDLE ON
>
> A BOLINE OR CARVING TOOL

This Ritual should be performed at the Full Moon.

Create your Sacred Space* and perform the Rite of Self-Blessing.* Take your candle and inscribe in it a Pentagram (five-pointed star within a circle) and place your initials in the centre. Offer it to the Goddess and the God saying,

'I call upon the Goddess and the God. Mother and Father of all Witches, I seek knowledge and understanding, guidance and companionship within the Craft. Aid me in my search for a Coven/mentor, give me the knowledge to find one and the wisdom to select one which is right for me. Blessed Be.'

Light the candle and place it safely in the centre of the Circle then sit facing it and the Altar (if your Altar is in the North, this will mean you are in the southern portion of the Circle). Look first at the candle, then, starting at the North, send your gaze Deosil around the Circle. As you do so visualize the boundary of the Circle glowing brighter and brighter, visualize it growing upwards and becoming a cone (this is the cone of power and is thought to be the origin of the pointed hat). Continue visualizing and make this cone of light spin. When it is revolving steadily and seems to be coming to a point, direct your energy to the peak and mentally release it. When you are sure that you have released all the pent-up energy, relax and take a few deep breaths to steady yourself. Place the candle in a safe place and burn it down over the next three nights.

The spell will start working after the third night, but do be aware that you still need to take sensible precautions about meeting strangers and in choosing a Coven which is right for you. Additionally, take a look at the section on contacts towards the back of this book.

FINDING COVENORS

Occasionally, a Coven finds it is having difficulty finding members, especially if they don't wish to advertise, although these days the problem is rare.

Perform the same Ritual as that for finding a Coven with the following small changes:

Place the Coven's initials within the Pentagram, and around it carve arrows pointing inwards.

When you present to the Goddess and the God, say,

'I call upon the Goddess and the God. Mother and Father of all Witches, we seek others to share knowledge and understanding, guidance and companionship within the Craft. Aid us in our search for Covenors who will make our Circle whole, who will be an asset to the Craft and who will bring honour to You. Give us the knowledge to find them and the wisdom to select those who will be right for both Coven and Craft. Blessed Be.'

Where there are several of you, the cone of power can be best raised by Circle dancing.*

Again, remember that a spell to attract the right people does not guarantee that one or two less right ones won't find you, so take the usual precautions.

FINDING AN OUTDOOR SITE

When it comes to locating an outdoor working site which is legal, sufficiently private and safe, there is no substitute for local knowledge and a few visits to check it out. However, if you are new to an area, or don't know of a good location, you might want to apply magic to the problem. The first step is to use the spell for Finding Things to locate potential places, but unless only one presents itself then you will need to take things a step further.

Prior to your Ritual, use a combination of divination, local knowledge and a good map to identify somewhere between three and six potential sites. Visit each site in turn and, assuming it still looks and feels good, take from it one fallen leaf, preferably from the centre of your likely Circle. Mark each leaf so that you know which site it came from. Place the leaves somewhere safe to dry out thoroughly.

You will need:

> YOUR MARKED LEAVES
>
> A THURIBLE
>
> SELF-IGNITING CHARCOAL
>
> TONGS FOR HOLDING THE CHARCOAL TO LIGHT IT

This Ritual should be performed at the Full Moon.

Name* each leaf for the location it came from. Light the charcoal around all the edges so that it will burn evenly and place it in the centre of the Thurible. Now place each leaf around the charcoal in such a way that each only just touches it. You need to do this quickly so that no leaf has the advantage! Focus your mind and watch the leaves carefully whilst chanting over and over,

'Lady show us the way, Lord show us the place.'

The last leaf to burn (or smoulder if they are damp) away is the best site to choose.

Note that when you first visit each of your potential sites it is a good idea to look out for signs that other Witches might be using it; even better would be to visit at the Full Moon or an Esbat. Otherwise you could find that the 'best' site is already taken.

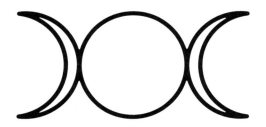

 COMING OUT

There comes a time in most Witches' lives when they wonder whether they should be making their beliefs known to friends and/or family and perhaps even to neighbours and colleagues. Generally speaking, I advise against it. However tolerant and understanding you think people are, there is always the chance that someone may turn out to biased, prejudiced, upset or offended, and once the secret's out you can never take it back. Furthermore, once you have told one person you have no control over who they might deliberately or accidentally tell.

I know this sounds strange coming from an extremely 'public' Witch, but I am fortunate in having a lifestyle which is not affected by it and a family who, having been sounded out thoroughly over a number of years, turned out to be supportive and accepting, rather than negative. However, I do know many others who have not been so lucky. Before you make your final decision I suggest the following:

Prior to your Ritual write a long list of everyone who may be affected by this: parents, grandparents, siblings, aunts, uncles, cousins, your children (and those you may have in the future) and their teachers, friends, colleagues, employers, customers, clients, neighbours, people who work in local shops and stores, and so on. Alongside these names make notes indicating the best and worst outcomes you can envisage happening. Take a couple of days to do this until you feel you really cannot add any more.

You will need:

> YOUR SHEET OF NAMES AND OUTCOMES
>
> ESSENTIAL OILS OF LEMONGRASS, BAY AND NUTMEG
>
> A SMALL DISH TO BLEND THE OILS IN
>
> A DARK BLUE OR DARK PURPLE CANDLE
>
> A FIREPROOF DISH

This Ritual should take place during the Waning Moon, preferably on a
Monday. Try to do it so that you can retire to bed as soon as you have finished.

**Create your Sacred Space,* inviting the Goddess in her aspect of Wise One.
Consecrate* the candle, asking the Goddess for wisdom, understanding and
knowledge. Blend the oils in the dish using 4 drops Lemongrass, 2 drops Bay and
1 drop Nutmeg. Anoint the candle and present it to the Goddess and the God
saying,**

*'I call upon the Goddess as Wise One and the God as Hunter to bring me wisdom and under-
standing. Guide me in this so that I choose aright, protect me and mine that I bring neither sorrow
nor harm. Blessed Be.'*

**Light the candle. Now take the paper and draw over it an invoking Pentagram, and
then anoint with the oil each of the five points of the star as you go. Light the
paper and place it in the fireproof dish to burn away.**

**Perform a Self-Blessing* using the blended oils, again asking the Goddess to bring
you understanding and wisdom. Remain and meditate for a few moments. Now
clear away and retire to bed, do not wash the anointing oils off until the morning.**

As you should not go to bed leaving the candle to burn away, extinguish it and put it to
one side. If you are still unsure the next day you can burn it for a further two evenings.
You may find that the right choice comes to you during the Ritual, but you should still
wait until morning before making your decision.

If after the Ritual, and considering the problem for three days, you are still unsure,
then the answer is that you should keep quiet. As I've said, once a secret is out it cannot
be taken back, whereas little harm can come from remaining private in your beliefs.

STAYING HIDDEN

For many Witches a prime consideration lies in keeping their beliefs to themselves, especially if they feel that someone else may be likely to let something slip. I have been challenged in the past in terms of, 'If you do nothing wrong why should you need to keep it secret?' In many cases I feel the question is rhetorical, as it is usually asked by someone who has just suggested that Witchcraft is some kind of evil! All I can add here is that many Witches choose to keep their path secret because of the problems it may cause for those near to them, perhaps their children at school, their elderly relatives in church, or perhaps themselves or their spouse at work. However, to help to keep your path hidden from those who have no need to know, try the following.

You will need:

A REASONABLY LARGE PIECE OF POLISHED HAEMATITE, PERHAPS AN INCH OR
TWO ACROSS, WHICH HAS BEEN CLEANSED

A BLACK CLOTH LARGE ENOUGH TO WRAP THE STONE

This is best performed during the Waning Moon. However, if you feel the Ritual is urgent, then work it at any phase of the Moon and repeat it at the next Waning Moon.

Perform the Rite of Banishing Unwanted Influences.* Consecrate* the Haematite through the elements. Hold it up to the Goddess and the God, saying,

'I call upon the Old Gods, upon the Goddess and the God, to bless and consecrate this stone; to make it a sanctuary, a place of safety and privacy for my Craft. May it keep my secrets safe, and protect me from the curiosity of others. Blessed Be.'

Now take the stone in your strong hand and place your weak hand over it. Close your eyes and breathe deeply and slowly. One by one visualize each of your Craft tools, until you can see it clearly and then, mentally, shrink it and place its image within the stone. Do this also with any books, notes and records you may have kept on the Craft. Lastly, visualize yourself as you are, working a spell, and place that image also in the stone. When you are sure you have included everything, hold the stone up again and say,

'I call upon the Old Gods, upon the Goddess and the God, to seal this stone, to make it a place of concealment that only I can access. I call upon them to seal it securely from the eyes, ears and minds of all, so that only when it is in Circle will its secrets be open, and then only to me. Blessed Be.'

After your Ritual wrap the stone in its cloth and place it in a safe place. Every time you wish to celebrate a festival, or to work magic, you will need to make sure that you place the unwrapped stone onto your Altar, so that you can properly use all the things you placed within it.

Remember, the best way to stay hidden and to keep secret is not to tell anyone, either verbally or by leaving your tools, equipment, books, etc. on view. Don't go in for loud chanting or strong incenses, as these will permeate even the thickest of walls. If you are careful, there is no reason why anyone need know that you work Witchcraft.

IN SUMMARY

There are as many potential spells as are there are events and changes in your life, or that of the person who comes to you for help. Therefore, there is no way I can list them all! You may by now have noticed that whilst some of the above spells talk in terms of working them for another, most are written as though you will be working them on your own behalf. This is because in the early days of magical working most of your magic will be either directly or indirectly for yourself. To change a spell which is written as though for you into one intended for another, you need to focus on that person and on the magic working for them. Similarly, most of the above are written as though you will be working on your own. Where you are working in a group everyone needs to focus on the intent and to add their energy, either by actually taking a role in the Ritual or by taking part in the raising of energy. Chapter 10 gives guidelines and ideas for ways you can adapt spells for other people, for group working and also ways of writing new spells and Rituals.

The next chapter, however, is concerned with the tools you use in spells. This does not mean the Altar equipment which was covered in Chapter 3, but the candles, oils, stones and other items you use to make the magic work.

SIX

MAGICAL RESOURCES

In Chapter 3 I talked about the equipment you might choose to have on your Altar, and how, whilst it is not essential to have a lot of tools and equipment, they do help to focus the mind, especially in the early days of working magic. The aids and tools I will talk about in this chapter are those which you use when working individual spells, for instance the candles, stones, etc. which you use to actually perform the magic, and how best to use them.

CORRESPONDENCES

The items used to work magic are not magical in themselves until you have worked on them, but they do have intrinsic energies of their own which can be used to enhance your working. These energies can be linked to colour, as in the case of candles, scent in incenses or the natural properties found in different crystals. In the Craft we call these links 'correspondences', meaning things which link, or correspond, with one another. There are correspondences associated with colour, sound, smell, shape, etc. There are also correspondences which relate to birds, fish, animals, plants, Deities, days, hours, astrological signs, Lunar phases and many more.

Correspondences are used to make it easier to work magic, but they are not magic in themselves. For example, a spell to increase self-esteem is enhanced by working at the Waxing or Full Moon, using a pink candle, Rose Quartz and Citrine, with scents of

Sandalwood and Ylang-Ylang. But these stones and scents, and even the Lunar phase, do not make the magic happen; the focus and energy of the Witch, together with their ability to harness and balance the internal and external energies are what make the magic work. The stones and scents add to the energy of the spell. Put it this way: if you are rowing from A to B along the river, it is easier to row with the tidal flow and with the wind at your back than it is to row against wind and tide. But if you need to row against wind and tide you can still get there, you just need to put in more personal energy. As you work in the Craft, your abilities will develop (just like the muscles of the rower in the example) and so there will come a time when the use of correspondences is less needful to work effective magic.

In the Craft we place rather less emphasis on some correspondences than do other magical systems. This is because as Witches we work within nature rather than separate from it; we utilize the elements both within and without, to create the changes we seek. Having said that, the use of some correspondences can be helpful and enhance your magic.

Correspondences can be thought of as coming in three kinds:

✴ *Timing*. Those linked to the timing of your magic; particularly the Phases of the Moon and the Wheel of the Year which in turn are linked to the cycles and aspects of the Goddess and the God. Remember, however, that whilst most spells can wait, there are some magics which will need to be performed as soon as you can. You will need to work at your Craft before you can be confident that you can work effective magic without utilizing the stronger tides, especially those of the Moon which represent the three aspects of the Goddess. This is why many of the spells in the preceding chapter advise working at the time of the problem and then reinforcing that magic at the more propitious phase. Astrological data, days of the week and planetary hours could also be included in this category, although only some Witches will use days, and very few will use planetary hours and other astrological data as these are closer to the province of the ritual Magician.

✴ *Identity*. Those correspondences which you use to identify who you are working for and are used to link the magic to the person. The most obvious are the use of photographs, locks of hair, etc, or the making of a fith-fath. Here, Witches will often use astrological data, such as sun signs, as well as a person's favourite colour, personal attributes, hobbies, etc. In the preceding chapter I have sometimes advocated using a sigil which you design for the purpose.

★ *Enhance the Magic.* Those correspondences which you might use to enhance your magic, in terms of colours, scents, and so on, which correspond to particular types of magic. There are many tables of these available; here I have given some of the more useful examples. Some people feel that days, planetary hours and the position of all the planetary bodies are essential, but most true Witches would disagree. If you wish to use correspondences, and I would certainly suggest that you do so at first, then, whilst you can start with those given it is a good idea to work from these and to develop your own. Witches tend to use this category of correspondence sparingly. There are no formal guidelines as to which, or how many of these to use, but I would say that one or two in any spell is quite enough. If you find yourself trying to relate Moon phase, day, hour, astrological data, colours of candles, scents in incense and more to enhance any one spell then you are working in the realm of the ritual Magician rather than that of the Witch.

LUNAR PHASES – THE TIDES OF THE MOON

I have already talked in Chapter 4 about the phases of the Moon, but to recap briefly they are:

★ *New Moon.* The time for magic which involves new things, fresh starts, new beginnings. The Rite of Naming, or Wiccaning, is often held at the New Moon.

★ *Waxing Moon.* This is the time of growth, and for magic which involves growth and increase.

★ *Full Moon.* This is the traditional time for magic and a particularly good time for magic and spells connected with healing, protection and fertility magic. The Full

Moon is also associated with all kinds of divination. Handfasting and Rites of coming of age are often held at the Full Moon.

★ *Waning Moon.* A time for sending things away: old habits, unwanted feelings. The late Waning Moon, a day or so prior to the Dark Moon, is often a time for holding the Rite of Withdrawal. Rites of Croning are also sometimes held at this phase.

★ *Dark of Moon.* The three days when there is no Moon visible in the sky. It is better not to work Magic or spells at the time when the Moon is hiding her face, as the energies at this time can be confusing and it is easier for things to misfire.

THE ASPECTS AND FACETS OF THE GODDESS

As I have said before, the Goddess is seen in three aspects; Maiden, Mother and Crone, and these three aspects are reflected in the phases of the Moon. Hence they are a primary influence not just in our magic but in all aspects of the Craft.

★ *Maiden.* The Maiden is represented by the New Moon. In times past a girl was considered a maiden until she actually gave birth to her first child, so the Maiden aspect continues well into the Waxing phase, until around three days before the Full Moon. The Maiden is the Goddess of youth, enthusiasm, new starts, fresh beginnings, of planning and preparing to bring into being.

★ *Mother.* The Mother is represented by the Full Moon. She is the Goddess of growth, fertility, ripening, fruitfulness, caring, nurturing and developing.

★ *Crone.* The Crone is represented by the Waning Moon and is also called the Wise One. In times past a Crone would be a woman past her time of childbearing, who therefore had the experience of life to know and understand her people, and to have learned the knowledge of herbs, plants, etc, so as to be skilled in healing. The Crone is the Goddess of knowledge and understanding, and hence all kinds of Divination. She is also the Goddess of reaping rewards for labours completed, and of rest.

Try not to see the three Aspects, or the phases of the Moon, as isolated individuals or times, remember that they blend into each other. Whilst the Goddess has many names, remember, they too are but facets of the whole. Having said that, it can be helpful to call upon different Goddess forms for different magics.

THE ASPECTS AND FACETS OF THE GOD

The phases of the God are less immediately obvious, as his cycles overlap in some respects:

✦ As *Lord of the Forest* he is Hunter from Samhain to Beltane, when he becomes the Hunted. In the former aspect his role is that of one who clears away all that has served its purpose and removes the old and outworn. As Hunted he is God of fertility, of fresh young life and growth.

✦ As *Oak King* he presides from Yule to Litha and then as *Holly King* from Litha to Yule.

✦ As the *Consort of the Goddess*, and her King, his aspects mirror hers through the seasonal festivals.

Like the Goddess, the God is also known by many names which emphasize different aspects, but are still part of the whole.

SEASONAL PHASES – THE WHEEL OF THE YEAR

Whilst the Sabbats are mostly times of celebration they have strong energies of their own. These energies can also be used to work magic, in tune with the phases of the Goddess and the God they represent, although it is preferable to reserve them as times for reflection and celebrating the Cycle of the Seasons where you can. There are Sabbat Rituals in Chapter 7.

★ *Samhain*. The Goddess becomes Crone. The God becomes Hunter. This is the time for Divination and Scrying. A time for reflecting upon what we have achieved and giving thanks, as well as for remembering what, and who, has gone before.

★ *Yule*. The Goddess is still Crone, and the God is still Hunter, but this is also the time of the Rebirth of the Sun and the time when Lord Oak takes over from Lord Holly. Whilst still the resting phase of the year it is a time for looking forward to what is to come.

★ *Imbolg*. The Goddess becomes Maiden, and the God becomes the young Hunter, in search of his bride and Queen. Here are the first signs of Spring and this is a time of new beginnings.

★ *Oestara*. A time of balance, to be rid of that which we no longer need and to take on the new.

★ *Beltane*. The Goddess becomes Mother and the God takes his place beside her. This is the time of the marriage of the Goddess and the God and a traditional time for Handfasting.

★ *Litha*. The Sun God reaches the height of his power before his decline into Winter. Lord Holly takes over from Lord Oak.

★ *Lughnasadh*. The first of the Harvest. It is the time of the Sacrificial King, as well as a time of personal sacrifice.

★ *Madron*. The height of the Harvest, it is also a time of balance, a time to assess whether we have paid for what we have been given, to redress the balance and to right wrongs.

COLOURS

The use of colour in magic is quite common, whether in candles, cloths, cords or stones, and the colours have many attributions, some of which are listed below.

★ *Red*. Fire, south, passion, anger, dispute.

★ *Orange*. Strength, confidence, health, honour, work.

★ *Yellow*. Air, east, thought, understanding, memory, communication.

★ *Green*. Earth, north, the physical, fertility, money.

★ *Blue*. Water, west, emotion, things of the sea.

★ *Indigo*. Inner knowledge, career, ambition.

★ *Violet*. Dreams, divination.

★ *Pink*. Affection, romance, self-respect.

★ *Lilac*. Peace, tranquillity, healing.

★ *Brown*. Animals and things of the land, grounding or bringing back down to earth.

★ *White*. Illumination, purity, and when the 'correct' colour cannot be discerned or obtained.

★ *Black*. Banishing, removing, concealing.

★ *Silver*. The Moon, the Goddess.

★ *Gold*. The Sun, the God.

CANDLES

Candles are probably the most frequent way in which colour is used for magic. However, there are certain things which should be borne in mind when using candles for magical purposes:

★ When anointing candles, always start at the centre and work towards the ends. Do not apply too much oil, as it burns very easily!

★ When carving or engraving candles, work in good light and on a secure surface so that you do not cut yourself. You do not need to make deep marks, just enough to imbue the candle with your intent.

★ Candles should be 'whole colour', that is, the same colour all the way through, not white ones which have been dipped in coloured wax. This is because when they burn, the candle colour, and the strength of that correspondence, will be diluted.

★ Where candles are scented you should ensure that the scent is that of an essential oil (in which case it may well not smell scented when burned) and not a created perfume. Created scents are rarely purely what they say on the label, so you cannot be sure what other influences you may be introducing. The scent should also be compatible with your intent.

★ Candles which are used for a spell should be allowed to burn all the way down. However, as you should *never* leave a burning candle unattended (not even for a minute!) you will need to either sit with the candle until it finishes, or ensure that you can complete the burning over the next two nights to complete the spell.

★ Candles which are used in Ritual but not for a spell or magic themselves, like Altar candles and quarter lights, can be re-used as their purpose remains the same from one Ritual to the next.

★ Please, always use a proper, secure, candleholder, as balancing a candle on a dish or saucer is highly risky!

★ Candles, magical or otherwise, should not be blown out, but extinguished with a snuffer or pinched out with your fingers, if you feel brave enough! This is because blowing can spray hot wax over everything and cause them to smoke, leaving soot on the walls and ceiling. If the candle is magical in intent, blowing it out will also negate or dilute the spell.

★ Magical candles do not have to be tall and thin like those sold as dining candles, but try to avoid any really fancy shapes which might distract you from your purpose.

★ The best candles for magical work are those which you make yourself. There are many candle kits available if you feel you would like to try your hand at this, and there is a wealth of information in *The Real Witches' Kitchen* too.

ASTROLOGICAL SIGNS

The signs of the Zodiac, which most people call star signs, are in fact Sun signs, as they indicate which house of the zodiacal wheel the Sun was in at the time of birth. Their sigils (special marks used to abbreviate them) can be readily found in most papers and magazines. Sun signs are often used in the Craft to identify a person, or to define a period of time. If you are one of those people born close to a cusp (the end of one sign and the start of another), it may be worth getting your chart produced professionally in order to be certain which sign is actually yours.

OILS AND OTHER SCENTS

There is a world of difference between choosing a pleasant-smelling lotion or perfume for personal use and selecting something for magical work. The scents used in magic are chosen for their properties, rather than the way they smell, so don't expect to enjoy everything you use in your magic. Furthermore, commercially produced scents are invariably blended with many other ingredients. For this reason you need to try to ensure that you get your scents from reliable suppliers. (Of course, you could make your own, but that is a science in its own right!) When buying oils try to find 100 per cent pure essential oils, and keep them in a cool dark place to prolong their life. When buying incenses look for those which burn without too much smoke – an indicator of poorer quality, or old stock. If using fresh plants or herbs, it is worth noting that the oil of a plant may have different properties from its leaves or stem, so be sure to read spells carefully and ensure you actually use that which is required. As there is a wealth of available scents, and I have written about them and their uses in some detail in *The Real Witches' Kitchen*, here I have given a short list of some of the ones I use most frequently:

✮ *Black pepper.* Protection, empowerment, mentally stimulating and penetrating.

✮ *Clary sage.* Uplifting, balances the mind.

✮ *Frankincense.* Spirituality, cleansing, purifying, clearing.

✮ *Jasmine.* The Goddess. Love, peace, spirituality, expression.

✮ *Lavender.* Healing of all kinds.

✮ *Lemongrass.* Strengthening, purifying, stimulating.

✮ *Neroli.* Spirituality, purification, relieves stress and anxiety.

✮ *Peppermint.* Purification, mental stimulation.

✮ *Rose.* Peace, romance, friendship, love, self-acceptance, cleansing.

✮ *Rosemary.* Healing and strengthening. Promotes mental powers.

✮ *Sandalwood.* The God. Meditation, purification, healing.

✮ *Ylang-Ylang.* Peace, love, acceptance, promotes confidence.

Scents, whether oils, incenses, herbs or flowers, should be kept carefully sealed and in a cool, dark place. Loosely stoppered bottles, jars or bags will allow the ingredients to 'contaminate' one another; warmth allows their essential properties to evaporate, and damp will mean that dry ingredients can start to rot or mildew! If you can keep your ingredients carefully they will more than make up for their original cost.

STONES AND GEMSTONES

Gemstones are a useful magical aid, especially when you wish to keep or give a tangible reminder of a spell. They are inexpensive, unobtrusive and attractive. The stones have intrinsic magical and/or healing properties created by their own resonance, which can be utilized or amplified in magical working.

Having said that, it is as well to be aware of the origins of your stones; many are ripped out of the earth by explosives, gathered and processed by harshly treated and poorly paid workers. Some are even chemically or electronically treated to 'improve' their natural colour. These stones do not resonate; they are dead. If you can, find out about the origins of any stones before you buy. Bear in mind that for magical purposes, size is rarely important; small works as well as large and the smaller 'low grade' (in terms of colour, shape and inclusions) stones are often those which have been gathered in a more gentle way. At the very least they will be the by-product of mining rather than the cause of it.

A far more nature-friendly way to get the stones for your magic is to find small pebbles, perhaps on the beach, which resemble natural gemstones, and learn how to feel their intrinsic magic. I make a point on visits to the coast of picking up a few small stones which catch my eye, bringing them home and getting to know them for use in my magic. These stones I usually return to the sea when the spell is completed or the magic has worked.

As with scents there are far too many different kinds of stone to go into here, so I have given a few of the ones I find most useful:

★ *Agate*. This comes in many varieties but all have links to hearth and home, strength, courage, love, healing (especially of rifts).

☆ *Amethyst*. Mental and physical healing, love, protection, courage, happiness.

☆ *Citrine*. Self-confidence, enhancement, protection.

☆ *Haematite*. Concealment, protection, deflection, defence, disperses.

☆ *Obsidian*. Concealment, protection, defence, divination.

☆ *Clear quartz or crystal*. Light, life, illumination, clarity, bonding, psychic powers.

☆ *Rose quartz*. Friendship, love, contentment, relationship, fidelity.

☆ *Smoky quartz*. Protection, defence, removes negativity.

☆ *Sunstone*. Success, honour, strength, energy.

☆ *Amber*. This is not a stone but a fossilized resin, but like any stone you should enquire as to where it came from. Healing, strength, beauty, attraction, love and protection (especially in childbirth).

In addition to checking the origins of the gemstones you use, you also need to ensure that you thoroughly cleanse them *(see page 47)* as they will almost certainly have been handled many times. If using stones you have gathered yourself then they only need cleansing if you feel they may have been handled, or cleaned if they are dirty.

CORDS AND THREADS

Cords and threads are used in magic involving knots, where they can be used to create a spell in several steps, like that for finding a job on page 98, or where something needs to be tied to secure it, either magically or physically. The former is often termed cord magic and can also be used when you want to create a spell which will be used at a later date, as in the tradition of sailors buying knotted cords to bring winds when they are needed. The colour of a cord or thread will often be selected according to its correspondence(s). However, there are other factors which need to be borne in mind:

★ Cords or threads should be made from natural fibres, cotton, hemp, wool or even silk. Man-made fibres do not work as well.

★ Cords used in magic should not be knotted apart from the knots which make the magic work. This includes any cord which the Witch might use to tie their robes; the ends of this should be over-sewn to prevent fraying (using adhesive tape is lazy!).

TALISMANS

A Talisman is any object imbued with magical power, which is intended to be worn or carried. It could be an item of jewellery, a coin, a bead, or perhaps a piece of paper inscribed with sigils. Talismans (and no it isn't Talismen!) are one of the forms of magic practised by a huge proportion of the population without even knowing it: engagement and wedding rings are not just tokens of love but are also designed to reinforce fidelity. Saint Christophers are given to ensure safe travel. Friendship bands are made by even the very young to bring about a continuing friendship. Even the crucifix is intended to avert evil and encourage goodness.

When working talismanic magic you can use whatever you feel will be most easily carried, so something which is already owned can easily be used for the purpose. The only thing I would add is that where someone asks you to prepare a Talisman for him or her, it is a good idea to get them to provide the object. Not only will you save the expense, but also it gives the person direct involvement in the spell.

DAYS OF THE WEEK

The correspondences for the days of the week are a way of linking several types of correspondence together as not only do they relate to the planets which rule over them, but also to the Goddesses and Gods, the elements, scents, colours, jewels, animals, plants, and so on. The correspondences below are by no means a complete list of everything which links with each day, particularly not the names of Goddesses and Gods, but should give you enough to start working with.

★ *Monday*. The Moon
Goddesses and Gods: Persephone, Diana, Hecate, Selene, Khonsu
Element: Water
Colours: white or yellow (New), red or blue (Full), black or purple (Waning).
    Silver
Scents: Jasmine, Poppy, Myrtle
Gemstones: Moonstone, Quartz
Magic associated with: dreams, fertility, illusion, divination, the feminine principle

★ *Tuesday*. Mars
Goddesses and Gods: Anath, Morrighan, Ares, Mars
Element: Fire
Colours: red
Scents: Pine, Cypress
Gemstones: Bloodstone, Carnelian
Magic associated with: defence, discord, battle, opposition

★ *Wednesday.* Mercury
Goddesses and Gods: Athena, Maat, Hermes, Mercury
Element: Air
Colours: Violet, indigo
Scents: Storax, Mace, Sandalwood
Gemstones: Agate, Opal
Magic associated with: communication, knowledge, exams, travel

★ *Thursday*. Jupiter
Goddesses and Gods: Isis, Juno, Jupiter, Thor
Element: Air/Fire
Colours: purple, blue
Scents: Cedar, Nutmeg
Gemstones: Amethyst, Chrysolite
Magic associated with: ambition, career, wealth, the male principle

★ *Friday*. Venus
Goddesses and Gods: Venus, Astarte, Eros, Adonis
Element: Water/Earth
Colours: green, rose
Scents: Rose, Jasmine
Gemstones: Amber, Jade
Magic associated with: friends, romance, beauty, self-respect, money

★ *Saturday*. Saturn
Goddesses and Gods: Nepthys, Rhea, Cronos, Saturn
Element: Earth
Colours: black, dark blue
Scents: Myrrh, Cinnamon
Gemstones: Onyx, Obsidian
Magic associated with: position, title, binding, banishing

★ *Sunday*. The Sun
Goddesses and Gods: Bast, Amaterasu, Lugh, Ra
Element: Fire/Air
Colours: gold, orange, yellow
Scents: Frankincense, Laurel
Gemstones: Topaz, Cat's eye
Magic associated with: honour, power, glory, work

You will notice that some correspondences seem to differ: you might find one scent recommended in the Scents list which does not appear under the day of the week with the same attributions. This is because there is an almost unlimited range of scents, and not room to list them all here. Correspondences may also appear to overlap. For example, a colour appears in the Days of the Week section with more than one magical use, but under candles the nature of the magic seems more specific. It is important to remember that the correspondence which feels right to your magical sense is the one which will work. Tables and lists like those above will consist of the things which work for the people who wrote them. If you feel at all unsure just focus on your intent, close your eyes and ask the Goddess and the God to guide you. Don't worry if the answer seems different from any list; work with what seems right to you.

In the next chapter I shall be looking at ways of devising your own Rituals and Spells and you may find it useful to be able to refer back to the tools, aids and correspondences here.

SEVEN

SABBAT

RITUALS

Witches celebrate eight seasonal festivals called the Sabbats, which together make up the Wheel of the Year. At these we mark the changes of the seasons and the stories of the Goddess and the God. Whenever possible, Witches will gather together to celebrate these festivals. We dance, sing, feast and honour the Goddess and the God by re-enactment of their stories. The Sabbats are divided into two main groups:

★ *The Major Sabbats* of Samhain, Imbolg, Beltane and Lughnasadh, which mark key points in the agricultural cycle. Originally these would have been celebrated at the times of their natural indicators, but nowadays they are usually celebrated on set dates.

★ *The Minor Sabbats* which mark the Equinoxes and Solstices in the Solar cycle. Before the introduction of accurate time keeping these would have been celebrated just after their associated Solar event, today they are sometimes celebrated on the dates below and sometimes on the actual date of the event.

Each of the Sabbats is associated with stories of the Goddess and the God, and in our Rituals we refer to these as well as to the relevance to our own lives.

Briefly, the eight Sabbats are:

☆ *Samhain*, 31 October. The most important festival of the year, the beginning and end of the year, the beginning of the resting season of the land and a time of remembrance of those who have gone before. A feast of the Goddess as Crone and Wise One.

☆ *Yule*, 21 December. The Winter Solstice, when the decreasing days give way to increasing life, and we celebrate the rebirth of the Sun. The Holly King is slain by his brother Lord Oak who now reigns as Oak King through the days of increasing light.

☆ *Imbolg*, 2 February. When the first signs of life are seen returning to the land. The Goddess changes her robes of Crone for those of Maiden. This festival is the herald of Spring.

☆ *Oestara*, 21 March. The Spring Equinox, when day and night are equal. The festival of the Goddess Eostar, who is derived from the Goddess Astarte, and whose symbols are the egg and the hare.

☆ *Beltane*, 1 May. The second most important festival of the year. The Goddess changes her robes of Maiden for those of Mother and we celebrate the marriage of the Goddess and the God.

☆ *Litha*, 21 June. The Summer Solstice. Here the Sun is at the peak of its power, and the lengthening days are replaced by those growing shorter again. The Oak and Holly Kings battle once more, with Lord Holly winning and reigning through the days of decreasing light.

☆ *Lughnasadh* or *Lammas*, 1 August. The festival of the first of the harvest. The feast of Lugh and of the Sacrificial King, who is these days most often represented by the gingerbread man.

☆ *Madron*, 21 September. The Autumn Equinox, once more a time of balance when day and night are equal, and the feast of the height of the harvest.

On the return to Samhain the year has turned full circle, hence the term Wheel of the Year.

As we have seen earlier, Sabbats are celebratory Rituals. Whilst it is possible, and sometimes necessary, to work magic at these times, it is good to have occasions when we can work Ritual which reflects the spiritual side of our beliefs, and which strengthens our inner selves. Sabbat Rituals usually take place within the following structure, which does not include Casting a Circle or working magic. Should you feel the need to work magic at these times you will need to make the appropriate changes.

Whilst most Witches would like to celebrate the Sabbats in the company of other Witches, this is not always possible. Solitary Witches still celebrate the festivals, although their Rites are usually less elaborate than those for a group. Many Witches will mark them in a low-key manner with their families, perhaps holding a dinner or party, and not necessarily placing any emphasis on the Craft as such.

SABBAT CELEBRATIONS

Generally, Sabbat celebrations all contain the following steps. Chapter 3 contains details for those steps marked.*

DEFINE THE PURPOSE AND COMMUNICATE IT*

PREPARE THE AREA*

SET THE ALTAR*

CREATE THE SACRED SPACE (WITHOUT CASTING A CIRCLE)*

SABBAT INTRODUCTION

CHANTING AND DANCING, TO RAISE ENERGY FOR CELEBRATION RATHER THAN
    FOR WORKING MAGIC*

CELEBRATE THE FESTIVAL

THE RITE OF WINE AND CAKES*

THE SABBAT BLESSING

REMOVING THE SACRED SPACE*

FEASTING

TIDY AWAY*

The main changes from working, and other celebratory, Rituals lie in the Sabbat Introduction, Celebration and Blessing.

✦ The Sabbat Introduction is a piece which explains the nature of the Sabbat, how it fits into the Wheel of the Year, and its relevance to our lives today. It should also refer to at least one of the tales of the Goddess and the God.

✦ The Sabbat Blessing comes after the Rite of Wine and Cakes*, and is a seasonal blessing which again refers to the Sabbat and to its relevance to our daily lives.

At the Sabbats, as at other celebrations, feasting is very important. These are occasions of joy and times when we enjoy the bounty of the Goddess and the God. Also important are the chanting and dancing, which should reflect the nature of the Sabbat.

Other Rites can also be included at the Sabbats. The Rite of Banishing Unwanted Influences* might be included if you feel the need to get rid of mental or emotional distractions. A Self-Blessing* would assist you to focus on the Divine and can be very empowering; it is especially useful for a Solitary.

Those of you who have read other books in the *Real Witches'* series will have found many ideas for the celebration of the Sabbats, some for Solitaries, some for families and yet others for groups and Covens. In the following Rituals I will focus on the Introduction, Ritual and Blessing which you can then fit into the basic outline above.

SAMHAIN

In my Coven we call the following Ritual The Night of the Crone. Its central focus lies around the Goddess changing her robes to those of the Crone and Wise One, and reflects the fact that, not only is this a resting time, but it is also a time for Divination. During the Ritual people will go, one by one, from the Sacred Space to visit the Crone in another location.

In advance, prepare an incense for Divination from:

> 2 PARTS SANDALWOOD
>
> 2 PARTS POPPY SEED
>
> I PART MYRRH
>
> I PART DRIED ORANGE PEEL
>
> I PART MACE
>
> ½ PART CLOVES

Grind and mix together thoroughly and leave for one month in a cool, dark place to allow the ingredients to blend. During that month, on the nights of the Full Moon and the nights of the Dark of the Moon, the incense should be placed on an indoor windowsill in the light and the dark of the Moon.

For your Ritual you will need:

> A CAULDRON, OR LARGE BOWL
>
> WATER
>
> BLACK INK
>
> A STICK TO STIR THE WATERS, PREFERABLY OF WILLOW
>
> BLACK CANDLE
>
> THE ABOVE INCENSE, A THURIBLE AND SELF-IGNITING CHARCOAL
>
> MATCHES
>
> A DARK CLOAK WITH A HOOD, OR A DARK CLOTH WHICH CAN BE USED TO
>   COVER THE CRONE

Prior to the Ritual, and preferably before anyone arrives, set aside a room or screened-off area. This is to be the House of the Crone and should be separate to the place where your Sacred Space is to be created. Try to choose somewhere you can make very dark and colder than other areas. It should not be possible for those in the Sacred Space to hear what happens in this other location. In this area place the cauldron on the floor with a cushion behind it. Place the candle on one side and the Thurible on the other. Ensure that the charcoal, incense and matches are ready to hand. Fill the cauldron with water and place enough ink in it to produce a black reflective surface. As my cauldron is iron and can rust, I place a glass bowl within it. This is one form of a Dark Mirror and for Witches is a very traditional form of Scrying, or Divination.

In this Ritual a Circle should be Cast,* not because you will be working magic but to define clearly the difference between the Circle and the area of the Crone.

SABBAT INTRODUCTION

A Priest or Priestess stands before the Altar and addresses everyone:

'Welcome. Tonight is the festival of Samhain, the greatest of the Sabbats in the Wheel of the Year. It is the end of the old year and the beginning of the new. Tonight is the first night of the resting season, when all that can be harvested has been gathered in. In times past these would be the supplies which would have to last us until new life returns to the land. All that would not survive would have been slain, and would provide the substance of our feast. From now the storms of Winter will be upon us, and the nights darken until the Sun is reborn again at Yule. It is a time for us to remember those who have gone before, who in the love of the Old Ones we will meet and know and love once more. Tonight the Goddess takes on her robes as the Crone, and the God rides out to start the Wild Hunt. It is a time of cold and of darkness, a time for us to reflect, and a time to seek the knowledge and wisdom of the Wise One. Blessed Be.'

SABBAT RITUAL

The High Priestess stands before the Altar and the High Priest gives her the Five-Fold Kiss.* He then invokes the spirit and wisdom of the Crone into her, in a similar way to Drawing Down the Moon.

The High Priestess stands with her hands slightly away from her sides until they are at the 5 and 7 points of the clock with her palms facing forward. Whilst he continues she should look over his head and focus on the Goddess as Crone and on allowing the spirit of the Goddess to enter her.

With the forefinger of his strong hand the Priest then touches the Priestess in the sigil of the First Degree; right breast, left breast, womb and right breast, whilst saying,

'I invoke thee and call upon thee Wise Mother of us all, bringer of all knowledge, wisdom and understanding. By seed and root, by stem and bud, by flower and fruit do I invoke thee to descend upon this the body of thy servant and Priestess.'

He then kneels and, spreading his arms outwards and downwards, says,

'Hail Hecate, from the realms of Old. Pour forth thy store of wisdom. I lowly bend before thee, I adore thee to the end. With loving sacrifice thy shrine adorn. Thy foot is to my lip.'

He kisses her feet and continues,

'My prayer upborn upon the rising incense. Then spend thine ancient love O Mighty One, descend to aid me who without thee am forlorn.'

The Priest then rises and faces the group. He calls upon one of the other Covenors to bring him the cloak and wraps the High Priestess in it, if it has a hood he pulls this down to screen her face, and says,

'Bow your heads and make way, for one walks before you who is in the care of the Wise One, the Dark Mother who brings the knowledge of life and death and rebirth, and who knows all, even that which we would hide in our hearts.'

He then precedes the High Priestess to a point in the Circle where he opens a doorway for her. She leaves the Circle and goes to the House of the Crone.

The High Priest then closes the doorway in the Circle and says,

'Tonight we will each have the chance to visit the Crone and ask wisdom of her. May our hearts be open and our minds be strong enough to listen and accept her words. Let us now prepare ourselves. Blessed Be.'

He leads the others in some chanting suitable to the occasion. One of the chants used by our group is:

Hecate, Ceridwyn,
Dark Mother take us in.
Hecate, Ceridwyn,
Let us be reborn.

Where there are a large number of people you might also want to have people take turns to tell tales of the Goddess and the God, and of the season, whilst they await their turns to visit the Crone.

Meanwhile, the High Priestess should complete the preparations in the House of the Crone by lighting the candle and incense, turning off all other lights and making herself as comfortable as possible on the cushion.

Back in the Circle the High Priest will wait a few moments and then send the first person to visit the Crone. He makes a doorway in the Circle to let them out saying,

'Go forth and seek the wisdom of the Crone. May the Goddess guide you in knowledge and under-standing. Blessed Be.'

He closes the doorway after them. The individual then goes to the House of the Crone and stands before her until acknowledged by the High Priestess. The High Priestess will ask the person to kneel and to gaze into the Dark Mirror. At this point it is up to the individual whether they have a question they want to ask, or whether they will simply wait to hear what is said. The High Priestess will stir the water with the stick, and when she is ready, tell the person what she sees, or feels, within her heart for that person.

When the 'interview' is over that person returns to the Circle where they wait to be re-admitted by the High Priest, who will then send the next person. They should not speak about their visit with the Crone until after the Ritual. This continues until everyone who wishes to has visited the Crone. After the last person, usually the High Priest himself, has visited, the High Priestess will put out the candle and incense and will return to the Circle.

The High Priest admits her and once again gives her the Five-Fold Kiss.* He next removes her cloak, and kissing her on each cheek, says,

'We welcome back to us our High Priestess who has travelled in the care of the Crone through the dark lands to bring us knowledge. May the Goddess watch over her, and over us all. Blessed Be.'

Some people have quite profound experiences during this Ritual. For others, messages and interpretations come later.

 ## SABBAT BLESSING

After the Rite of Wine and Cakes,* the High Priest steps forward to give the Blessing:

'I call upon the Old Gods, upon the Hunter and the Crone who preside at this the dark part of the year. May they watch over each and every one of us, may they guard, guide and protect us in all that we do. Within their care we know that although the days continue to darken the light will yet return to us. And so the Wheel of the Year turns. Blessed Be.'

After the Ritual an extra place is laid at the feast in order that we might remember those who have gone before.

YULE

In this Ritual we will Rise to Greet the Reborn Sun and enact the Battle of the Oak and Holly Kings. Hence it is better if it can take place outdoors, preferably away from a residential area! When working outside you do not have to have a full Altar, with representations of the elements, etc, as you are to be out there in the midst of them. If you cannot find a reasonably remote outdoor location then you can hold this Ritual in your garden, or even indoors, but you will need to ensure that you do not disturb the neighbours. On the morning, you will need to set off in good time to have Created your Sacred Space* before Sunrise, which takes place in the UK at around 8am. Ideally, you will time your Ritual so that the chanting starts just before sunrise. If you have drummers and/or other acoustic musicians in your group then get them to bring their instruments with them.

Remember that the Oak and Holly Kings are brothers, and facets of the same archetype. Strictly speaking the ruling brother is termed King and the other is known as Lord, so prior to Yule you have Lord Oak and King Holly, after Yule they become Lord Holly and King Oak.

You will need:

      A GOLD CANDLE

      A WIND-PROOF GLASS VESSEL TO PUT THE CANDLE IN, AN EMPTY JAR WILL DO
         IF YOU HAVE NOTHING MORE DECORATIVE

      OAK AND HOLLY CROWNS

      MUSICAL INSTRUMENTS (OPTIONAL)

Prior to the Ritual assign the roles of Oak and Holly Kings to two people, preferably male. Get them to practise/rehearse their battle, to try to minimize the possibility of injury, and to ensure that the 'right' person, the Oak King, wins! Make crowns of Oak and Holly for each of them.

SABBAT INTRODUCTION

Remember that this will be given whilst it is still dark, so it needs to be memorized.

'Welcome. This is the festival of Yule. Today, after the days of decreasing light, the Sun is once again reborn. Even now in the midst of Winter, whilst the Wild Hunt is at its peak, a spark of light is born which brings to us the promise of Spring, of light and heat, of growth and fruitfulness. This is the season of hope and the time for looking forward to what will come and what we will achieve. Today, Lord Oak challenges his brother the Holly King, for rule over the land and the light half of the year. Should he win, as he surely must, he will bring new growth and fertility and life afresh. Blessed Be.'

 ## SABBAT RITUAL

Everyone stands in the Sacred Space, facing the point where the Sun is to rise. Together they chant, to the accompaniment of any musicians in the group. Chanting should start off slowly and quietly and build up as the Sun appears over the horizon. One of the chants we favour is:

> *Return, return,*
> *by Earth, by Air,*
> *by Fire and by Water.*

Save any dancing until the Sun has started to rise, so that you have enough light to see by.

Once the Sun is well on its way, the chanting should stop and a Priestess says,

'The Sun is rising and a spark of light is reborn to the land.'

She lights the Gold candle in its wind-proof container and says,

'*Even as the spark of life is lit, so this candle is our hopes for the promise of the new season. Blessed Be.*'

The candle is passed to everyone in the Circle who makes a wish for the new season.

The chanting and dancing resume. The Holly King puts on his crown of leaves, and at an agreed signal, the brothers Oak and Holly interrupt the chanting with an argument:

Oak Lord: '*Holly King! You are old, your time has passed, your rule over the land is ended. Brother, give up your crown and your throne.*'

Holly King: '*Never! Younger brother, you are usurper; you are young and green and untried. Take my crown if you can, but I will never give it up for you.*'

Oak Lord: '*Brother, I would that we do not fight, that we shed not our blood. Give up your crown, for now the new Sun has risen and it is rightfully mine.*'

Holly King: '*Brother, it saddens me that you should wish to take from me that which I hold. Never will I give it up for you. Care of the land can only belong to he who wins it by right of might and strength.*'

Oak Lord: '*That which you hold is no longer rightfully yours. Brother Holly, I challenge you to battle, and our spilt blood will be taken up by the land, which is in our care.*'

The Holly King removes his crown and hands it to the High Priestess, who will hold it and the Oak crown for the duration of the battle, saying,

'*Then take my crown if you dare, if you can! Let us see to whom the land belongs!*'

Everyone else should be moving away a little during this exchange, so as to give the two combatants room. As the battle is being fought the others should start by cheering on the Holly King, but switch allegiance so that towards the end they are cheering for the Oak King.

Once the Oak King has won, the High Priestess calls him over. He kneels at her feet and she says,

'Once again Holly and Oak have fought, and as is rightful at Yule, Lord Oak has won. Lord Oak I crown you, King of the lightening days.'

She places the Oak Crown on his head and says,

'Hail and Welcome to the Oak King.'

Everyone except Lord Holly repeats,

'Hail and Welcome, the Oak King.'

Lord Holly steps forward and says,

'Victor of this day you might be, but my time will come again, and you will kneel at my feet once again.'

The Oak King replies,

'But for now, kneel before me Lord Holly, for this is my time.'

Lord Holly kneels and says,

'Hail, the Oak King.'

The High Priestess says:

'Now is the time of the Oak King, but even as the year grows so it will once again become time for Lord Holly to step forward. For as we need light we also need darkness. As we need day, we need night. As we need Summer, we need Winter. For both are as the two sides of a coin, and without the one, the other cannot be. And so the Wheel turns. Blessed Be.'

The High Priestess and the Oak King perform the Rite of Wine and Cakes.*

 ## SABBAT BLESSING

The Oak King gives the blessing:

'I call upon the Old Gods, upon the reborn Sun and the spirit of the Oak. May the spark of light reborn this day, grow ever stronger. May its fire light and heat the land. May it bring forth new life and new hopes. As it grows in strength from day to day, may we also be made stronger. As it brings growth and life, may we also grow and bring forth the new in our lives. And so the Wheel turns. Blessed Be.'

IMBOLG

In advance of your Ritual the women should prepare a figure of the Goddess Bride (pronounced Breed). She should have a womanly figure and be dressed in the white of Spring, with white and yellow flowers in her hair and on her dress. They also make a thin white veil, which will completely cover her until she should be unveiled. They should also make bedding in the same colours. The men should prepare a bed into which the figure will fit, and a phallic wand of the same length as Bride. Whilst some collusion will be needed to ensure that bed, figure and wand are compatible, the men should not be allowed to see Bride, nor the women to see the bed and wand until the appropriate point in the Ritual.

You will need:

YOUR BRIDE IMAGE

BRIDE'S BEDDING

BRIDE'S BED

THE PHALLIC WAND

13 TEA LIGHT CANDLES, WITH HOLDERS

A SMALL BOWL OF FLOWER PETALS, FROM SEASONAL BLOOMS, BUT, PLEASE,
   NOT PICKED FROM THE WILD

Prior to the Ritual the Priestesses should bring Bride and her bedding, concealed under a cloth, and place them before the Altar. The men should do likewise with the bed and wand. The tea lights in their holders should be evenly spaced around the outer edge of the Circle.

The Ritual should begin with the room lit only by one candle. If you still have your Yule candle, this would be ideal.

 ## SABBAT INTRODUCTION

'Welcome. This is Imbolg, the festival of the first of Spring. Imbolg means 'in the belly' and at this season the first lambs are born. The first buds are on the trees, the first plants show through the frozen earth. The breath of air which comes to us holds the promise of the future. Here we clearly see the signs which tell us that the Winter will pass and the land will be fertile once more.

'The Goddess changes her robes to those of the Maiden, and the God is once more the virile youth who walks the land.

'This is the festival of Bride, known also as Brighid, Bridget, Brigandu, Brigantia and by many other names. Triple Goddess of poetry and inspiration, smithcraft, healer and muse, Bride is one of the greatest of the Celtic Goddesses. At this time we make her bed that the God might join her and she may, once again, become fertile in the name of the land. Blessed Be.'

 SABBAT RITUAL

The High Priestess says,

'At Yule a spark of light was born, now in the sight of the Goddess and the God of Spring, we would see that flame blossom and grow. We seek within it the warmth and light of the Summer Sun to come.'

She lights a taper from the Yule candle and lights one of the tea lights, then continues,

'We call upon Bride, Goddess of Spring to be with us.'

Everyone repeats,

'Bride be with us.'

She passes the taper to the next person Deosil in the Circle who lights their tea light and says (if male),

'We call upon the young God, Lord of the Spring to come among us.'

Everyone says,

'Lord of the Spring be with us.'

As the women light their tea lights, they say,

'We call upon Bride, Goddess of Spring to be with us.'

Everyone says,

'Goddess of Spring be with us.'

The taper is passed around until everyone has lit their candles and the Circle is now a circle of light.

The High Priestess leads the women to the Altar, where they hold up the Bride image, still covered with her veil. She holds it up to the men, with the women crowding around her, and says,

'Behold the image of the Bride, Goddess of Spring. In her, new hope resides. In her, new life may blossom and grow. But how shall this come to be?'

The women now step back from the High Priestess although they do not resume their places in the Circle.

The High Priest now leads the men to the Altar and says,

'Only together with the God will the Goddess bring life and fertility to the land and the people. For as light needs dark, and day needs night, woman and man, Goddess and God need one another, to bring life into being.'

The men then unveil the bed. The High Priest holds it up and says,

'This gift we offer that they may join together for the good of all.'

He places the bed onto the Altar. The men now withdraw to the other side of the Circle, where they group together with their backs to the Altar.

The women, keeping their backs to the men, and making sure they cannot peek, make the bed and place Bride, now unveiled, within its covers. When all is ready they place Bride in her bed in the centre of the Altar. The High Priestess says,

'Bride is abed, and like the sleeping Spring she waits only for the God to awaken her. Let the God seek his Goddess, let them unite in the promise of new life to come.'

All the women return to their places, one of them taking the bowl of petals with her.

The men now approach the Altar with the wand, still wrapped. Once there they gather round and unveil the wand, placing it within the covers with Bride. The High Priest then moves Bride and her bed to the centre of the Circle and says,

'As surely as the Goddess is here the God is also, for, ever does he seek to be with his Lady and his love. Blessed Be.'

The men return to their places and the female Witch passes the bowl of petals around so everyone can take one or two. Everyone dances and chants:

Lady of the Moon, Lady of the Moon,
Come to us be with us, Lady of the Moon.

As they dance each person in turn floats their petals down onto Bride in her bed, and makes a wish for something they wish to start in the coming season.

When the chanting is finished, usually after many repetitions, Bride and her bed are replaced on the Altar. After the Ritual they are set in a safe place until the next Sabbat when they can be put away.

The Rite of Wine and Cakes* can be performed by the High Priestess and High Priest or they can help the newest female and male Witches to do so.

SABBAT BLESSING

The Blessing should be given by the youngest, or newest, female Witch:

'I call upon the Old Ones. Upon the Goddess and the God of Spring, upon Bride and her Consort, return and be once more with us. Spread your love and your blessings upon us and be with us and those we love. Take our offerings and bring new life and hope to the land, bring inspiration and energy to us, bring fertility and growth to all. As Winter turns once more to Spring, new life begins again. And so the Wheel ever turns. Blessed Be.'

OESTARA

This Ritual focuses on the duality of men and women. Ideally, you will have an equal number of men and women for this Ritual. However, life is rarely ideal, so where there is an imbalance some people will have to double up in the Ritual.

You will need:

> A NUMBER OF DARK CLOTHS, ONE FOR EACH OF THE MEN
>
> A NUMBER OF WHITE CLOTHS, OR SHAWLS, ONE FOR EACH OF THE WOMEN
>
> ENOUGH WHITE CANDLES, IN HOLDERS, SO THAT EACH OF THE WOMEN MAY HOLD ONE
>
> A NUMBER OF EGGS, EITHER HARD BOILED AND DECORATED (OR CHOCOLATE IF YOU REALLY CAN'T RESIST!)
>
> A CAULDRON OR LARGE BOWL OF WATER

SABBAT INTRODUCTION

'Welcome. This is the festival of Oestara, sacred to the Dawn Goddess Eostar, she whose symbols of birth and life are the Hare and the Egg.

'This is a festival of the dying and rising Gods, of Attis, Mithras, Tammuz, Adonis and Osiris and many more. It is the time when the Goddesses Persephone, Inanna, and others have returned from the underworld, bearing the knowledge of life, of death and of rebirth. All these, and many others, have been renewed and refreshed, even as we seek to be renewed and refreshed in our lives.

'This is also the Spring Equinox, when day and night are equal and in balance. This balance we seek in our own lives too, for each must seek to cast off the outworn to make way for the new. Blessed Be.'

SABBAT RITUAL

The Ritual commences with everyone chanting, the women will Circle dance around the men who stand in a smaller circle within the Circle.

For the first verse everyone sings:

We all come from the Goddess
And to her we shall return
Like a drop of rain
Flowing to the ocean.

For the second, third and fourth verses the women continue to sing:

We all come from the Goddess
And to her we shall return
Like a drop of rain
Flowing to the ocean.

At the same time, in the second, third and fourth verses the men sing:

We all come from the Horned God
And to him we shall return
Like an Autumn leaf
Floating to the forest floor.

Men and women should sing competitively, each group trying (tunefully?) to drown out the other.

As they proceed through verses 3 and 4, the women should, one by one, cover the men's heads with the dark cloths. As his head is covered each Priest should sink to the floor, and lie as though dead. (The women will avoid treading on them!) When all the men are on the ground the women continue singing softly. They go to the Altar where they each take a candle and light it from the Altar candle. All lights and candles other than those of the women and the Altar candle are extinguished. The women, still chanting softly, then walk in procession out of the room. Once outside of the area they drape the white shawls around their shoulders.

After a few minutes they change their chant to:

'Return, return, the Earth, the Air, the Fire and the Water.'

They process back into the room and circle the group of men three times. One by one each woman will place her candle on the Altar, or around the outer edge of the Circle if that can be done safely. She will select a man and remove his dark cloth, replacing it with her white shawl and, drawing him to his feet, say,

'As man is to woman, so the God is to the Goddess, without both there can be no life. As the Goddess descends to free her love, and the God rises to give her his strength, so do I call upon you, rise once more, be with us and among us. Blessed Be.'

Once all the men are standing the white shawls are removed by the women, and one by one the women will each give a man the Five-Fold Kiss.*

The High Priest then places the cauldron of water in front of the Altar and says,

'This is the time of the dying and rising God, who lives and dies and is reborn. Like him, to be reborn we must first die, to live fully we must release that which holds us back. This is the cauldron of Ceridwyn, the symbol of life and death and rebirth. Into these waters we may cast off all that is not needful to us.'

He consecrates the water in the same way as the Banishing of Unwanted Influences,* and each person steps forward to dip their fingers in, rather than the bowl being carried around the Circle as usual.

The women then each take their candle and an egg from the Altar and give one to each man saying,

'From darkness into light, from death into life. Take this symbol of the love of the Goddess, that she may ever walk with you. Blessed Be.'

The men then present the candles back to the women saying,

'The Goddess leads the God from darkness to light and so I return this flame to you. This is the symbol of the light of Sun, may he ever brighten your way. Blessed Be.'

The candles and eggs should be placed safely on the outer edge of the Circle until the Ritual is completed.

After the Rite of Wine and Cakes* the Sabbat Blessing is given.

 ## SABBAT BLESSING

A Priestess starts the blessing:

'I call the Dying and Rising Gods, they who have lived and died and been reborn, to bring life to us and fertility to all the land.'

A Priest continues:

'I call upon the Goddess Eostar to bring her gifts of life and strength to us.'

They finish together:

'For the cycles of life and death and rebirth go ever on, the seasons come and go, each in their turn. And so the Wheel turns. Blessed Be.'

BELTANE

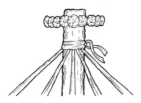

This Ritual combines elements of the traditions of the Bel fires and of the chase of the Stag Lord. The chanting and dancing take place in the early part of the Ritual, rather than before it starts. Clapping and chanting are encouraged but it is best not to have any drumming as this will impede the chase. Similarly, the Rite of Wine and Cakes* takes place within the body of the Ritual, rather than just after it.

You will need:

> 2 FIRES. IF YOU CAN WORK OUTSIDE THEN YOU CAN HAVE SMALL FIRES IN
>   CAULDRONS OR SIMILAR; IF YOU ARE INDOORS THEN YOU NEED 2 SHORT
>   FAT CANDLES, ONE RED AND ONE GREEN, ON SAFE HOLDERS
> A CANDLE FOR EVERY PERSON PRESENT, RED FOR THE WOMEN AND GREEN FOR
>   THE MEN

Before you create the Sacred Space, place your two fires approximately 2 feet apart, in the centre of your working area. It should be possible to pass safely between them, but not too easy to do so.

SABBAT INTRODUCTION

'Welcome. This is the festival of Beltane, the Great festival of fire and fertility. Now is the time when the Goddess sheds the robes of Maiden and takes on those of the Mother. Now the God stands at her side, and rules as her Consort, and their marriage is for the fertility of all the land.

'In the past the young stag Lord, chosen at birth, would run with the deer, challenge and be challenged, and if he won through would win the maiden. Thus was the Great Rite celebrated to bring fertility to all.

'This is the festival of the Fire God Bel, known also as Belennos, Beli-Mawr, Belinus, and by other names from times and places far away. In times past the old hearth fires would be extinguished and a new flame sparked from the embers. Two fires would be lit on a high point where they could be seen by all. Livestock would be driven between them and the people would leap them to purify, strengthen and bring fertility to all.

'This is a time of great joy, a time to love, sing, dance and make merry, for the Old Ones lead us in the dance of life. Blessed Be.'

 SABBAT RITUAL

The High Priestess lights the two fires from the Altar candle saying,

'In days past, we would have lit our fires in the centre of our village community, and so I light these in the centre of the community of our Circle. May they purify and strengthen, inspire and bring forth fertility, even as the fires of old. Blessed Be.'

Everyone should start Circle dancing around the outside of the two fires, starting slowly and building up pace and volume. They should not hold hands.

One of the chants we use for this is:

Cernunnos, horned one,
Cernunnos King of the Sun,
Herne the Hunted and Hunter,
Stag Lord of the Earth.

After the Circle dancing has been going on for a while the High Priestess taps one of the Covenors on the shoulder. He or she then breaks from the Circle, and picks a group member of the opposite gender. The 'hunter' will chase the other person in and out of the dancers and finally between the two fires, where the 'quarry' is 'caught' and given a kiss. That Covenor then selects someone else to chase, catch and kiss. This goes on until everyone has been chased between the fires, including the High Priestess.

People should be very careful passing between the fires, holding long skirts or robes safely away from the flames! Energetic types can even jump the flames if they wish.

After everyone has been between, or over, the flames, there is usually a short pause while everyone gets their breath back!

The High Priestess and High Priest now start the Rite of Wine and Cakes,* but instead of passing the Chalice and plate around the circle, they will walk around the Circle together with the High Priest offering to the women and the High Priestess to the men.

The High Priestess and High Priest now take the red and green candles from the Altar. She will give a green one to each male, and he will give a red one to each female, and they each say,

'Take this symbol of the fires of life and fertility, take it home and burn it in the names of the Mother Goddess and of the Father God. May it bring light and heat, life and fertility into your lives, and into the lives of those around you. Blessed Be.'

SABBAT BLESSING

The High Priestess says,

'I call upon the Goddess and the God. Mother and Father of us all, bring your blessings upon each of us. May these candles take the light and heat of the Bel fire into our homes and our lives. May we too bring light and warmth into the world around us. Even as the God hunted his Goddess, he is now in turn caught by her. The Maiden is Mother now, and the God takes his rightful place by her side. And so the Wheel turns and life goes ever onward. Blessed Be.'

LITHA

This Ritual should take place on the seashore. You will not need robes, an Altar or many tools, but it might be advisable to take a change of clothing. Find a location where the tide comes in reasonably steadily, and where you will not get cut off by the incoming waters. Check the tide tables to ensure that you can start your Ritual about one hour before high tide. Also check the location to ensure that it is reasonably private at the time you intend to use it. If you can find a very secluded location, there is no reason why you should not work the Ritual during the day. Alternatively, you might like to time it so that you can be present to mark sunrise prior to starting, although this may well mean staying up all night! If you really cannot arrange to do this on the coast then you will need to give thought as to how to bring about a suitable amount of the element of surprise into your Ritual.

Prepare a series of small cards each with a question about, or linked to, the Craft on it. There should be four or five cards per person. The questions do not have to directly involve magical knowledge, so you could, for example, ask, 'How do you spell Myrrh?' or 'Describe the leaves of the plant Rosemary', and so on. Questions can be simple or hard; some can even be 'trick' questions. Note that one person, usually the High

Priestess, has the final say as to whether an answer is right or wrong, and this person is the arbiter.

Tell everyone who is attending to bring a single yellow or gold flower. It is worth mentioning here that it is not a good idea to pick wild flowers as these may well be protected or endangered, even if prolific in your area.

You will need:

> A BAG WITH SEVERAL SLIPS OF PAPER, ONE FOR EACH PERSON, WITH THEIR
> NAME ON IT
> THE QUESTION CARDS
> A SMALL PRIZE FOR THE WINNER

Before the Ritual actually starts, get everyone to find small stones and other natural beach debris to mark the outline of the Circle, which should be below the high tide mark. The Circle should be large enough that people will be well spread out. Also collect some driftwood for a small fire, which will be in the centre of the Circle. Please ensure it is very small, as you do not need the coastguard alerted! Once the Circle is marked and the fire started, take the first name slip out of the bag; this person stands to the right of the high tide mark. Continue pulling slips until everyone has their place, selected at random, in the Circle. You will probably need to spread them out evenly, as there is usually some reluctance to be at the lowest tidal point! Assign the roles in creating the Sacred Space in such a way that people do not have to move away from their allotted places.

 ## SABBAT INTRODUCTION

'Welcome. This is Litha, the Summer Solstice, the longest day and the height of the Sun's power. But herein lies the paradox. For even as the Sun reaches the height of its power, it begins to decline. From this point the nights will lengthen and the days shorten.

'At this time Lord Holly once more challenges his brother the Oak King, and wins. From now he will preside over the darkening half of the year.

'This is also the time of the trickster Gods, the time of Pan, Puck and Loki, and of the Goddesses and Gods of humour and jest. And in keeping with this we celebrate with mirth and joy, as well as with reverence. Blessed Be.'

 ## SABBAT RITUAL

The High Priestess says,

'We have gathered to celebrate the Summer Solstice, to mark the height of the Sun even as he starts his decline. This is the festival of Fire and of Water, so it is in keeping that we should meet both in our Rites. Tonight/today we will pit our knowledge of the Craft against the incoming waters, in honour of the Sun King. Blessed Be.'

The High Priest now shuffles the question cards and deals them out evenly amongst everyone, except the arbiter. Starting to the left of the High Priestess, each person takes it in turn to ask a question of another in the group. Where it is answered correctly the answerer chooses whether to exchange places, where the answer is incorrect the questioner can choose.

After each answer everyone chants:

Cernunnos, horned one,
Cernunnos King of the Sun,
Herne the Hunted and Hunter,
Stag Lord of the Earth.

Everyone then moves one place to his or her left, and the next person asks his or her question. Anyone moving before the chant is completed is 'out'. Where a questioner has moved, it is the person to their left after the move, who asks the next question. The High Priestess can intervene if she feels things are becoming unfair.

If the weather is clement and the participants are fairly hardy, you might like to denote someone as being 'out' only when the water reaches their knees. Or you may prefer to declare 'out' as soon as their feet become wet. As people fall foul of the waves, they can change into dry clothes or you can set them to preparing the post-Ritual feast, until you reach the second phase. As you can probably see by now, the people closest to the water will want to get away from it, whilst those further up the beach will want to retain their places. When there is only one person in the Circle, in addition to the arbiter, that person is the winner.

Everyone should now gather round, above the tide line, with his or her flowers. The High Priest now stands facing the waves and, raising his arms up to each side of his head, says,

'I call upon the Sun King, in whose honour we have gathered, to witness that … (name of winner) has today met the challenge of the waters and has prevailed. In recognition of this I present him/her with this. Blessed Be.'

The prize is handed over. The High Priest continues,

'Mighty Lord of the Sun, who brings heat and light to the land, who causes all things to be fruitful and flourish. Mighty Lord of the Sea, whose waters pour out upon the land, who causes all things to grow and be fertile. Great Mother Goddess from whom all life proceeds and to whom all will return. Accept our offerings and our thanks. Blessed Be.'

He casts his flower into the waters. Everyone else also casts their flowers into the waters and sings the above chant once again.

The Rite of Wine and Cakes* can be performed either by the winner and their chosen partner, or by the High Priestess and High Priest.

SABBAT BLESSING

This should be given by the winner of the competition:

'I call upon the Old Gods, and the elements of Fire and Water, Earth and Air, which are all around us and within us. Pour forth your blessings on all here present. Lord of the Sun whose cycle now turns, be with us each and every one. Great Mother, watch over us and guide us well. The lightening days are over, the darkening days are here. And so the Wheel turns. Blessed Be.'

LUGHNASADH/LAMMAS

JOHN BARLEYCORN

There were three Kings into the East
Three Kings both great and high,
And they hath sworn a solemn oath,
John Barleycorn must die.

They took a plough and ploughed him down,
Put clods upon his head,
And they hath sworn a solemn oath
John Barleycorn was dead.

But cheerful spring came kindly on,
And showers began to fall,
John Barleycorn got up again,
And so surprised them all.

The sultry suns of summer came
And he grew pale and wan,
His head well armed with pointed spears,
That no-one should do him wrong.

The sober autumn entered mild,
When he grew tall and pale,
His bending joints and drooping head,
Showed he began to fail.

His colour sickened more and more,
He faded into age,
And then his enemies began,
To show their deadly rage.

They took a weapon long and sharp
And cut him by the knee,
They tied him fast upon a cart,
Like a rogue of forgery.

They laid him down upon his back,
And cudgelled him full score,
They hung him up before the storm,
And turned him o'er and o'er.

They filled up the darksome pit
With water to the brim,
They heaved in John Barleycorn
And let him sink or swim.

They laid him out upon the floor,
To work him further woe
And still as signs of life appeared,
They tossed him to and fro.

They wasted o'er a scorching flame,
The marrow of his bones,
But old miller used him worst of all,
And crushed him mid two stones.

And they have taken his very heart's blood,
And drank it round and round,
And still more and more they drank,
Their joy did more abound.

John Barleycorn was a hero bold,
Of noble enterprise,
For if you do but taste his blood,
'Twill make your courage rise.

You will need:

SEVERAL COPIES OF THE POEM JOHN BARLEYCORN BY ROBERT BURNS, PRINTED
    IN A REASONABLE SIZE FONT

A FEW EARS OF BARLEY, OR CORN, WITH THE STEMS AND LEAVES STILL
    ATTACHED, TIED INTO A BUNCH

A KNIFE

3 SHORT STICKS

SOME WATER

A SMALL DISH

2 STONES

A CLOTH TO COVER THE FLOOR

THE CHALICE WITH A GOOD QUALITY BEER IN IT

A PLATE OF FRESHLY BAKED REAL BREAD, NOT THE MASS PRODUCED SLICED
    STUFF!

Before the Ritual commences, choose three people to be the 'kings'. If you can, choose people who will throw themselves into their roles! Give everyone else a copy of the poem with the verses they are to read clearly marked. Try to ensure an even division of verses.

The Rite of Wine and Cakes* which takes place immediately after the central Ritual will take place using the beer rather than wine, and bread rather than the usual cakes or biscuits.

 ## SABBAT INTRODUCTION

'Welcome. This is the festival of Lughnasadh, the feast of the Solar God Lugh. It is the feast of the first of the harvest, when the land begins to yield its abundance. In times past this was a time of sacrifice, to repay the land in blood or wine, for that which will be taken. It was believed that the first sheaf cut must be repaid before the land awoke to prevent the harvest continuing. Today our sacrifices are of time and energy, and so we gather together to celebrate and to honour the Goddess and the God from whom all life flows. Blessed Be.'

 ## SABBAT RITUAL

The High Priestess takes the barley and holds it out before her, saying,

'Behold the first of the harvest, symbol of the bounty of the land and of the Great Mother who sustains us. Let us give thanks for the fruitfulness of the land. Blessed Be.'

The three 'kings' now step forward and take the barley from the High Priestess, and as the readers read their assigned verses of John Barleycorn, the 'kings' go through the actions in the poem. The readers should proceed slowly in order that all the steps can be accomplished.

SABBAT BLESSING

The High Priest gives the blessing:

'I call upon the Old Gods, upon the Mother and upon the Sun God. Your bounty flows out upon the land, it sustains it and makes it fruitful, so that it is fertile and brings forth life. Smile upon us also, that we might have knowledge of you and walk in your ways. Ever watch over us, guard, guide and protect us. May we likewise be fruitful and bring forth life. And so the Wheel turns. Blessed Be.'

MADRON

In advance, everyone should be asked to give some thought as to what they have been 'given' by the Goddess and the God during the preceding year. This includes personal achievements, friends, health, new skills, good times, and so on. They should also reflect on any unresolved issues they may have in their lives; outstanding disagreements and arguments that should be brought to a close, and how they might resolve these. Hopefully, none of these should affect other Coven members, but if they do they really should be resolved before the Ritual.

With these thoughts in mind, each person should create and bring to the festival some kind of home-produced harvest offering. It could be something they have made from natural ingredients, something they have grown in their garden, a picture, poem or other artistic endeavour, so long as it is something they have expended their personal energy on. Each item should be presented as nicely as possible and wrapped so that it cannot be seen by the others.

You will need:

I WHITE AND I BLACK CANDLE FOR EACH PERSON AND CANDLEHOLDERS TO
PUT THEM IN

Prior to the Ritual the packages should be placed on a tray, covered with a cloth and placed under, or behind the Altar out of sight.

 ## SABBAT INTRODUCTION

'Welcome. This is Madron, the Autumn Equinox when day and night are equal once again. The harvest is well under way and we are seeing the results of our efforts. Even as we reap the rewards of our labour we must ask whether we have indeed paid for that which we have been given.

'As we see the Wheel turn towards Autumn our hearts and minds too turn to hearth and home. We seek the resolution of quarrels, and reconciliation with those we love, for this is the time of forgiveness and reunion. A time for the payment of debts and the release of prisoners. And so we must ask ourselves whether we have indeed paid for what we have been given, and whether we still hold prisoners in our minds and hearts. For all must be set into balance lest the storms of Autumn come and nothing survive. Blessed Be.'

 ## SABBAT RITUAL

Everyone stands in a Circle. The High Priestess says,

'This is a time of balance and it is fit that we should seek balance within ourselves. Within the hearts and minds of each and every one of us there is that which is no longer useful. We have guilt which is outworn, regret which should be put behind us and feelings which are past their time. Let us first put these from us. Let us open our hearts to the Goddess and the God, that they might bring us the balance which we seek. Blessed Be.'

She turns to the Altar and lights the first of the black candles. Each person now steps forward and takes a turn to light a black candle and state which feelings they have finished with.

Everyone chants four times:

We are the flow, we are the ebb,
We are the weavers, we are the web.

The High Priest now says,

'The Goddess and the God have smiled upon us, each and every one. Let us recall their gifts and give thanks.'

One by one each person steps forward to the Altar, states the things that they have received in the preceding year, and lights a white candle. As they light their candle they say,

'I give thanks to the Goddess and the God for their bounty, may I ever be aware of their gifts and worthy of them. Blessed Be.'

Again everyone chants four times:

We are the flow, we are the ebb,
We are the weavers, we are the web.

The High Priestess now steps forward again and says,

'It is meet and fit that we should cast off that which is no longer needful and that we should give thanks for that which has been given. But also we should seek to repay the gifts of the Goddess and the God, and the companionship of the Circle to which they have brought us. Bring forth the gifts.'

The High Priest brings the covered tray forward and says,

'Each of us has worked on one of these, has placed their energy into it in token of repayment to the Old Gods. Let each now receive the gift of another that it may serve to remind us to strive ever towards balance. Blessed Be.'

The High Priest now takes the tray around the Circle and everyone should take a gift which they did not provide.

The gifts should not be opened until after the Ritual. Should someone end up with the gift they brought, they can exchange it with someone else.

The High Priest and High Priestess now perform the Rite of Wine and Cakes.*

 SABBAT BLESSING

A Covenor gives the blessing:

'I call upon the Old Gods, to bless us. At this time of harvest we ask that they guide us in the sowing of our seeds for the future, aid us in reaping the harvest we seek, and help us to remember the life of the land, and the love of friends. May they bring us balance in our lives. For all things strive towards balance, night and day, male and female, dark and light, Summer and Winter. And so the Wheel turns. Blessed Be.'

There are many themes which can be taken as the centre of your Sabbat Rituals, although I have only been able to include some of them here. To make your celebrations meaningful you will need to examine the festivals in more detail and to reflect upon the way in which each of the Sabbats is reflected in your life. It is also helpful to look at some of the stories of the Goddess and the God, to help you see how all the pieces go to make up the whole.

EIGHT

RITES OF PASSAGE

Rites of passage are those celebrations and Rituals we perform at key stages in our lives. They usually mark the birth of a child, marriage and death. Some people also celebrate coming of age and retirement. In the Craft we have similar Rites which have different names:

☆ *Wiccaning.* This is the Rite of Naming performed to welcome a new child. The child is presented to the Goddess and God, the Elements, and the assembled guests. They are not dedicated or promised to any specific path in the same way as in a Christening.

☆ *Handfasting.* The Rite or Ritual where two people declare their love for each other and their intention to be a partnership. A Handfasting differs from the better known Wedding in several respects: the couple comes to the Circle as equals, neither is given to the other; they make their own promises to each other, there is no set formula; they can choose to unite for life, or for a year and a day. Indeed many couples choose the latter, not because they intend to split up at the end of that time, but so that they may make fresh promises and declarations of love every year.

☆ *Withdrawal.* This Rite (or Rites) is intended to actively celebrate the life of someone who has died, and may be held some time after burial or cremation. This is often done to spare the feelings of non-Pagan relatives. For some, this Rite may be enacted several times as different groups of friends and family gather at different times to celebrate their loved one. The Rite of Withdrawal can also be held for much loved pets.

★ *Naming*. This Rite is often held when an adult chooses a new or Witch name to denote their entry into the Craft. It is sometimes held as part of the second degree Initiation and sometimes as a Ritual on its own. In some Covens the Initiate is given their new name by the High Priestess, but in most cases the person chooses their own Witch name.

★ *Puberty*. In the secular world people celebrate their 16th, 18th or 21st birthdays as coming of age. This replaces rites of puberty which would have been held when a woman first menstruated or when a boy passed his first test of manhood. However, many Craft families have revived these Rites as more young people seek to celebrate them. Rites of Puberty are generally single gender affairs as these days there is still a certain amount of shyness regarding puberty and adolescence!

★ *Croning and Wizzening*. Originally Croning would have taken place at the end of menopause and Wizzening at the time when a man was accepted as too old to hunt or fight. The closest we come to these in the world outside Paganism is the retirement party with its gold watch, and even this is rare in these times of changing employment practices. However, as with the Rites of Puberty, many are seeking to revive these customs. Croning is sometimes enacted at the end of menopause and Wizzening at around the age of 70 when health is beginning to fail. As these Rites are intended to indicate that the physical activity of a person is of far less importance to the group or family than the wisdom of age, people may choose to celebrate them at any time from around 50 onwards.

The key thing to remember about any of these Rites of Passage is that their format is not established by some kind of outside authority; it is for the participants to devise their own ways of celebrating them. In the case of Wiccaning and Withdrawal it will be the wishes of the near and dear which influence the format of the Ritual. In all the others the person to whom it is happening should have some input, even if they do not wish to write their own Ritual. Even in the case of someone being Named during their Initiation Ritual, they should at least be aware that the Rite is to take place. In all except the last, the Ritual does not have to take place within a Cast Circle, you can simply assemble a ring of your friends and family, and you do not have to have a formal Altar. You do not need to have the event led by a Priestess or Priest, although most prefer to as they can act as mistress or master of ceremonies.

The next thing that needs to be borne in mind is that you should think carefully about who you invite. It is highly probable that not all your friends, let alone your relatives, will feel kindly about having a Witchcraft Ritual thrust upon them. You will either have to give them enough information to enable them to choose whether to attend, or hold a second, non-Wiccan, Ritual where you know they will feel comfortable. There can be similar difficulties with venue, catering and so forth, although these are less of a problem now than, say, ten years ago, and are usually solved by 'shopping around'.

Here are some other points which you need to take into account. Where there are likely to be children present you will need to be ultra careful that the Altar equipment, especially candles, incense, etc, are well guarded by adults. If you are using a hired venue, check in advance that candles and incense are acceptable, and will not set off the fire alarms.

I shall lay out each of the following Rituals in a fairly full version, thus enabling you to choose what to include and remove. The Rituals will therefore assume that you have a High Priestess and others in the Coven to create the Sacred Space, etc. Where there are aspects already covered in Chapter 3, they will be noted by*.

WICCANING

Ideally, you will hold this Ritual when the child is at an age where the mother is able to carry her child for an hour or so without tiring (even if both parents are taking an active part, this is a good indicator that she has recovered from the birth), but before it is active enough to want to get down and move about. This is more for the sanity of the parents than any Craft reason! It is also a good idea to keep your Ritual short, to give you the best chance of completing it before the child becomes bored, hungry or whatever.

At a christening, close friends of the parents are usually selected as Godparents whose duty it is to guide the spiritual development of the child. In the Craft we do not believe that a child should be indoctrinated into any spiritual path, but some people do select Guardians or Sponsors, whose purpose is often to guide a child in more practical aspects of their upbringing. For example, you may know someone with considerable outdoor knowledge, sporting skills, or even mechanical expertise, who you would like to have a close association with your family.

If you have enough Witches present you may like to have them define the boundary of your Circle, thereby effectively keeping those with little or no Circle knowledge from stepping across the boundary. Otherwise you can mark that boundary with flowers, stones or even candles in jars.

Prepare the area.*
Set the Altar.*

Unless everyone is a member of the Craft, or has stood in Circle before, you will need to perform the above two steps before they arrive. Once everyone is present, get them to form a Circle around the room. We have found that if you mark the Circle on the floor, perhaps with flowers, you can then get them to gather on the outside.

The parent(s) and child enter the ring of friends.

Define the purpose and communicate it.* **This should take the form of a welcome to everyone present, with guidelines on what is about to happen and how they should behave. Include asking them not to move around, talk amongst themselves, break the Circle, or pop to the bar for a drink! In other words, you are reminding them that this is an event just as solemn as a christening.**

The High Priestess says something like,

'Welcome everyone. We have come here today to welcome and formally name ... (name of child) the son/daughter of ... and ... (parents' names). This celebration is an occasion of great joy to all of us for we welcome a new life to our circle of family and friends. Whilst it is perhaps not in the style you are used to, it is every bit as meaningful as any religious rite which welcomes a child. I would ask that whilst the ceremony is underway that you respect the beliefs and wishes of ... and ... (the parents' names) and maintain your places. Please do not cross the Circle, or move around it. Thank you.'

She may also outline the Ritual so that everyone knows what is going to take place.

Create the Sacred Space.* Again, unless everyone is accustomed to the Craft you may find it best to keep the invocations short.

The High Priestess then takes the parent(s) and child to each of the quarters, starting at the East, saying,

'Oh element of Air behold this child ... (name of child), son/daughter of ... and ... (names of parents), who has now come amongst us. Watch over him/her, guard, guide and protect him/her through all his/her days. Blessed Be.'

If you have enough Witches so that one may stand at each quarter, you might like to have one stand for each element, in which case they can then welcome the child, saying:

'In the name of Air I bid thee welcome ... (name of child). Blessed Be.'

This is repeated for Fire, Water and Earth. The High Priestess then leads the parent(s) and child to Altar, where she says,

'I call upon the Goddess and the God to recognize ... (name of child). May they watch over, guard, guide and protect him/her through all things. Blessed Be.'

The High Priestess then turns to face everyone assembled and says,

'I call upon each and every one of you to welcome … (name of child), son/daughter of … and … (names of parents). May he/she grow healthy and happy, joyous and wise, loving and loved (you can add other attributes here if you wish). Hail and welcome … (name of child).'

Everyone should then say,

'Hail and welcome … (name of child)'

The High priestess then says, *'Blessed Be.'*

If the parents have nominated Guardians or Sponsors this is the time for them to step forward and announce what area of knowledge they will try to impart to the child.

The Rite of Wine.* If everyone is of the Craft then you can hold the Rite of Wine and Cakes in the usual way, but where some guests are not of the Craft it may be better to omit the Cakes. The wine is shared firstly with the parents, then with any Witches in Circle. You may choose to then decant it into a number of glasses and have your Witches take it around to everyone else, although some people may be less than comfortable with the idea of sharing from one glass. Alternatively, the High Priestess can ask everyone to charge their glasses and raise a toast to the newly named child.

Removing the Sacred Space.* Again this should be kept short. At the end of this the High Priestess can take a moment to thank everyone,

'On behalf of … and … (names of parents), and of … (name of child) I would like to thank everyone for being here today. Could I please ask you to give some space to those who are tidying the Altar, thank you. Our ceremony is over, let the feasting begin!'

Feasting.*
Tidy away.* Unless everyone present is familiar with the Craft it is a good idea if one or two people are responsible for ensuring that the Altar is cleared and the equipment safely packed away as soon as is possible.

You can incorporate music, singing and dancing into your Ritual but you do need to take into account the fact that the central figure (the child) may not be used to loud sounds and is quite capable of kicking up a huge fuss if their preferences are not put first!

HANDFASTING

There are many traditions associated with the joining of two people. Some of these, whilst Pagan in origin, are referred to in daily speech, for example:

☆ *Tying the knot*. In a Handfasting we do this literally, the partners' hands are tied together, usually with coloured cords.

☆ *Jumping the Broom*. This symbolizes the leap from one life (that of being single) to a new one (that of being partners), and in a Handfasting we do actually jump the broom. Usually the broom in question is decorated with flowers and ribbons, and perhaps even bells. It is held horizontally across the Circle and the couple jumps over holding hands. Often the two people holding the ends will raise it slightly as the couple jumps, hence the saying 'taking the plunge'!

Handfasting is a great opportunity for exercising your imagination in dressing not only the participants, but also the room and the Altar. You may choose period costume, circlets of flowers, floral loops, knots, and so on.

As in a Wiccaning you may be holding a Ritual to which non-Witches are invited and so you need to give consideration to their lack of knowledge as to what actually happens. When my partner and I were Handfasted we sent a letter out with the invitations which outlined the Ritual, and to reassure our guests that we were not going to be doing anything untoward!

Many people getting Handfasted like to nominate a Supporter each, rather in the manner of Best Man and Maid of Honour. These two are there to help the partners get ready, to soothe their nerves, perhaps even to slip them a much needed drink and generally to ensure that they actually get where they should be, together, at the right time. If the couple have decided to exchange rings or other tokens of their relationship, the supporters should ensure that these are to hand, placed on the Altar Pentagram.

One of the key points of a Handfasting is the promises the couple make to each other. These should be written by the parties concerned, in their own words. An obliging High Priestess may try to help them put their thoughts into words, but ultimately they should say whatever is in their hearts. As many couples are nervous enough without the thought of having to learn their promises by heart, you might like to have these held in such a way that they can read them.

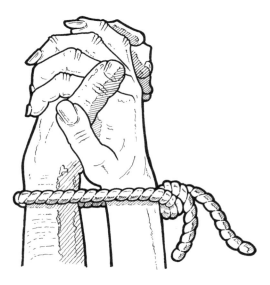

Prepare the area.*
Set the Altar.* In addition to the usual tools you will need anointing oil and the **Handfasting cord. Place the broom to one side of the Altar. The rings or other tokens should be placed on the Altar when they arrive at the Circle.**

Define the purpose and communicate it.* Again the High Priestess needs to welcome everyone and to give them an idea of what to expect and what to do. **Create the Sacred Space.***

The couple then enter together, followed by their Supporters. The High Priestess says,

'I welcome … and … (names of the parties) who have come here today to join hands and celebrate their love of one another in the company of us all.'

The High Priestess then invites the couple to kneel before her* and she anoints each of them on the forehead with oil, saying,

'I do anoint thee that the Goddess and the God may smile upon you and your union. Blessed Be.'

The couple then stand* and the High Priestess says,

'You have come here together today, is it your wish that you be Handfasted one to another?' **Presuming that they say yes, she continues,** *'Then I bind your hands in token of the bond you would make with each other.'*

She takes the cord and ties the right hand of the man to the left hand of the woman. She then says,

'What promises of love do you make?'

The man then makes his promises to the woman.

The woman then makes her promises to him.

The High Priestess then unbinds their hands and, where there are tokens, the couple exchange these. The High Priestess then says,

'Let all present bear witness that … and … have exchanged vows and have declared their love of each other. Henceforth let all know that they are joined together as man and wife, equal and supporting one another. Let the Goddess and the God bring blessings upon them and on their union together. Blessed Be.'

Two people, who could be the Supporters, then take the broom and hold it horizontally cross the Circle, at a height sensible for the couple to jump. The couple hold hands and jump the broom together. There is usually cheering and clapping at this point.

The High Priestess then takes the couple around to each of the quarters and presents them to the elements,*

'Oh element of Air, I present … and … (names of couple) who today have Handfasted. Watch over them, guard them, guide them and protect them in all they do. Blessed Be.'

If you have enough Witches to have one stand at each quarter then that Witch will say,

'I bid thee welcome in the name of Air. Blessed Be.'

This is repeated at each quarter. The High Priestess then leads them back to the Altar and, raising her arms to the North, says,

'I call upon the Goddess and the God to bear witness that here today … and … (names of the couple) have exchanged promises and are forthwith as one. Welcome them, watch over them, guard, guide and protect them. Blessed Be.'

She turns to face everyone and says,

'I here present to you … and … (names of the couple), Handfasted here today in the sight of us all. I bid you welcome them. Hail and welcome … and … (names of the couple).'

All should echo her *'Hail and welcome'.*

She then says, *'Blessed Be'.*

The Rite of Wine and Cakes.* Where the couple are Witches they should conse-crate the wine and then share it with the other Witches in Circle. As with the Wiccaning you may prefer to ask the High Priestess to lead everyone in a toast, rather than passing the Chalice, or a series of glasses, around to everyone present. Once again you may find it simpler to omit the Cakes.

Remove the Sacred Space.* Once again at the end of this the High Priestess can take a moment to thank everyone,

'On behalf of … and … (names of the couple) I would like to thank everyone for being here today. Could I please ask you to give some space to those who are tidying the Altar, thank you. Our ceremony is over, let the feasting begin!'

Where either or both of the couple have worn a circlet of flowers they may choose this moment to throw them into the group to see who catches them.

Feasting.*
Tidy away.* As before, it is best to get the Altar packed away safely as soon as possible.

 WITHDRAWAL

Rites of Withdrawal can take many forms. Many Witches like to prepare for their own passing by writing a meditation, which they will follow when the time comes. But the bulk of these Rites are those performed by their near and dear after death. As mentioned above, it is common for Rites of Withdrawal to be held later than burial or cremation, as these latter are almost certainly going to attended by those who are not of the Craft and it is at the least insensitive to insist that the newly bereaved take part in Rites of which they have no understanding.

A Rite of Withdrawal can be as simple as two or more people sitting together and remembering the departed, or it can take the form of a Ritual:

Prior to the Ritual ask everyone to give some thought to what they remember about the one who has passed on. If you wish you can invite them to bring photos, a favourite piece of music, perhaps a gift. Ask them to try to bring specific memories as well as general thoughts.

Define the purpose and communicate it.* This is the time to remind everyone that whilst we are sad for our own loss, we are gathering to remember the good times, the gifts of personality we have been given, and generally to celebrate as that person would have celebrated were they with us. It is also a time to remember that, as Witches, we believe in the Summerlands and in reincarnation, so that we are thinking of our loved one as having moved on to a new life, rather than simply having stopped living in this one.

Prepare the area.* If you are going to play music which you shared with the departed then ensure you have the appropriate equipment to hand.
Set the Altar.* You may find it useful to ensure that tissues are to hand, as this is a time when emotions can be keenly felt.
Create the Sacred Space.*
Chanting and dancing.* This raises energy, not for magical work but to sustain everyone in Circle.

The High Priestess says,

'We have gathered here today to celebrate the life of … (name of departed) who meant a lot to each of us and whose passing we grieve for. But even as he/she has gone from us, he/she has left something behind. And within the hearts of us all he/she lives on. Let us therefore remember him/her with love and laughter, with gratitude for the things he/she brought to us and the memories he/she left behind. Blessed Be.'

Each person then takes it in turn to say something about the departed. This can take the form of a short tale, perhaps something amusing which you shared together. I find that once a couple of people have started then it becomes easier for everyone to join in. It's important to give everyone a chance to share their thoughts and memories, even if some may be more amusing than totally flattering!

Once everyone has finished, or when the High Priestess considers it is time to wind down she says,

'Each of us has memories of … (name). He/she will be sorely missed, but so long as we remember, he/she will live on in our hearts and our lives. And we know that in the love of the Mother Goddess and of the God we will meet and know and love once again. Blessed Be.'

The Rite of Wine and Cakes.* This is performed in the usual way, although the High Priestess, or the departed's closest friend, may wish to take a second 'helping' in the name of the departed.
Removing the Sacred Space.*
Feasting.* It is usual for tales about the departed to continue and indeed more is usually said after the Ritual than during.
Tidy away.*

The above Ritual is just as suitable for a pet as for a human, and can take place on more than one occasion, perhaps even years after the event, when someone feels the need to celebrate the life of that loved one.

NAMING

This is the Rite where an adult takes a 'Witch name', either through choice or as part of their second-degree initiation. It is believed that Witch names originally served the purpose of making it difficult for Witches to give one another away, and if this were the case then the names used would have certainly been used at all times during meetings and Rituals. These days Witch names are often reserved for within Circle or just for major Rituals.

Whether you are choosing a name for yourself or for another, the choice of name needs careful consideration. This is because your Witch name should stay with you, it is not something you should be changing later on. It is thought that choosing the name of a major deity is somewhat presumptuous, however choosing a lesser known one means that you need to check carefully for any unintended associations. For example, Deirdre might have been most beautiful of face and manner, but she also caused war and family division, and ultimately killed herself. Some names are oversubscribed; there are a great many Merlins, Morganas and Morrighans about! Some names are too unwieldy, such as She Who Walks by the Rivers in Moonlight, and some cause rather more mirth than might have been intended (I'll leave you to discover those for yourself!). Wherever possible it is also a good idea to select something which you can not only remember, but also spell!

Where the candidate is choosing their own name they should discuss it with their High Priestess in advance of the Ritual, and she should make sure that she can remember it and pronounce it properly.

I have said that the Rite of Naming can take place as part of the Ritual of Initiation, but here I am going to write it as a Ritual on its own. Later in this book you will find Rituals of Initiation and you can take the central part of this Ritual to insert at the appropriate point.

Define the purpose and communicate it.*
Prepare the area.*
Set the Altar.* You will also need anointing oil and possibly a slip of paper with the new name on it.
Create the Sacred Space.*

The High Priestess says,

'I call upon … (usual name of person) to step forward.'

The candidate moves Deosil around the Circle and stands before the High Priestess. She kisses him/her on each cheek and says,

'Welcome sister/brother in the Craft. Is it your wish to take a new name at this time, to signify your commitment to the Craft and to be known by us and the Gods for all time?'

The candidate answers. The High Priestess then asks the candidate to kneel and anoints his/her forehead with oil, saying,

'Therefore in this Circle and before the Old Gods, I do name thee … (Witch name). May you grow in it and in the sight of the Goddess and the God.'

She causes them to stand, and says, *'What is your name?'* They answer.

The High Priestess then pushes them out into the Circle where they are gently shoved from person to person, each one asking, *'What is your name?'* to which they answer. Once everyone has thus questioned them, they return to stand before the High Priestess.

She then takes the candidate to each quarter in turn and presents them,

'Hail Air, I present before you … (old name), henceforth to be known as … (Witch name).'

Where there is a Witch at each quarter they will then say,

'Welcome … (Witch name) in the name of Air. Blessed Be.'

Once the candidate has been presented to each of the quarters* they return to the Altar where the High Priestess stands behind the candidate, both facing North. She holds up their arms and says,

'I call upon the Goddess and the God to acknowledge … (Witch name). May they watch over him/her and may he/she ever be faithful in their service. Blessed Be.'

She releases the candidate's arms and both turn to face the group. She says,

'Behold our brother/sister in the Craft, henceforth known as … (Witch name).'

The High Priestess then welcomes* the candidate saying,

'Welcome … (Witch name).'

She kisses him/her on each cheek and says, *'Blessed Be.'* The candidate then proceeds Deosil around the Circle and is likewise welcomed by everyone present. The Rite of Wine and Cakes.* The candidate should be the first to partake of the consecrated wine.

Removing the Sacred Space.*

Feasting.*

Tidy away.*

 ## PUBERTY/COMING OF AGE

Traditionally, these Rites of Passage would have been marked in ways which we may well not find acceptable in this day. Girls would have marked their first menses by changes in clothing and hairstyle, which announced to the world that they had become a woman. They might have been secluded for this and all following cycles, and many would have been quickly married off. Boys would mark their entry into adulthood by taking part in the hunt and celebrating their first kill, much as still happens in the fox-hunting fraternity.

Both genders would put away childhood, all games and toys, and become adults in every sense. But our young are likely to be still attending school and we can allow a longer apprenticeship to adulthood before they must sever all childhood links. Hence our Rites are likely to be less overt.

As mentioned above, Rites to mark puberty are often single gender affairs as the young are often shy about the physical changes which take place at this time. Girls know their fathers and brothers are aware of menstruation but may not want their first period marked openly. Boys know their mothers and sisters understand their bodily changes but do not necessarily feel happy with them being broadcast aloud. Additionally, it is harder to choose one single event which marks puberty in a boy; is it his first shave, is it when his voice finally breaks?

Another consideration at this time is whether the youngster actually wants to mark the event at all. I know of several parents in the Craft whose fond hopes of a Ritual at this time have been dashed by the young person's reluctance to be the centre of such attention. And I know of a couple of youngsters who went along with it only to please their parents, which rather negates the meaning of the Ritual. As a result you need to consult the young person as to what their wishes truly are and, where they would actively like a Ritual, what form it should take. There is no doubt that you could hold a Ritual in Circle, but as the most important person may never have been in Ritual before, as few Covens accept under 18s anyway, it may be better to hold something rather more low-key.

Girls are often slightly less shy than boys so an all-female party where she is welcomed into the sisterhood of women, perhaps by being given gifts which are all red and wrapped in red, would be both appropriate and acceptable. In my youth this event was often marked by being first allowed to wear high heels and make up!

Boys may prefer an event with only male guests where the emphasis is perhaps aligned to sport, a camping trip or some other shared interest. It used to be believed that the time when a man first took his son to the pub was the accepted indicator that he could regard himself as a man, but today few of us would consider condoning under-age drinking as an acceptable Rite of Passage.

All in all, Rites for puberty are difficult issues which are perhaps best resolved by the people concerned. If, however, you still feel that you would like to hold a Ritual to celebrate this then I would suggest a single gender Ritual along the following lines:

Define the purpose and communicate it.*
Prepare the area.*
Set the Altar.*
Create the Sacred Space.*
The parent welcomes* the youngster into the Circle saying,

'Today we welcome my daughter/son … (name) who has taken a major step on the road towards being an adult. She/he joins our sisterhood/brotherhood of women/men. From now she/he starts to put aside the toys of childhood and looks towards taking her/his rightful place in the world of women/men. May the Goddess and the God watch over her/him, guard, guide and protect her/him. Welcome … (name) and Blessed Be.'

The parent kisses their child on each cheek.

The parent then performs the Five-Fold Kiss* on their daughter/son.

The youngster is then taken Deosil around the Circle* where each individual welcomes them with a kiss.

The Rite of Wine and Cakes.* As this is a single gender affair obviously both parties will be of the same sex.

Removing the Sacred Space.*
Feasting*. In order to emphasize the sisterhood/brotherhood it is best that this remains single gender rather than inviting the other half of the community. I also feel that gifts should be given which in some way or another are a tangible indicator of the progress towards adulthood.
Tidy away.*

 ## CRONING/WIZZENING

Just as the traditional Rites for puberty are no longer appropriate, the Rites for Croning and Wizzening are as inapplicable to today's world. Few of us live in an environment where there is a Council of Elders to which we are invited. And those Witches who do attend a Council of Elders, in that they each run a Coven, are as likely to be in their prime of life as they are to be getting on in years! The marker of becoming a grandparent does not really have the same meaning as it used to, as people start their families at vastly different ages and are living longer, so that one woman might be Croned in her thirties and another not until her eighties! Additionally, many women do not pass through a menopause as such, as surgery and HRT have blurred the boundaries. Neither can retirement be used as a marker as some will retire early and some (including writers!) may never retire.

Within the Craft, and especially within Coven working, the time of Croning and Wizzening is taken by some to be the point at which the individual decides they can no longer be fully active in Circle. They may step down from being High Priestess or High Priest and possibly choose to attend Sabbats only. They will probably take no active role in creating the Sacred Space, and will to all intents be present in the same way as a newcomer to the Craft. This taking a permanent step back is not to be confused with 'time out' caused by ill health, outside commitments, exhaustion or even pregnancy. This has to be a final decision, although occasionally a person might be asked back to cover emergencies, or asked to provide the advice and guidance you would expect from a Wise One.

Many Witches find that Croning or Wizzening is something which takes place in two stages. First, their knowledge in the Craft is sought after by experienced Witches and thus they find themselves being treated as Wise One long before they expect to stand down. Secondly, there comes a time when they simply do not have the energy to fulfill all their Coven duties as well as to be a sounding board for others. At this point they may choose to formally declare this by holding a Rite. It is therefore inevitable that anyone choosing to hold such a Rite will have considerable knowledge, not to mention their own ideas on what should take place.

If the person involved is High Priestess or High Priest they are likely to 'retire' with their partner, although this is not always the case. Either way there will need to be a handover of the Coven to the person or persons who will replace them. In the following Ritual I am going to assume that the retiring Witch is the High Priestess. In this case she may also wish to invite Witches from outside of her own Coven, perhaps from daughter groups, to attend.

Define the purpose and communicate it.*
Prepare the area.*
Set the Altar.*
Create the Sacred Space.*

The departing High Priestess addresses the Coven:

'This is the last time I shall stand in Circle with you as your High Priestess. The Goddess and the God have smiled upon me and have placed you in my charge over these many years. I have witnessed your first steps on the path and I have seen many of you come to fulfilment, with others yet just stepping out. I have seen birth and death, joy and sadness, chaos and order, and you have become like children unto me. You have been the joy that makes me rise in the morning; you have been the sorrow that I have taken to my pillow at night. But yet you are my legacy and I am proud to have known each and every one of you. Tonight I step down from my role as your High Priestess and become just a Priestess of the Craft. So for one last time, before another takes my place, I ask you to join with me in the ways of the Old Gods. So I bid you all, Hail and Welcome. Blessed Be.'

Dancing and chanting.* In the same way as the Rite of Withdrawal this is to provide energy for the Coven, rather than for any magical purpose.

Drawing Down the Moon.* In the case of a Priestess this is almost certainly going to be the last Drawing Down she takes part in, and it is likely to be one of the aspects of the Craft which she is most going to miss. She may well choose to give her own Charge rather than the traditional one. A retiring Priest would also perform the Drawing Down but upon the Priestess rather than being the subject of the Rite.

The Rite of Wine and Cakes.* The High Priestess personally takes the Chalice to each Covenor and likewise the cakes.

Blessing. The departing High Priestess gives a Blessing to the Coven:

'I call upon the Old Gods, I call upon the Elements and upon all Witches of the past, present and future, to bear witness here. For whilst this is an ending it is also a beginning and so the Wheel of Life, like that of the Year, turns. May the Old Ones watch over you, may they be ever present with you, may your hearts and minds be ever in their care. Blessed Be.'

Handover. She then calls forward the new High Priestess and presents her to the Coven,

'Behold … (name) for this is your new High Priestess. May she guide you well, may she love you and care for you even as I have done. Show her honour and respect her well, for even as she will care for you, she is yours to care for. Mark well that you and she are known to the Old Ones who are ever present.'

The outgoing High Priestess then gives the Five-Fold Kiss* to the incoming High Priestess.

Note: where both High Priestess and High Priest are changing over the High Priestess will give the kiss to the incoming High Priest and vice versa.

The outgoing High Priestess then takes the new one and presents her to each of the quarters and to the Goddess and the God saying,

'Behold here is … (name) who is now High Priestess of the Coven of … (name of Coven). Blessed Be.'

The new High Priestess then goes to each Covenor in turn, who welcomes her saying, *'Welcome and Blessed Be'.* **She kisses them on each cheek and wishes them** *'Blessed Be'.*

The outgoing High Priestess may well give the new one any items of Coven equipment which are not personally owned, usually together with a ring or necklace of 'office'.

Removing the Sacred Space.*

Feasting.* **It is to be hoped that the Covenors will have made more than the usual effort in the feasting department and that they will have felt moved to bring gifts for the departing High Priestess to the Ritual!**

Tidy away.* **Under no circumstances should the outgoing High Priestess be expected to take the burden of this on this occasion!**

Where the candidate for Croning or Wizzening is not the High Priestess or High Priest it is usual for them still to take the major role in Drawing Down the Moon, and in the Rite of Wine and Cakes. Obviously they will not be handing the Coven over.

As mentioned above, all Rites of Passage can and should be altered to suit the person(s) taking the central role(s). However meaningful you make a Handfasting Ritual it is no good if it is not what both parties want. As with all Rituals, these should be approached with much thought, so run through the content and the actions and ensure that you truly understand what is to happen and why. Unlike other Rituals, there should be much consultation to ensure that everyone gets what they really want. I have written detailed instructions for the preparation, organizing and holding of Rites of Passage in a series of booklets which are listed in the Recommended Reading at the end of this book. I also work closely with the Children of Artemis to conduct workshops on writing and organizing Rites of Passage.

NINE

RITUALS OF INITIATION

The Rites of Initiation are generally those which mark a person's progress within a Coven and the Craft. The only exception is the Rite of Self-Initiation or Self-Dedication which is usually conducted by the Solitary Witch outside of the Coven system. They are the Rituals which cross the divide between working and celebration as they contain elements of both. Whilst no spells are worked, a Circle is cast and power is raised.

My previous book, *The Real Witches' Coven*, contains advice and guidance on the preparation and training of candidates for Initiation within a Coven, together with advice to the High Priestess on the preparation needed to perform these Rituals. In this chapter I have included the content of those Rituals, together with a few notes to aid understanding. I have also included a Rite of Self-Initiation, or Self-Dedication, as it is sometimes known, and the Coven Oath. But what do all these terms refer to?

THE COVEN OATH

Some Covens, who introduce newcomers to Circle work before their First Degree, will also ask them to make a commitment to the Coven when they first join. This is known as the Coven Oath, and marks formal entry to the Coven. It helps to ensure that the newcomer understands the requirements of the Coven, especially regarding secrecy. I would emphasize that this is the Candidate's promise, made on their honour, to the Goddess and the God, and that neither the High Priestess nor the Coven has any power to enforce this, other than asking the person to leave the Coven.

THE DEGREES OF INITIATION

Within a Coven there are usually three Rites of Initiation, known respectively as the First, Second and Third Degree Initiations. In each of these steps the Witch makes promises of commitment to the Craft. Although the High Priestess or High Priest may be the Initiator, the promises made in these Rituals are made to the Goddess and the God; the Coven simply facilitates this. The Degrees mark the Witch's progress and correspond to many of the key aspects of the Craft, thus:

* ✫ *The First Degree* – The Aspirant's statement of beginning to learn and walk the Path of the Witch. Here they start to learn. This relates to the New Moon, the Maiden aspect, youth and enthusiasm, knowledge of life, knowledge and understanding of the self.

* ✫ *The Second Degree* – The Initiate is considered ready to take the next step, that of learning to teach. It relates to the Full Moon, the Mother aspect, maturity and fruitfulness, knowledge of death, knowledge and understanding of others. Many Witches also choose to take a new or Witch name at the time of their Second Degree and this can be found on page 221.

* ✫ *The Third Degree* – The Initiate is ready to start their own Coven when the circumstances are right. This is linked to the Old and Dark of the Moon, the Crone aspect, age and wisdom, understanding of the cycles of life, death and rebirth, combining the knowledge and understanding of self and others. Teaching to learn more oneself, for as we teach so we learn.

SELF-INITIATION

A Witch who chooses to work on their own as a Solitary may choose to make their own promise to the Goddess and the God, and this is termed Self-Initiation, or Self-Dedication. Sometimes a Coven will allow a Solitary who is known to them to perform this Rite within Circle, but their role is simply that of supporters and witnesses.

THE COVEN RITUALS

The basic format of any of these Rituals is similar to that of the Sabbats:

DEFINE THE PURPOSE AND (WHEN WORKING WITH OTHERS)
    COMMUNICATE IT*

PREPARE THE AREA*

SET THE ALTAR*

CREATE THE SACRED SPACE*

BANISH UNWANTED INFLUENCES AND/OR SELF-BLESSING

DRAWING DOWN THE MOON

THE INITIATORY RITE*

THE RITE OF WINE AND CAKES*

REMOVING THE SACRED SPACE*

FEASTING

TIDY AWAY*

Those steps in the *list* marked * are essential. Details of those marked * in the *text* can be found in Chapter 3.

 **THE COVEN OATH**

This takes place with the whole group standing in Circle. After the Sacred Space* has been created, the Candidate will be called to kneel before the Altar and will repeat the words after the High Priestess:

"I … (candidate's name), undertake this Oath of my own free will, in the presence of the Old Gods and before all here present: I will not reveal the secrets of the Craft, nor use the knowledge I gain to impress the foolish, nor to frighten the childish. I will follow the Old ways, in humility and obedience, to the best of my ability, and uphold the Craft as best I may. I will not reveal the secrets of the Circle; the nature or detail of its workings, nor the names of its members.

'As I do will, so mote it be. Blessed Be.'

The group will, as is usual, echo the *'Blessed Be'*.

After they have given the Oath they are considered an Aspirant and are greeted by each of the other Covenors in turn. As this is a short Rite it often takes place within a Ritual, usually one to celebrate one of the Minor Sabbats in which case the rest of the Sabbat Ritual then follows.

 ## THE FIRST DEGREE

This usually takes place at least a year and a day after the candidate has been introduced to the Coven. Only those Witches who have taken their First Degree will stand in Circle, this is to prevent those who have yet to do so from seeing the Ritual.

Prior to any Initiation Ritual, the Aspirant or Initiate should have fasted for at least 6 hours, unless there are medical reasons why this period should be shorter. You might also like to insist that they have drunk nothing other than water or milk for 24 hours, to free the body of all stimulants such as caffeine, etc. Immediately before the Ritual they should wash their hair and bathe, using no cosmetics, lotions, unguents, etc. They should also remove all jewellery, including sigils of the Craft, although you may have to allow any rings which cannot be physically removed!

In addition to your usual Altar equipment you will need:

> 1 x 9-FOOT AND 2 x 4-FOOT-6-INCH LENGTHS OF RED CORD, FOR BINDING
> THE ASPIRANT
> 1 FINE WHITE CORD 9 FEET IN LENGTH, FOR THE MEASURE
> ANOINTING OIL. MAKE YOUR OWN BY BLENDING THE FOLLOWING ESSENTIAL
> OILS IN 5ML OF BASE OIL: 2 DROPS JASMINE, 2 DROPS FRANKINCENSE,
> 1 DROP ORANGE, 1 DROP ROSEMARY

A FULL SET OF WORKING TOOLS

A BELL. I FIND THE BEST RESULTS ARE GAINED IF YOU REMOVE THE CLAPPER
FROM A HANDBELL AND THEN STRIKE IT WITH AN ATHAME THE REQUIRED
NUMBER OF TIMES. THIS STOPS ANY UNWANTED SOUNDS WHEN HANDLING
THE BELL

The First Degree is usually performed at, or just after, the New Moon.

When the Aspirant arrives at the Covenstead they are not permitted to meet the
other attendees, but are kept separate and are prepared. If they are to be skyclad,
as is usual, then this is the time for them to remove all their clothes, jewellery, etc.
Bind them and blindfold them, and leave them sitting; if your location is seriously
cold you might like to cover them with a cloak or blanket. The traditional method
of binding the Aspirant requires three red cords, one 9 feet long and two 4 feet 6
inches long. The long cord is used to tie their wrists behind their back with the
centre of the cord. The ends are then brought over the shoulders and knotted
loosely in front, in such a fashion that the Aspirant cannot strangle her/himself!
One of the short cords is knotted around the right ankle, the other just above the
left knee. They should be instructed to meditate on why they seek Initiation and
upon the Goddess and the God. Whilst the Aspirant is being prepared the other
Covenors should be getting themselves and the Altar ready, if they have not
already done so.

After the Sacred Space is created and Energy raised,* the Initiator opens a
doorway in the Circle and the Sponsor leaves to collect the Aspirant. The doorway
is closed, and the Coven waits in silence. The Sponsor brings the Aspirant to the
doorway, guiding them from behind, usually with their hands upon the Aspirant's
shoulders. En route to the Circle the Aspirant should be gently disorientated to
increase the feeling of going from the mundane world to that of the Craft. We
achieve this by making them walk a circuitous route, sometimes going in and out
of a room more than once. You can also turn them around several times, so that
they cannot tell which direction they are going.

At the edge of the Circle the Aspirant and Sponsor halt.

Initiator: '*Who stands at the gateway of the Circle?*'

Sponsor: '*Here stands … (Initiate's name), seeking Initiation to the First Degree.*'

Initiator: '*Who stands for this person?*'

Sponsor: '*I … (Sponsor's Witch name or name), Witch and Priest(ess) of the Third* (or Second, if that be the case) *Degree.*'

Initiator: '*Have they been properly prepared?*'

Sponsor: '*On my honour as a Witch I vouch that they have.*'

Initiator (challenging the Aspirant): '*O thou who standest on the threshold between the world of man and the domain of the Old Gods, hast thou the courage to make the assay?*' **(Places the point of his/her Athame to the Aspirant's breast)** '*Better you should fall upon this blade than enter this Circle with fear in your heart.*'

Aspirant: '*I have two passwords: Perfect Love and Perfect Trust.*'

Initiator: '*All who have such are welcome, I give thee a third to pass through this dread door.*' **(Kisses the Aspirant on each cheek.)**

The Initiator hands the Athame to the sponsor, goes behind the Aspirant and pushes them gently into the Circle. The Sponsor closes the gateway in the Circle and returns the Athame to the Initiator. The Aspirant is then presented to each of the quarters in turn. The Initiator says,

'*Take heed ye Lords of the East (South, West and North), that … (Aspirant's name), here presented, is properly prepared to be initiated as Priest(ess) and Witch.*'

The handbell is rung three times and the Aspirant is led to stand before the Altar, where the Initiator gives the Aspirant the Five-fold Blessing:

'In other religions the postulant kneels while the Priest towers above him. But in the Craft we are taught to be humble and we kneel to welcome him and say: Blessed Be thy feet (**kisses right foot then left**), that have brought thee in these ways. Blessed Be thy knees (**kisses right knee then left**), that shall kneel at the Sacred Altar. Blessed Be thy womb (**where the Aspirant is female** or phallus **for a male**), (**kisses the lower belly**), which brings forth the life of man. Blessed Be thy breasts (**kisses right then left**), formed in strength and in beauty. Blessed by thy lips (**kisses once on lips**), that shall utter the Sacred Names. Blessed Be.*

'Now we shall take your measure, that thou shalt be known to us and to the Old Gods for all time.'

The Sponsor takes the fine cord from the Altar and measures the Aspirant around the head and ties a knot in the cord, around the chest and ties another knot. Lastly, with the help of the Initiator, the Aspirant is measured from head to toe and the Sponsor ties a final knot. During this process they say,

'These are the measurements of your body in life, so that in death your shroud and coffin will be fit.'

The cord is then placed on the Altar. The Initiator asks,

'Before thou are fully sworn, art thou ready to pass through the ordeal and be purified?'

The Aspirant will hopefully give a positive response. There are a number of ordeals which you may choose to put the Aspirant through, and as High Priestess you can select one or several, or add variations of your own. Please remember that this is intended to emphasize the meaning and solemnity of this step, it's not an excuse to vent the frustrations of the last day, week, month, etc. Nor is it an excuse to terrorize your Aspirant! You could try, or adapt, one of the following:

☆ **A series of light symbolic lashes with the Scourge, usually administered with the Aspirant kneeling and the number of strokes being indicated by the ringing of the bell. The traditional number is 3, 7, 9 and 21 lashes. The Initiate should feel the scourge, but not be marked by it. To get it right, practise on your own leg in advance and then err on the side of caution.**

✸ Pushing the Aspirant from person to person and questioning their ability to keep the secrets of the Craft, their willingness to learn, their potential conduct as a Witch and so on.

✸ Splashing them with very cold water and even some flecks of melted wax; again practise on yourself first.

✸ Asking searching questions about why they wish to enter the Circle and become a Witch.

✸ Some traditions used to prick the Initiate and place a drop of their blood onto the measure. These days this really is unnecessarily risky, both for the Initiate and for you.

Once the ordeal(s) is (are) over the Aspirant is made to kneel before the Altar. The Initiator asks,

'Thou hast bravely passed the test. Art thou ready to swear that thou wilt always be true to the Art?'

After a positive response from the Aspirant, the Initiator asks,

'Art thou always ready to help, protect and defend thy brothers and sisters of the Art?'

After a positive response from the Aspirant, the Initiator says,

'I hereby sign thee with the Triple sign, I consecrate thee with oil. (Anoints the Aspirant with oil on the belly, right breast and left breast.) *'I anoint thee with wine.'* (Anoints with wine.) *'I anoint thee with my lips.'* (Anoints with kisses.)

The Initiate is unbound and the blindfold is removed. The Initiator says,

'I hereby salute thee … (name of Initiate), **(kisses on each cheek)** *in the name of the Old Gods, newly-made Priest(ess) and Witch. Art thou ready to take the Oath?'*

After a positive response from the Initiate, the Initiator says,

'Then repeat after me (Note: it is a good idea to read this line by line and let the Initiate repeat each bit after you.):

'I … (Initiate's name), duly consecrated Witch and Priest(ess), here in the presence of the Old Gods, do, of my own free will and accord most solemnly swear; that I will keep secret and never reveal the secrets of the Art, except it be to a proper person properly prepared, within a Circle such as I am in now. And that I will never deny the secrets to such a person, if he or she has been properly prepared and vouched for by a brother or sister of the Art. I swear that I will not use the Craft to impress the foolish or to frighten the childish, and that I will uphold the Craft in health or sickness, weary or bright, in dark days and light days till I reach the Summerlands. All this I swear by my hopes of a future life, mindful that my measure has been taken and that my weapons will be turned against me if I break this my solemn oath. Blessed Be.'

The Initiator now takes the Initiate around and presents them to each of the Quarters, saying,

'Hear ye Lords of the East (South, West, North) … (Initiate's name) is now consecrated Priest(ess), Witch and child of the Goddess.'

The Ritual now pauses while the Initiate is welcomed by everyone in the Circle.

The Initiator now presents the Initiate with each of the working tools. It simplifies the process if the Initiator takes the tool from the Altar, hands it to the Initiate whilst explaining its purpose, then the Sponsor takes it from the Initiate and replaces it on the Altar. The tools you should have are the Sword, Athame, Boline, Wand, Chalice, Pentacle, Censer of Incense, Cords and Scourge (even if you do not use it). This is because the Scourge is symbolic of suffering and its presentation is usually accompanied by the statement and question, *'For it is written that to learn one must suffer and be purified. Art thou ready to suffer to learn?'* **To which the Initiate should answer in the affirmative.**

If you choose to give the Initiate a gift, perhaps the sigil of the First Degree, this is now the time to do so. Some Covens pause here and allow the Initiate to consecrate their own Athame, if they have one and have not already done so.

The High Priestess and High Priest now perform the Rite of Wine and Cakes,* the Initiate should stand to the left of the High Priestess in order to be the first Covenor to whom the Chalice is handed after consecration.

The Circle is now removed. It is usual for an Initiation to be followed by a feast.

 ## THE SECOND DEGREE

The Second Degree takes place when the High Priestess considers that the individual is ready to take on the responsibility of passing on their knowledge of the Craft. Only those Witches of Second Degree and above will be present in the Circle.

A significant part of the following Ritual represents the Initiate's own journey to the realm of Death. For this you will need to assign a number of people to play the roles of Portal Keepers (referred to in the text of the Ritual as PK1, PK2, etc) and of Death. This journey commences on the arrival of the Initiate at the Covenstead where they are met by a senior Covenor who plays the role of the first Portal Keeper. Where you do not have enough Witches of Second Degree or above then you may need to assign this role to the Initiator, and double up on subsequent roles.

In the period approaching the Ritual, the Initiate should be encouraged to read and reflect on these legends and their inner meanings, and also to meditate upon how this is reflected in everyday life. Close attention to these legends will enable the Initiate to answer the questions of the Keepers of the Portals and Death during the first part of the Ritual.

Some Covens work this Ritual with everyone skyclad, others with only the Initiate skyclad, yet others prefer to provide the Initiate with a special 'Initiation Robe'. This represents the garment that the Initiate wears when they meet Death. As such it is better that it is loose fitting, made of coarse cloth and roughly finished. Something in the way of a knee-length shift is ideal.

In addition to the usual Altar and Ritual equipment you will need:

> A HOODED ROBE OR CLOAK FOR THE FIRST PORTAL KEEPER TO WEAR. IDEALLY, THIS SHOULD COMPLETELY COVER THEM AND MASK THEIR IDENTITY. SUBSEQUENT PORTAL KEEPERS AND DEATH SHOULD STAY OUT OF SIGHT UNTIL THE INITIATE HAS BEEN BLINDFOLDED
>
> BLINDFOLD
>
> A CUP OR GLASS WITH SOME STRONG-TASTING LIQUID. THIS SHOULD NOT BE THE SAME AS THE CHALICE. THE DRINK NEED NOT NECESSARILY BE PLEASANT, BUT SHOULD NOT ACTUALLY BE TOXIC!
>
> INITIATION ROBE, IF BEING USED

ANOINTING UNGUENT, WHICH YOU CAN MAKE YOURSELF. TAKE AROUND A
TEASPOONFUL OF PETROLEUM JELLY AND ADD THE FOLLOWING ESSENTIAL
OILS: 4 DROPS LAVENDER, 2 DROPS FRANKINCENSE, 1 DROP MYRRH,
1 DROP CLARY SAGE
A GUIDED VISUALIZATION OF THE DESCENT OF THE GODDESS

This Ritual is best performed at the Full Moon.

As in the First Degree the Initiate should be kept apart from the other Covenors
until they actually enter the Circle. Ideally, the Initiate will arrive last, after the
Circle has been cast* and energy has been raised, and will commence the Ritual
literally on the doorstep.

The Initiate is met at the entrance to the Covenstead by the first Portal Keeper
who commences the Initiate's preparation. Key to this preparation is the Initiate's
ability to answer the questions to the satisfaction of each Portal Keeper, Death and
the Initiator. This means giving honest answers as the Initiator will, by this point,
have a good idea of the Initiate's personality and actions in the Craft and will have
communicated to the others the answers he or she deems acceptable. If you have
insufficient Witches of Second and Third Degree to take all these roles, then you
can have individuals taking multiple roles.

While the Initiate is being prepared, the remainder of the Covenors present will
prepare the Altar and Create the Sacred Space,* taking care to invite* the Goddess
in her Aspect of Crone and the God in his aspect of the Hunter. Although the
Initiator may not be playing a role, they may wish to step in to the preparatory area
to hear the Initiate's answers. Note that each Portal Keeper should go to the
Circle as soon as they have completed their allotted role. In order to prevent
multiple opening and closing of a gateway in the Circle it is a good idea to hold off
actually Casting the Circle until the sixth Portal Keeper arrives.

PK1: '*Who are you?*'

Initiate: '*I am … (Initiate's name), Witch, Priest(ess) and child of the Goddess.*'

PK1: *'Why do you come here?'*

Initiate: *'I seek Initiation to the Second Degree.'*

PK1: *'By what right do you seek such?'*

Initiate: *'I come by right of Initiation to the First Degree.'*

PK1: *'How do you come?'*

Initiate: *'Freely, by my own will and accord.'*

PK1: *'Then enter the underworld and begin your descent, for this is but the first of seven portals which you must pass, before you attain that which you seek. Do you have the courage to make this journey?'*

Initiate: **'(Answers in own words.)'**

PK1 then admits the Initiate into the Covenstead, blindfolds them and leads them to the next portal.

Note: Where you have limited space you may have to select one or two points in a room and lead the Initiate to and fro in order to increase the perception of distance in the 'journey'. Alternatively, you may choose to lead them from room to room, even into the garden. Also spinning a person around, or leading them backwards and forwards, can add significantly to their disorientation and the drama of the rite.

PK2: *'I am the keeper of the second portal and I challenge you. Do you have the strength to make this journey, for the weak will surely wither and fade away?'*

Initiate: **'(Answers in own words.)'**

PK2: *'You may only succeed by your own strength of will. If you wish to continue you must remove all sigils of protection and all other finery, for it has no place here.'*

(The Initiate removes all jewellery, including Craft symbols and talismans, and is then disorientated.)

PK3: *'I am the keeper of the third portal and I challenge you. What have you given of yourself to the Craft?'*

Initiate: *'(Answers in own words.)'*

PK3: *'If you would continue then you must go barefoot along a path of thorns, for the way you seek is hard and beset with difficulties.'*

(The Initiate removes footwear and is disorientated.)

PK4: *'I am the keeper of the fourth portal and I challenge you. Do you believe that you can succeed upon a quest that many fail, for with failure may come madness and despair?'*

Initiate: *'(Answers in own words.)'*

PK4 (handing the Initiate the cup or glass mentioned above): *'Then take this cup and drink, but be aware that it contains a powerful potion that brings madness and incomprehension to those who are not ready, and having partaken of this you pass the point of no return.'*

(The Initiate drinks and is disorientated.)

PK5: *'I am the keeper of the fifth portal and I challenge you. Are you prepared to be changed? For this journey will change you and your perceptions, and you will never again, be the same as you are now.'*

Initiate: *'(Answers in own words.)'*

PK5: *'Then cast off your outer garments for you must leave all that you are behind you.'*

(The Initiate removes outer garments and is disorientated.)

PK6: '*I am the keeper of the sixth portal and I challenge you. I believe that you are selfish and unworthy, and fear to look upon Death. What say you to Death?*'

Initiate: '**(Answers in own words.)**'

PK6: '*None may come before Death unless they are naked and bowed, remove all that remains to you.*'

(The Initiate removes remaining garments and is again disoriented. The Initiate remains temporarily skyclad, even if you do intend to use an Initiation Robe.)

Death: '*I am the keeper of the seventh and final portal and I challenge you* (puts Athame to Initiate's breast). *Do you have the passwords, for if not then this blade shall end you here and for all time?*'

Initiate: '**(Answers in own words.)**'

Death: '*Kneel before me for I am Death, the keeper of the dark realms. I hold the secrets that you seek, if you have the wisdom, the courage, the strength and compassion to pass the tests of the underworld. Do you have these qualities?*'

Initiate: '**(Kneels and answers in own words.)**'

Death: '*I recognize you as a Witch of the First Degree and bid thee welcome to my realm. Are you willing to accept the Death of the body, of the mind and of the spirit?*'

Initiate: '**(Answers in own words.)**'

(Death now hands the Initiation Robe to the Initiate, who puts it on. Where the Initiator has also been present to observe the Initiate's responses, they will return to the Circle at this point.)

Death: '*I anoint thee with an unguent that will give your spirit flight to face the dangers and to accept the knowledge of the spirit realms.*'

(Anoints the Initiate on the wrists, ankles and temples with the unguent.)

Death: '*I bind thy body for the sacrificial altar, where your lifeblood may be spilled to attain the blessings of the Old Ones.*' **The Initiate is bound with the 9-foot cord in the same way as for the First Degree, but the two shorter cords are not used.** '*I shall lead you to the temple of the Crone where your faith will be tested and where you will be judged to be suitable, or not.*'

(Death leads the Initiate to the Circle, which has been prepared and where everyone is waiting. The Initiator waits on the edge of the Circle for Death and the Initiate to arrive.)

Initiator: '*Identify yourself so that all present may know you.*'

Death: '*I am … (Witch name), Witch of the Third Degree, and stand here as Death. I have one here who seeks to journey in the realms of the underworld.*'

Initiator: '*By what right do they seek entry?*'

Death: '*By right of the First Degree and the courage to make the assay.*'

Initiator: '*Are they properly prepared?*'

Death: '*By my word, honour and all that I hold true.*'

Initiator: '*Then both be welcome.*'

(The Initiator opens a gateway in the Circle and then kisses Death as he/she enters. Death then leads the Initiate into the Circle. The Initiator closes the gateway. Death disorients the Initiate and makes him/her kneel facing one of the Quarters.)

High Priestess: *'Behold here you find the Dark Mother, the Lady of the darkest night, Keeper of all that men shun and cower from in the light. Death is my servant and if you wish to seek me you must first suffer the pain of death, the fear of death, and cross the abyss. If you have the substance to pass the tests of the elements, then you may enter my realm and seek my wisdom. Are you prepared?'*

Initiate: '**(Answers in own words.)**'

Initiator: *'A sigil is marked upon you. Greet the element it signifies with its proper name and ask its blessing upon you.'* **(Inscribes invoking Pentagram of the appropriate element upon the Initiate's back.)**

Initiate: '**(Answers in own words.)**'

(The Initiate is made to rise, led around the Circle and made to kneel before a different Quarter. The question is repeated and the Initiate should answer. This process continues until the Initiate has visited and identified each Quarter in turn. The High Priestess may also wish to add, or substitute, other tests in the same way as was done for the First Degree.)

Initiator: *'You have borne the tests of the elements, but now you must face the final and greatest test, the test of the spirit. Do you believe you are worthy?'*

Initiate: '**(Answers in own words.)**'

(The Initiate is untied and lain across the Circle with their head to the North. The blindfold is left on.)

The High Priestess reads the Second Degree Pathworking, which takes the form of one of the stories of the Descent of the Goddess.

After the Pathworking, the Initiate is made to kneel in the centre of the Circle and receives each, or a smaller selection, of the working tools. They must identify and describe the use of each.

The Initiator raises the Initiate to their feet and says,

'Before you seek that which you attain, you must answer one last question: If granted the Second Degree what will you do with it?'

Once again, the Initiate answers in his or her own words. Assuming each test is passed, the Initiate is then sworn to the oath of the Second Degree, and is anointed with oil, wine and kisses in the sigil of the Second. Now the blindfold is removed and the Initiate is greeted by the High Priestess and everyone else in the group.

The Rite of Wine and Cakes* is then conducted by the High Priestess and High Priest with the Initiate being the first to receive the Chalice as in the First Degree Initiation. The Sacred Space is now removed* and a celebratory feast* is held.

 ## THE THIRD DEGREE

The Third Degree Initiation is given when the High Priestess considers that the Initiate is ready to take on the responsibility of running a Coven. It is not, however, to be inferred or assumed that this means that they know everything! None of us in the Craft ever stop learning; in fact the more you learn, the more you become aware of what there is still to learn. I am not giving the full text for this Ritual, as it should not be read by anyone who is not already a Third Degree Witch. There are some published Third Degree Rituals, a few in whole, more in part, but if you want to maintain the secrecy of this Ritual you will need to alter those anyway.

You will need:

ANOINTING OIL

This Ritual often takes place during the Waning Moon to honour the Goddess in her aspect of Wise One. This reflects the third aspect of the Goddess as well as the third stage of Initiation.

The main steps in the Third Degree Initiation are the Great Rite,* the Anointing of the Initiate, the Willing of Power, the giving of the Secret Names of the Goddess and the God, and the Rite of Wine and Cakes.* Unlike the First and Second Degree Initiations there is no reason for the Initiate to wait in order to avoid meeting the other Covenors who will be attending, as these can only be of the Third Degree anyway. Not only can the Initiate be present when the Circle is created, but also they can take an active part in this.

After creating the Sacred Space* and raising energy,* everyone other than the Initiate and Initiator leaves the Circle and does not return until they are called after the Anointing.

After the Great Rite,* the Initiate is anointed in the symbol of the Third Degree with water, wine and kisses. After this the rest of the celebrants are invited to return.

For the Willing of Power, the Initiate kneels and the Initiator places one hand on the Initiate's head, the other under their right knee. The Initiator focuses all their energy, and calling upon the power of the Divine which was invoked into them, then focuses and directs that power into the Initiate. With that energy also comes knowledge and instinct for the Craft.

The Initiator then whispers the secret name of the Goddess and that of the God into the ear of the Initiate.

Initiator and Initiate then perform the Rite of Wine and Cakes,* with the Initiator's partner being the one who receives the Chalice first. The Sacred Space is removed as usual, and celebrations can commence.

THE RITUAL OF SELF-INITIATION

In advance of your Ritual you should meditate on your reasons for taking this step as it should represent as deep a commitment to the Goddess and the God and to the Craft as any Initiation taken within a Coven. I recommend that for the three nights preceding the Ritual you perform a Self-Blessing* and then spend around 10 minutes in contemplation of the step you are taking. Also, take time to phrase the wording of the promise you intend to make to the Goddess and the God. I have included a suggestion below, but you may wish to rephrase this. You might like to write this out clearly so that you are not struggling to remember it at the time.

Take time to consider whether you will choose to take a Witch name, and what that might be. In addition, you might like to select special clothing and/or jewellery which you will consecrate in Circle, and reserve for your Craft workings. All your Altar equipment and your Athame should be consecrated in advance.

You will need:

ANY SPECIAL CLOTHING

ANY SPECIAL JEWELLERY

This Ritual should be performed at the Full Moon.

After creating your Sacred Space,* perform the Rite of Banishing Unwanted Influences.* Next perform a Self-Blessing,* during which you should focus on the strength and energy of the Mother Goddess being directed into and around you. This should be sufficient for you to feel empowered, but you can also chant a little if you feel this adds to the energy of your Circle.

Kneel in front of the Altar, facing North. Raise your arms up to each side of you and visualize the Goddess and the God, standing before you. When you feel ready say,

'I ... (your usual name), call upon the Goddess and the God, upon the Elements of Earth, Air, Fire, Water and Spirit, and upon all the Witches of past, present and future to witness that I choose the path of the Witch. I dedicate myself and all my works to the service of the Goddess and the God. I promise that I will not use the Craft, nor the knowledge I gain, to impress the foolish or to frighten the childish. I promise to uphold the Craft, and the Wiccan Rede to the best of my ability, and to keep silent about the secrets I may learn and the knowledge I gain. I undertake that I take this promise of my own free will and accord and that I will hold myself to it, come what may. As is my will, so mote it be. Blessed Be.'

If you choose to take a Witch Name, continue,

'In token of my promise I take unto myself a new name, that of ... (Witch name). May I grow in its likeness and may it aid me in my service of the Goddess and the God. May the Old Ones know me by this name and help me always to be faithful to it. Blessed Be.'

If you wish to consecrate* any clothing or jewellery, stand up again and do so in the usual way. Hold it up before the Goddess and the God, saying,

'I dedicate this ... (name the item/s) to the service of the Goddess and the God, that it may serve to remind me of this my sacred promise. Blessed Be.'

Immediately put the item(s) on.

Now perform the Rite of Wine.* After you have taken a sip replace the Chalice on the Altar. Kneel again and dip the forefinger of your strong hand into the wine and anoint yourself on the forehead in the shape of a pentacle, saying,

'With this wine, consecrated and blessed by the Goddess and the God, I anoint myself in earnest of the promise I have made this day. May the Old Ones watch over me, guard me, guide me and protect me in my chosen path. May they bring enlightenment and understanding, knowledge and control. Blessed Be.'

Remain and meditate for a few moments before removing the Sacred Space.*

If you have performed this Rite in Circle with other Witches then they should also share in the Rite of Wine and follow it with the Cakes.* If you are on your own then make a point of having something to eat and drink to ground yourself fully.

Rituals of Initiation do not usually take place all that often, so you might like to consider doing as we do in my Coven. Prepare a special book, which contains the full 'script' of each of the Rituals, in a font and format which will make reading by candle-light easy. Prior to the Ritual, have a rehearsal with all the active participants (except the Initiate, unless this is a Self-Initiation) where you 'walk through' all the actions. This helps to ensure that you have everything you need to hand and that you are familiar with the Ritual. Either have the book of the script placed on the Altar in such a way that it can be read, or appoint a 'book holder' who carries it, together with a candle, throughout the Ritual in case it is needed.

TEN

WRITING RITUALS AND CREATING SPELLS

However comprehensive a book on Witchcraft, Magic and Spells is, it can never contain every spell you may need, or every Ritual you may wish to work. The nature of spells and magic changes with time; I doubt my ancient predecessors gave a lot of thought to protecting motorcycles! Rituals also alter to reflect the changing needs of our times, and so that you can ensure everyone takes an active and meaningful role. This is as it should be – for the Craft to be meaningful, it needs to develop and grow to meet the needs of the Witches of today and, in time, those of tomorrow. One of the sayings I frequently repeat is, 'Witches should be a part of the world, not apart from it.' In order to make the spells and Rituals in this and any other book meaningful to you and appropriate to your needs, you will need to learn how to change Rituals without losing their meaning and how to write effective spells and magics.

In an established Coven this learning takes place in a fairly straightforward way: As an Aspirant and First Degree you spend at the very least two years taking part in Rituals and seeing magic performed. This period means you will have participated in one or more full turn of the Wheel of the Year. Occasionally, you might see how your High Priestess adapts spells and Rituals to answer a specific need, perhaps one you yourself approached her with. You might even be involved in making these adaptations. After your Second Degree you will almost certainly be asked to write some Rituals for the group, and to devise some spells. Your High Priestess or another experienced Witch will guide you in this, to help you avoid some of the more common pitfalls. After you have taken your Third Degree you will still have access to this guidance, even though by then you may feel less in need of it. However, for those of you in newer groups, or who are starting out on your own, the prospect of creating your own magic can be quite daunting. Here then are some guidelines on writing Rituals and creating Spells.

WRITING AND ADAPTING RITUALS

As we saw in Chapter 2, a Ritual is made up of a series of Rites focused around the magical working or celebration, which is the purpose of that Ritual. There are two main categories of Ritual: those which contain a magical working or spell, and those which are celebratory. In the former you need to cast a Circle and raise power, in the latter you do not. Initiations are an exception as they are both a magical working and a celebration.

There are several key steps in writing and constructing meaningful Rituals, which can be thought of as the questions you ask yourself. They are the same questions I would be asking were you to come to me for help!

PURPOSE AND NATURE?

Without a purpose there is no point in holding a Ritual. You need to define what exactly you intend to celebrate or achieve.

CELEBRATION OR WORKING?

In most cases it will be easy to decide whether this is a celebration or a working, but it is as well to give some thought to this as occasionally the lines can become blurred. For example, you might wish to give thanks for the safe delivery of Anne's child and yet seek the help of the Goddess and the God as Anne is still poorly. These two steps can be combined in a working Ritual, but resist the temptation to also try to present the child to the elements, the Goddess and the God, as that falls into the category of Wiccaning and is a celebration. Of course, you could work a spell for Anne's recovery in a working Ritual and then take a token of that spell to the Wiccaning to give to Anne at the end of the celebratory Ritual.

WHO AND HOW MANY?

It is far easier to write a Ritual when you know exactly who will be there, and their level of experience and understanding. In the absence of this level of information you need a rough idea of numbers and at least some idea as to whether all, or any, have been in Circle before. As I have said before, everyone should have some kind of role in a Ritual and it should be meaningful for everyone, but there are obvious differences in the kinds of roles you can entrust to an experienced Third Degree and an Aspirant attending their first Ritual. As a rule of thumb I entrust active roles to those with experience and get the least experienced to stay with chanting, dancing and reinforcing roles until they grow in confidence and the Craft.

An idea of numbers is also helpful when deciding whether everyone is going to reinforce a spell. For example, you may intend to anoint six magical candles. If there are 20 people in Circle and each candle has to pass through everyone's hands before the next is started, you are going to be there a long time! But knowing there are a lot of people you can write your Ritual so that several candles are circulating at once.

Another point to consider here is whether the people can actually do what you plan? Energetic Circle dancing is out unless you have enough fit people to do it. A person can be well enough to stand in Circle with a broken arm, but will not want to leap around the room!

WHERE?

If indoors, do you have, or can you make, enough room? Will your Ritual be so noisy that it disturbs the neighbours?

If outside, can everyone get there? Some of us older Witches do not easily climb steep hills and rock faces, and still have enough energy to perform magic afterwards! Not only that, but can you get everything you need to your site? Is it physically safe? Check your site for broken bottles, rusty metal, rabbit holes, etc. Is it both legal and private? Ritual is rarely a spectator sport. Nor do you want to attract the attention of the police! What will you do if there's really bad weather?

WHEN?

Some Rituals are best performed at certain phases of the Moon, or on particular days of the week, and so on, but it is still a good idea to look at other factors. Is everyone you need going to be available? Will your location be free? Have you chosen a sensible hour, or will the place be overrun with small children? And so on.

ARE THE ROLES FAIR?

I repeat, everyone should have a meaningful role, the Craft is a participatory belief system, and there should be no spectators. Whilst you cannot please all of the people all of the time, I have seen a surprising number of Rituals which seem designed to give one person (usually the writer) the starring role, whilst everyone else is not far from being cast as 'the admiring audience'! If you find yourself designing a Ritual like this, give some thought to whether you are writing for a purpose or because you enjoy being centre stage.

WHICH RITES?

Some steps in a Ritual cannot be ignored: preparation, those creating and removing the Sacred Space, and so on. Other steps should be selected because you need them, not because you 'like the idea'. Ask yourself, do you need to Banish Unwanted Influences, perhaps because you are working a spell for defence, or because everyone is upset about something. Do you need to raise energy? And would dancing and chanting work better than Drawing Down the Moon, because it more fully involves everyone?

ARE YOU HAPPY WITH YOUR RITES?

The basic steps in casting a Circle are not fixed in stone. Yes, you do need to prepare the space, set the Altar, Bless the elements, invoke the quarters, invite the Goddess and the God, and so on, but you do not need to stick rigidly with the wording you have been using or with the actions you normally perform. Now, I would not suggest that you change the wording of, for example, invoking the elements, at each and every Ritual, as this is just going to confuse everyone. But you might like to consider adapting it slightly, especially for a celebration. For example, when invoking the elements for a Handfasting you might like to change the usual invocation to, '*I do summon, stir and call ye O element of Air. Raphael, guardian of the gateway of the East, attend with us for this Ritual for the Handfasting of Jane and John, guard us, guide us and protect us in these our Rites. Hail and welcome. Blessed Be.*' And you might like to change the banishing to, '*I do banish thee O element of Air. Raphael, guardian of the gateway of the East, we give thanks for your presence at the Handfasting of Jane and John. Continue to guard, guide and protect them in all they do. Hail and Farewell. Blessed Be.*' Obviously, if you do this with one element you will need to do likewise with all the others, and perhaps adjust the invitation of the Goddess and the God too. Similarly, you might like to expand the actions of invoking so that when Air is called the person walks Deosil to the Altar, collects the incense, walks it around the circle and finally places it in the East quarter, and likewise with all the elements.

HOW LONG IS IT?

Whilst there is no ideal length for a Ritual, it is important that it is neither too long nor too short. Over-long Rituals are energy draining and, if not totally fascinating, result in people losing focus. Too short and your Ritual may feel rushed and incomplete. I cannot give you definitive timings but would suggest that anything under 30 minutes or over 90 minutes is worth looking at. Where a Ritual is over long, consider reducing the number of Rites, or their individual length, etc. If a Ritual seems too short ask yourself if you have missed or shortened any steps, or whether you need to spend more time raising energy, or in establishing focus.

CAN YOU DO IT WITHOUT PAPER?

Lots of people in Circle trying to read from pieces of paper, rustling them, dropping them, trying to read by flickering candlelight and losing their place, is the bane of any High Priestess's life. It is one thing to have a 'book of the script' available to one or two people at an Initiation, or a list of the steps handy on the Altar; it is quite another to have a dozen individuals all clutching sheets of words. If a Ritual is that complex then perhaps you need to rethink it, or at the least provide copies in advance so people can prepare. Ask yourself if you are trying to put too much in, or if you are trying too many new things at one time.

DOES IT FLOW?

You should be able to recall the steps in a Ritual because they make sense to you. For example, Banishing Unwanted Influences logically would come before, not after, Self-Blessing, if you feel the need for both. Try to avoid sudden changes in direction; these usually happen when you are trying to put quite different spells or Rites together in one Ritual.

EQUIPMENT?

Do you have, or can you get, all the tools, equipment and aids you need. It's little good to decide fresh sunflowers are a 'must' in the depths of Winter. You can usually overcome these problems by checking in advance and substituting alternatives.

If you have asked others to bring essentials, remember to check with them a day or so before. It's surprising how many forget or don't bother to tell you they couldn't find the right things.

HAVE YOU THOUGHT IT THROUGH?

As you can see from the above questions, planning a Ritual is not just about writing a list of actions, there are many other things which need to be considered. One of the best ways of checking your Ritual is to 'walk it through'. Visualize each of the steps taking place, what everyone is doing, where they are standing, the tools and equipment they will need.

When I used to do a lot of business presentations I was advised that you should take three times as long in preparation as you do in presentation, and I find this is a good rule of thumb when preparing Rituals.

DOES EVERYONE UNDERSTAND?

Part of the preparation for Ritual lies in communicating the Ritual to everyone who will be there. For complex Rituals you might like to contact people to give them advance information. But whether you do that or not, you do need to take time before the Ritual to ensure that everyone really understands, not that they are just too stunned by it all to ask!

As you can see from the above questions, writing Rituals is not just about producing a list of actions, there are many other things which need to be taken into account, not least the practical ones. But the key to writing working Rituals lies in choosing or devising the spell(s) or magic(s).

DEVISING SPELLS

Devising spells is really not that difficult. The most important thing to remember is that it is your focus and intent which make the magic work. All the tools, equipment, aids and correspondences help you to achieve it, they don't do it for you.

Once again there are some fairly simple steps which you need to go through and, once again, I have covered them in the form of the questions I would ask you.

WHAT IS THE PROBLEM?

You absolutely have to establish the nature of the problem. It is no use working magic for 'Jack' if you don't establish what it is you want to do for him.

WHAT IS THE UNDERLYING CAUSE?

Having defined the nature of the problem, look to see if there is an underlying cause. Say Jack is experiencing conflict at home, there are arguments all the time and he feels unhappy there. If you simply work to 'resolve home conflict' it might result in his wife leaving him, making him more unhappy. Perhaps the conflict is caused by lack of money, which is in turn caused by his compulsive gambling. In this case you might like to work towards encouraging Jack to give up his addiction.

HOW MUCH OF THE PROBLEM IS YOU?

Personal honesty is very important in the Craft and especially in any kind of magical working. Say you have fallen out with a friend – instead of jumping straight in to work to make them more tolerant and understanding, give serious thought to how much you may have contributed to the problem. Are you being stubborn, or accusative? Perhaps you should be working towards making both of you more tolerant?

WHAT OUTCOME DO YOU SEEK?

In some cases this appears obvious; for Jack you seek to break his addiction to gambling. However, at other times it can be less so. For instance, were you to consider working to give Jill confidence for an interview, you would want to focus on her getting the right job, not just this job.

Also give some thought to whether the outcome you seek will go against the Wiccan Rede, in word or in spirit! Working magic to make someone love you will interfere with their freedom of will, is definitely against the Rede and, as a result, is quite likely to misfire in some way.

ARE YOU TRYING TO ACHIEVE TOO MUCH?

Some problems need to be broken down into steps and each step addressed separately. For example, to try to achieve a pregnancy, ensure a safe pregnancy, ensure safe delivery and the protection of the infant, all in one spell is too much. It's far better to work several really powerful spells, than to create one huge one which tries to cover everything.

WHEN SHOULD IT BE WORKED?

Ask yourself, is this really an urgent problem or can it wait until the appropriate phase of the Moon? Few magics apart from healing are really urgent, and indeed many will benefit from the extra thought you put into them if you plan and think ahead. If the problem needs addressing immediately and the Moon is in a less propitious phase, then can you redirect your focus to achieve the same results? In healing you could work to banish an illness at the Waning Moon, rather than waiting for the Full to work to speed the healing processes.

WHO IS IT FOR?

When you are working magic for other people you need to be sure that you can identify who the magic is for, and direct it appropriately, so you need to make sure that you have enough information to do this properly. When working magic for those who come to you, you need to consider if a tangible object will give them more confidence in the spell. Of course, when working for someone who is not of the Craft you also need to give thought as to what item(s) you could give which would be acceptable. It's no use empowering a Pentagram to give to your maiden aunt if she considers it to symbolize the devil; it'll just end up in the bin! Perhaps a pot plant would be more acceptable.

WHICH MAGICAL AIDS WILL YOU USE?

Magic can be worked using candles, cords, stones, mirrors, etc., as seen in Chapter 6. To choose between them, focus on what you are trying to achieve and consider which is most appropriate. Mirrors are good for reflecting things; cords are good for things which have several steps and so on.

Also consider which is best for your personal and working circumstances. I like to scry into a real fire, but I wouldn't try it in a house with no fireplace! If you want to work magic to help heal a housemate with strong anti-Witch views, then leaving a fith-fath with their photo on it lying around, will be counterproductive. If six of you are going to imbue something with energy at the same time, you're going to need something larger than a bead to work on.

Do you need any aids to maintain focus? A picture of your subject perhaps?

ADVANCE PREPARATION?

No point in deciding now, to perform a spell tonight which requires water left in moonlight for three nights, unless you have already prepared the water.

Also, do you really have everything you need? Many's the time when I've been certain I have something in the cupboard, only to find that actually I haven't. Don't just believe it's there, go and check!

WHAT PREPARATION NEEDS TO BE DONE IN CIRCLE?

In theory you only need clay to make a fith-fath. In practice you will also need: something to put it on, or it might just stick to your Altar cloth; something with which to inscribe it with any sigils you have chosen; and a damp cloth to wipe off the excess clay from your hands before it gets onto all your working tools.

Also give some thought to how long your in-Circle preparation will take. If you're working with others you don't want to keep them hanging around for two hours because that's how long it takes you to draw the sigil of your choice. Even on your own your time in Circle preparation does not need to be too lengthy as you may lose focus.

HOW ARE YOU GOING TO WORK THE SPELL?

It is important to ensure that everyone in Circle agrees with the magic. Just one person who is unsure can dilute or negate the spell. Even when working on your own, if you have even the slightest doubt about the wisdom of doing the magic, or that it will work, you will effect the outcome. If in doubt, don't do it!

Also, give some thought to the practical moves which need to be made. Who will need to do what and when?

HOW WILL YOU PAY FOR THE MAGIC?

Life, and the world, work on the exchange of energies; you have to burn the wax to get light from a candle, you have to water a plant to make it grow, you have to be pleasant to someone before they will like you. In magic, some of the energy comes from within, but some also comes from outside, and this should be repaid. After a Ritual some people like to place a little of the wine and cakes on the land as an offering, but I feel that something more practical is probably more effective. It could be tending plants, clearing litter or maybe helping a neighbour. You might like to devise a Ritual of thanks, write a poem, or paint a picture to honour the Goddess. Whatever your skill, try to utilize it to benefit the land, honour the Divine, or just to put some of your energy into saying 'thank you'. For every act of magic, successful or not, you should put something back; you are not making a deal with the Goddess and the God!

Whether you are writing a Ritual or devising a spell, don't be afraid to use things already in existence. Take ideas from others or from books and adjust them to suit your needs. You won't get any extra 'points' for re-inventing the wheel!

Finally, whenever you feel stuck for ideas, or confused from too many options, ask the Goddess and the God for guidance. They are, after all, the Mother and Father of us all, and what they don't know about magic, you will not find elsewhere.

WHAT WITCHCRAFT REALLY IS

Witchcraft may be one of the faster growing spiritual belief systems in the world today, but there are still a lot of misconceptions and prejudices surrounding it. Some have been generated by modern films, books and TV programmes; these portray the Craft as anything from glamorous and fun, to a satanic devil worship of the worst kind. Other prejudices, and even fears, have a deeper origin in the propaganda of the Church of Rome which sought to superimpose its faith, along with taxation and political control, on the beliefs of rest of the world. As a result, the perception of many people is confused, to say the least.

The following is a brief introduction to Witchcraft, as it really is, and as it is practised by millions of people in the world today.

Witchcraft is one of a number of belief systems whose roots pre-date Christianity and which come under the 'umbrella' heading of Pagan. Indeed, Witchcraft has roots which go back to Palaeolithic times, as illustrated by the cave paintings of our ancient ancestors. Having said that, the Craft is a living religion and has as much relevance to us today as it had to its practitioners in the past. We still seek healing of our bodies and minds, strength to deal with our daily lives, understanding and compassion to help us relate to those around us, and to develop ourselves.

So what do Witches believe in and how do they express these beliefs? First, you have to understand that, unlike the more 'orthodox' religions, the Craft has no paid or formal priesthood; in the Craft we are each our own Priest or Priestess and therefore make our own decisions as to the expression of our beliefs. As a result there is no 'one true way' to being a Witch. This gives rise to a great diversity in our daily practices, and indeed enables the Craft to grow and adapt to the real world in a way that other paths find difficult because of their interpreted doctrine. Having said that, there are many beliefs and practices that most Witches hold in common:

WE BELIEVE THAT THE DIVINE IS BOTH MALE AND FEMALE

We believe that the Divine is male and female in perfect balance, and that we should seek that balance in ourselves and in our lives. Put simply, this means that we believe in the Goddess and the God, and they may be referred to by many names, according to the needs of the individual or indeed their personal preference. It helps to think of the Divine as being like a mirror ball, with each facet having a different identity, although all being part of the Divine. As a result you may find that the Goddess is referred to as, for example, Isis, Astarte or Hecate, and the God referred to as, perhaps, Osiris, Herne or Pan. Some Witches will simply refer to the Lord and Lady or the Goddess and the God, others will call them the Old Ones or the Old Gods, or even just the Gods.

The Goddess is seen as having three aspects: Maiden, Mother and Crone (or Wise One). These aspects are reflected in the cycle of the Moon, and in our daily lives, for everything has its beginning, middle and closing phases. The God also has different aspects, but these are more clearly defined through the festivals of the seasons and the Wheel of the Year.

WE ARE EACH OUR OWN PRIEST OR PRIESTESS

As mentioned above we have no formal Priesthood in the Craft, although those Witches working in a group or Coven setting will have a High Priestess and High Priest who are the leaders of that group. This does not make them better Witches; it simply denotes their standing and authority within that group. Having no formal priesthood means we do not rely on others to interpret or intercede with our Gods for us, we are each entitled to make our own connection with the Divine, in our own way. This might be through ritual, meditation and/or magic, and most Witches will use a combination of different techniques at different times.

WE HAVE NO 'BOOK OF INSTRUCTION'

There is nothing written in Witchcraft in the way that Christians have the Bible or Muslims the Koran. There are a great number of books on the Craft and it is up to those who wish to read some of these and make personal decisions as to their relevance. Each individual can choose the complexity of their Rituals, and the form that their path will take. For some this may mean working in a group or Coven, while others may prefer a Solitary path. Some will seek to work formalized magic whilst others prefer the Hedgewitch approach, working closely with nature and using herbs to achieve their magics.

EVERYONE IS ENTITLED TO THEIR OWN, INFORMED CHOICE OF SPIRITUAL PATH, SO LONG AS THEY HARM NO ONE ELSE

Witchcraft is a non-proselytizing belief system; we do not feel the need for everyone to believe as we do in order to feel secure in our faith. There is plenty of room in this world for everyone to find their own way of relating to the Divine. In fact, all religions have as much, if not more, in common than in difference. Hence there is no reason why we should not encourage and celebrate a diversity of beliefs. As Witches we encourage our young to examine many paths and to make their own decisions, based on their own needs. We do not seek to convert others to our beliefs, but neither do we wish to be indoctrinated in turn.

WE BELIEVE THAT WE SHOULD RESPECT NATURE

This means not taking more than we need and indeed trying to recompense for that which we have taken. This involves trying to live not only in the modern world, but also in balance with the planet. Witches tend to shop second-hand, make at least some of the things they use and to recycle where they can. This does not mean that we are all 'green warriors' campaigning against the building of roads or houses. It does mean that we try to tread lightly on the world.

WITCHES UTILIZE THE ELEMENTS IN THEIR WORKINGS

It is not just that we respect nature, we also see ourselves reflected by the elements of Air, Fire, Water, Earth and Spirit. Whilst these elements are all around us in nature they are also within us; Air is our thoughts, Fire is our passions and enthusiasm, Water is our emotions, Earth is our bodies and Spirit is our selves. These are the energies we harness in working magic and in order for this to work effectively we must be able to achieve balance between them. These elements also have reflections in daily life. For every project to work it must have its phases of thought, enthusiasm, emotional involvement and formation, and must also be imbued with its own spirit. These elements are represented by the five-pointed star, or Pentagram, which when placed in a circle becomes the Pentacle worn by many Witches as a symbol of their beliefs.

WE BELIEVE IN AND PRACTISE MAGIC

Magic has been defined as the ability to create change by force of will and in some respects is not dissimilar to a belief in the power of prayer. However, in magic it is our personal intervention which creates the change around us. Magic is not like cookery, just a matter of following a recipe and getting a result. True magic requires a deep understanding of ourselves and the energies that are around us, and the ability to control and focus our own energies. One of the greatest keys to this is the ability to visualize. It also requires a study and understanding of the elements of Earth, Air, Fire and Water, not just in the world, but also within us. The magic we practise is not that of stage conjuring or of the special effects that you see so often in modern films. It is practised to heal, protect and enhance our lives. It is worked for ourselves, our near and dear, and for those who come to us with requests for help. Magic should always be practised with the Wiccan Rede in mind and also with regard to the law of three-fold return which states that whatever you do, good or ill, will be returned to you three times over. This latter is not confined to magical working, but should be borne in mind at all times. There are other concerns which should be taken into account before starting any magical working, and these are detailed in *The Real Witches' Handbook*. However, if you are careful to harm no one and not to interfere with anyone's freedom of will, then you have the basic guidelines for good magical practice.

WITCHES CELEBRATE THE WHEEL OF THE YEAR

The Witches' calendar contains eight key festivals, called Sabbats. At these we mark the changes of the seasons and the stories of the Goddess and the God. Whenever possible Witches will gather together to celebrate these festivals. We dance, sing and honour the Goddess and the God by re-enactment of their stories. Solitary Witches also mark the Sabbats, and ways of doing this can also be found in *The Real Witches' Handbook*. At the end of these rituals we celebrate by feasting with food and wines. Many of the Sabbats have a familiar feel to non-Witches as they have been taken over by newer belief systems and incorporated into their calendars. The Sabbats are the festivals of Samhain, Yule, Imbolg, Oestara, Beltane, Litha, Lughnasadh and Madron and details can be found in Chapter 7 Sabbat Rituals. Taken together they form the Wheel of the Year.

WE TAKE PERSONAL RESPONSIBILITY FOR OUR LIVES

The main 'rule' in the Craft is called the Wiccan Rede; 'An it harm none, do what thou will.' This in itself includes not only our respect for others and the world around us, but also respect for ourselves. We do not believe that we can blame external forces or other people for our thoughts, words and deeds, and that if we do wrong it is up to us to do our best to rectify it.

WE SEEK PERSONAL DEVELOPMENT

There is much to learn in the world and in the Craft, but we do not expect others to feed us this information. We actively seek to expand our knowledge and extend our skills by personal effort. All Witches are aware that they will never know enough, let alone all. This personal development also includes expanding our personal skills and attributes, 'ironing out' our personal misconceptions and problems, and each working to become the best self we possibly can. Witchcraft has been called, and rightly so in my opinion, 'a thinking person's belief system', as it involves a course of personal exploration and general study which never ceases.

THE SUMMERLANDS AND REINCARNATION

Witches believe that we live many lives and between them we return to the Summerlands, a resting place where we review the lessons we have learned in the life we have just completed, and select the lessons to be learned in the life to come. When we speak of reincarnation we do not mean that we come back as the same person but rather that our spirit is born again. Whilst it can be interesting to research previous incarnations, and the information we acquire may illuminate aspects of our current lives, it is necessary to remember that the personal responsibility we also believe in means that we cannot blame our past(s) for our current problems. We must live in the present and work towards achievement in this life.

WITCHES PRACTISE HERBLORE

We utilize the properties of plants and nature for healing and self-improvement, and in the course of our magic. Herbs, plants and spices can be used in food and drink, lotions and ointments, sachets and talismans, incenses and candles. They can be used in their natural state (as I write this I have Rosemary on my desk to aid my thoughts and concentration), dried or in oil form, as in aromatherapy which has become so popular in recent years.

WITCHES CREATE THEIR OWN SACRED SPACE

Witches do not have special buildings in which they worship, in fact most Witches do not even have a room or even a space set aside for working. The Witch creates his or her own working space wherever and whenever it is needed, and this can be inside or out. This space is called the Circle, and it is created in several steps, briefly speaking they are:

✱ The invocation of the elements of Air, Fire, Water and Earth, which are the energies on which we draw. They are always called in this order as Air represents thought, which should precede all our actions. We bring the element of Spirit to the Circle through ourselves and through the Divine.

✱ The invitation of the Goddess and the God: the Divine, whose assistance we need to perform our working, and in whose honour we gather.

✱ The drawing of a Circle large enough to contain those taking part and the actions they are there to perform. This is usually done on the psychic level rather than on the physical, although some will place markers to visibly show the boundary. The Circle is drawn clockwise (or Deosil) from the North-East point of the area, between Earth and Air, and overlaps at that point in order to ensure that it is complete. The Circle is there to contain the energy raised, until it is ready to be released, and to protect those within its boundaries from outside energies and distractions.

These steps can be formal and relatively elaborate in group working, or very simple and performed using visualization when created by a Solitary Witch. Any action which takes place within the Sacred Space will have more effect and potency than the same action performed outside of the Sacred Space. In addition, things can be made outside of the Circle and then taken into it to be magically enhanced or empowered, and then Blessed and Consecrated for use.

WITCHES AND WITCHCRAFT

There are many different branches of today's Craft:

⭐ *Gardnerian* – This tradition was founded by Gerald Gardner, who is sometimes known as the Father of Modern Witchcraft. Gardnerian Witchcraft is strongly based around Gerald Gardner's own *Book of Shadows* and his Rituals are closely adhered to.

⭐ *Alexandrian* – This branch of the Craft was founded by Alex and Maxine Sanders. It is less rigid and more flexible than Gardnerian Craft.

⭐ *Hereditary* – This, as the name indicates, is Witchcraft which is passed down from one generation to the next through the family line.

⭐ *Traditional* – This term relates to Witchcraft which is not so much learned as remembered. Traditional Witches are those for whom the Craft comes instinctively. They often work magic and understand the precepts before discovering Witchcraft.

⭐ *Hedgewitch* – These are Witches whose Craft is almost entirely based around the land and nature. They work almost exclusively through herbs and plants.

Witches may work within these traditions on their own as Solitaries, or in groups which are often called Covens.

The term Coven is used to describe a group of Witches who meet and work together on a regular basis. Despite the common misconception, a Coven does not have to be 13 people, but is essentially any number from three upwards. A Witch on his or her own is termed a Solitary Witch. Witches may be Solitary through choice – it can be easier to get things done if you don't have to take account of others – or because they are unable to locate a suitable Coven. Two Witches working together are usually termed a Partnership, even when of the same gender. More than two and it is termed a group or Coven. As with any group, the Coven has to have a leader and this is usually the High Priestess, either supported by the High Priest or on her own. In some cases a Coven will be run by the High Priest, but this is usually because there is no Priestess of sufficient rank and experience to take the role of High Priestess.

Just as there are many different kinds of Witch there are different kinds of Coven. There are Gardnerian, Alexandrian, Hereditary and Traditional Covens, and even some which combine these and other aspects of the Craft. There are even cyber-Covens, although unless very well directed, these tend to be more of a forum where Solitaries can share ideas, seek magical assistance and generally discuss the Craft. There are some Covens which are single sex, although the majority are mixed. Some are dedicated to specific pantheons of Gods; others are more eclectic. Some will take newcomers (often called Aspirants or Neophytes), some don't. Generally speaking, most Covens will initially follow the path that was learned by their High Priestess, although their practice will almost always evolve and differ from this in time. This is one of the reasons for the diversity of practice which can be found in the Craft.

There is no 'right' type of Coven, but it is important to find, or create, the kind that is right for you.

Witches who have joined a Coven hold the same beliefs, celebrate the same festivals and work magic together. This is not to say that those in a Coven don't work on their own, but solitary work by Coven members is supported by the High Priestess and the rest of the Coven.

SEEK TO KNOW MORE?

If you would like to know more about today's Witchcraft I would recommend reading *The Real Witches' Handbook* and some of the other books mentioned in the Recommended Reading at the end of this book.

TERMS AND DEFINITIONS

Some of the words in here may have only been touched upon briefly in the text. However, they are words which are in common use in the Craft and may well crop up in other books you have read or will read. Other words are also in common usage but have a particular meaning within the Craft, and that is the meaning I have given here.

Asperger	A small bundle of twigs tied together to form a mini-brush. An Asperger is used to sprinkle water, and sometimes oil, around an area.
Aspirant	A person who has joined the Coven and has taken their Coven Oath, but has yet to take their First Degree Initiation. These are sometimes referred to as Neophytes.
Athame	The Witches' knife or blade. Traditionally a black-handled knife with a double-edged blade nine inches long, the Athame is used when invoking and banishing the elements and other energies. The only thing an Athame should cut is air, or the wedding cake at a Handfasting. Some traditions hold that iron should not be taken into the Circle and hence, if they have an Athame it will not be made with that metal.
Besom	The traditional Witches' broomstick. This symbol of fertility is literally jumped during a Handfasting to signify the leap from one 'life' to the next. The Besom is also used to symbolically sweep the circle.

Boline	The white-handled knife. This is the working knife of the Witch and is used whenever any cutting, say of herbs, or carving of symbols is required.
Book of Shadows	A personal record or journal of all your magical workings, and the thoughts, feelings and results that come from them. Gardnerian Witches refer to *The Book of Shadows*, which was written by Gerald Gardner together with some of his senior Coven members.
Candidate	A person who wishes to join the Coven, about whom the High Priestess has yet to make a decision. Some Candidates may be Initiates, where they have self-initiated, or in some cases the Initiates of other Covens.
Censer	A heat-proof container for burning incense. A censer usually has a perforated lid, to let the heat and vapours out, and chains so that it can be hung from a convenient hook, or even swung so that you can circulate the perfume.
Chalice	The Chalice is a symbol of the Goddess and can be made from wood, stone, glass or metal. It can be plain or ornate; what is important is that is contains the wine used in the Rite of Wine and Cakes, or in the Great Rite.
Circle	This defines the Sacred Space of the Witch. It is created whenever and wherever it is needed. Casting the Circle is just one part of creating the Sacred Space. A Coven would traditionally cast a Circle nine feet across; however, when working on your own it should be as small or large as your needs.
Coven	A group of three or more Witches (two would be a partnership). Coven size varies considerably, although some consider that a 'proper' Coven should be made up of six men, six women and the High Priestess. The Coven is the family group of the Witches.
Covenor	Any member of the Coven who has taken their Coven Oath, from Aspirant to High Priestess.

Covenstead	The home of the Coven, where most of the indoor meetings and Rituals will take place. The Covenstead is usually the High Priestess's house.
Craft	One of the terms for Witchcraft, which has been rightly described as both an Art and a Craft.
Daughter Coven	The term used for a Coven which has been formed by a member of the original Coven, and is hence directly descended from the Mother Coven.
Deity	A Goddess or a God. The term 'Deities' is often used generically for all Goddesses and Gods, wherever they have come from.
Deosil	Clockwise or Sunwise. When setting up and working in your Sacred Space you should always move Deosil, unless you are undoing something.
Divination	The techniques and ability to discover that which might otherwise remain hidden to us. The Tarot, Crystal Ball, Astrology, reading tea leaves, and many others are all forms of Divination. Witches tend to use the term Scrying, although strictly speaking this refers to the Dark Mirror, Cauldron, Fire or Witches' Runes.
Divine	A broader term than Deity, the Divine encompasses both the Goddess and the God and includes those aspects which do not have a gender or a name.
Elements	The term Elements is often used to refer to Earth, Air, Fire and Water. However, it is important that the fifth element, that of Spirit, which we ourselves bring to the Circle, is not forgotten. The Elements are the keystones of the Craft and also refer to aspects of ourselves as well as energies around us.
Esbat	The Witches' term for Full Moon meetings or workings.
Fith-fath	An image, usually created from wax or clay, of a person, made so as to direct magic towards that person.
Goddess and God	The female and male aspects of the Divine. However, the term 'the Gods' is often used to denote both.

Great Rite	This is the symbolic union of the Goddess and the God. Generally it is performed with the Chalice and Athame; the exceptions to this are between working partners and in some forms of initiation.
Handfasting	One of many Rites of Passage, Handfasting is the name for the Witches' wedding. It differs from most 'orthodox' kinds of wedding in that both parties enter as equals and make their own individual vows to each other. Handfastings can be of different prearranged durations.
High Priestess/High Priest	The leader of a Coven is usually the High Priestess. She may lead jointly with her High Priest, but holds ultimate authority and responsibility. Some groups are run by the High Priest alone, usually where there is no female of sufficient experience to take this role.
Hive Off	The process by which one or more Witches from the Mother Coven set up their own group, with the blessing of the High Priestess of the Mother Coven.
Initiate	An Initiate of any degree, including the High Priestess.
Initiation	Initiation literally means 'to begin'. However, in the Craft Initiation is seen as the permanent declaration an individual makes to their Gods. Many of the paths within the Craft refer to three degrees of initiation, each denoting a different level of attainment and ability.
Lore	Knowledge handed down from generation to generation. Originally oral tradition, a lot of the old lore is now finding its way into books. Much ancient lore which was thought, in our scientific age, to be superstition, is now being proven and accepted.
Magic	The ability to create change by force of will. It is worth remembering that many things we take for granted, like electricity, would have been considered magic by our ancestors.
Mother Coven	The Coven that the High Priestess came from and/or the Coven from which the new Coven descends.

Occult	Literally the word means 'hidden'. In medicine, 'occult blood' simply means blood that has been found through testing because it cannot be seen with the naked eye. Today, Occult is often used as a semi-derogatory term for anything which is not understood and is therefore feared.
Orthodox	A term I have used to identify those beliefs which people tend to think of as older than the supposedly new age beliefs, when in fact the reverse can be said to be true. For example, people tend to think that Christianity is an older belief system than the modern Pagan beliefs, when in fact the origins of Paganism (including Witchcraft) vastly pre-date it.
Pagan	This is a generic term for a number of pre-Christian religions – Druids, Witches and Heathens to name a few. 'Pagan' probably comes from the word *paganus*, referring to those who didn't live in the towns, a version of country-bumpkin if you like! Alternatively, it could come from the word *pagus*, being an administrative unit used by the occupying government. Either way, it was originally used as an insult, now it is a 'label' worn by many with pride.
Partnership	Two Witches who work together. They are frequently, but not always, a couple who are partners in daily life too.
Pathworking	A form of guided meditation in which you take a journey, which leads to an opportunity to discover more than you already know. Sometimes also referred to as 'interactive guided meditation'.
Pentacle	This is a five-pointed star with the points touching but not overlapping a circle. It symbolizes the five Elements together with the Circle of power. The Pentacle is worn by many Witches, but is also currently very fashionable, so you cannot be sure whether the wearer is of the Craft or not.

Pentagram	This is a five-pointed star not enclosed in a circle, which also symbolizes the five Elements and, like the Pentacle (above), can also be worn. However, the main uses of the Pentagram are in invoking and banishing. Whilst there are different invoking and banishing Pentagrams for each of the elements the most commonly used is the invoking Pentagram of Earth which is drawn by starting at the top point and moving deosil and continuously around the whole 5 points. As the invoking Pentagram must be complete, six lines are drawn, the last being a repeat of the first.
Priest and/or Priestess	In the Craft we are each our own Priest or Priestess, and need no one to intercede with or interpret our Gods for us.
Quarters	The four cardinal points of the compass – north, south, east and west – which are linked to the directions of the Elements.
Reincarnation	To believe in reincarnation is to believe that we return to this world many times, as many different individuals.
Rite	A small piece of Ritual which, although complete in itself, is not generally performed on its own, such as the Rite of Wine and Cakes. A series of Rites put together are a Ritual.
Rites of Passage	These rites are specific to marking the change from one stage of life to another, such as birth, marriage and death. Their names in the Craft – Wiccaning, Handfasting and Withdrawal – are different from those in current use, which reflects the different emphasis that Witches place on these events. There are other Rites of Passage but they are less common even in the Craft today.
Ritual	A series of Rites put together to achieve a specific result.

Sabbat	A seasonal festival. There are eight Sabbats in the Witches' calendar, which together are often referred to as the Wheel of the Year. Sabbats are traditionally times of great celebration and festivity. Many of the old Sabbats are still celebrated, under more modern names, for example, Yule is known as Christmas, Samhain as Halloween, and many more.
Sacred Space	For many religions their place of worship, or religious centre, is a building. Witches create their Sacred Space wherever and whenever they need it, and their magical workings, and some of their celebrations, take place within its boundaries.
Scrying	The Witches' term for Divination, especially when carried out using a Dark Mirror or the Witches' Runes.
Sigil	A symbol devised to indicate someone or something. A Sigil can contain a lot of information, for example two people's names and their Sun signs. It is better to devise your own Sigils rather than to use those made by others.
Solitary	A Witch who works on her or his own.
Soul mate	This is a term used to describe a person with whom you have continuing links which persist from one lifetime to another. It does not, as is commonly misconstrued, imply that these two people will always be lovers or romantic partners through different lifetimes. A Soul mate could just as easily be found in a parent, relative or even a really close friend.
Spells and Spellcraft	A spell is a set of actions and/or words designed to bring about a specific magical intent. Spellcraft is the ability, knowledge and wisdom to know when, as well as how, to perform such actions.
Strong Hand	For a person who is right handed this will be their right hand, for someone who is left handed it is their left. The strong hand is sometimes called the 'giving hand'.

Sun sign	The sign of the Zodiac under which a person is born. It is the Zodiacal house that the Sun was in at the time of birth and therefore their Sun sign. Other planets will be in other houses and can therefore be thought of as Moon sign, Mars sign, and so on.
Summerlands	The Witches' name for the place our spirit goes to between incarnations, where we rest and meet with those who have gone before us, and where we choose the lessons we will learn in our next life.
Thurible	Also sometimes called a Censer, this is a fireproof container designed to hold burning charcoal and loose incense. Unlike a censer, it does not have to have either a lid or chains, as it is intended to sit on the Altar.
Training Coven	A Coven which will take on newcomers, including those with no experience of the Craft, and actively encourage them to learn, grow and develop in the Craft.
Visualization	This is seeing with the mind's eye, so strongly that it appears no different from 'reality'. Visualization is not just about seeing though; when you are skilled at it, all your senses will be involved. For example, when visualizing the Element of Air you will feel the wind touch your hair and skin, hear its passage through the trees and smell the scents of Spring. Visualization is one of the key factors in working the Craft and performing magic.
Wand	A piece of wood the length of its owner's forearm. In some traditions the Wand is only used where the Athame is not; in others the Wand and Athame can be interchanged.
Wheel of the Year	This is the term used to describe the Eight Sabbats as a whole and refers to the fact that they form a complete and repeating cycle.

Wicca and Wiccan	Wicca has been largely adopted as a more 'user friendly' term for Witchcraft. Personally, I do not describe myself as a Wiccan as it simply leads to the question, 'What does that mean?' and any explanation will sooner or later end up leading to the word Witch. There are some who consider that those who call themselves Wiccans are less traditional than Witches.
Widdershins	Anticlockwise and the opposite of Deosil.

FURTHER READING AND POINTS OF CONTACT

There are a great many excellent books available today on the Craft. I have not tried to list them all here but have selected some of those which I have found useful. This might be in a general way, or because they specialize in a particular area which is too complex to be covered in an all-round text. Many of these books are intended to be used as reference, rather than to be read as literature. If a book is not listed here it does not mean it is not a valuable work, nor is it intended as a slight to the author. Equally, not every book here will suit every reader, as each has his or her own requirements in terms of content, and preferences when it comes to style. If you find yourself reading something you find tedious or 'heavy going', do not feel that you have a problem, it may simply be that you and that work are not compatible. You may find some of these books are out of print, however, it should be possible with perseverance to locate them through the library system. In any case, I would always recommend trying to get hold of a book through a library, at least in the first instance. In this way you can see if you like it before deciding to own a copy.

OTHER WORKS BY KATE WEST

Real Witchcraft: An Introduction, co-written with David Williams, 1996. A basic introduction to the Craft. Reprinted 2003 by Mandrake Press (formerly published by Pagan Media Ltd as *Born in Albion*).

Pagan Paths, Pagan Media Ltd, 1997. Six Pathworking cassettes covering the Elements, the Goddess and the God. These are available from the Children of Artemis, see below.

Pagan Rites of Passage, Mandrake Press, 1997. A series of booklets giving information and Rituals for the Rites of Passage of Handfasting, Naming and the Rites of Withdrawal.

The Real Witches' Handbook, Thorsons, HarperCollins, 2000. Real Witchcraft for real people with real lives, this book shows how to practise the Craft in a way sensitive to those around you.

The Real Witches' Kitchen, Thorsons, HarperCollins, 2002. Oils, lotions and ointments for Magic and to relieve and heal. Soaps and bathing distillations for Circle and Magical work. Magical incenses, candles and sachets to give or to keep. Food and drink to celebrate the Sabbats, for personal wellbeing and to share with friends.

A Spell in your Pocket, Element Books, HarperCollins, 2002. A handy pocket-sized gift book for the Witch on the move.

The Real Witches' Coven, Element Books, HarperCollins, 2003. A complete guide to running a Coven. Problems and solutions, and real-life examples of what can, and does, happen. For the new, or would-be, High Priestess and/or High Priest this covers all the aspects you need to know. For the experienced High Priestess/High Priest, there are new insights and stories you will relate too. For the would-be Coven member, this tells you what to expect!

Forthcoming: *The Real Witches' Garden*, Element Books, HarperCollins, 2004. Witchcraft in the environment it belongs. Whether you have a windowsill or several acres, let Kate help you to take your Craft into your bit of nature.

GENERAL BOOKS ON THE CRAFT

J W Baker, *The Alex Sanders Lectures*, Magickal Childe, 1984. A perspective on Alexandrian Witchcraft.

Rae Beth, *Hedgewitch*, Phoenix, 1990. Solitary Witchcraft, written as a series of letters to newcomers.

Janice Broch and Veronica MacLer, *Seasonal Dance*, Weiser, 1993. New ideas for the Sabbats.

Janet and Stewart Farrar, *A Witches' Bible* (formerly *The Witches' Way* and *Eight Sabbats for Witches*). Phoenix, 1996. Alexandrian Craft as it is practised.

Gerald Gardner, *The Meaning of Witchcraft*, Rider & Co, 1959; reissued by Magickal Childe, 1991. Gardnerian Witchcraft.

Pattalee Glass-Koentop, *Year of Moons, Season of Trees*, Llewellyn, 1991. Information on the Tree calendar and ideas to incorporate at the Full Moons.

Paddy Slade, *Natural Magic*, Hamlyn, n.d. A perspective on Traditional Witchcraft.

Doreen Valiente, *ABC of Witchcraft*, Hale, 1973. Gardnerian Craft written in 'dictionary' form.

Doreen Valiente, *The Charge of the Goddess*, Hexagon Hoopix, 2000. A collection of the poetry and thoughts from the 'Mother of Modern Witchcraft'. Compiled and published after her death, this work gives a unique insight into the development of the modern Craft.

BOOKS ON PARTICULAR ASPECTS OF THE CRAFT

Anne Llewellyn Barstow, *Witchcraze*, HarperCollins, 1995. Detailed history of the persecution of Witches.

Jean Shinola Bolen, *Goddesses in Everywoman*, HarperCollins, 1985. A guide to finding the Goddess within, and a wealth of tales about the aspects of the Goddess.

Scott Cunningham, *Cunningham's Encyclopaedia of Magical Herbs*, Llewellyn, 1985. Magical uses, and tales surrounding most common herbs.

Scott Cunningham, *Cunningham's Encyclopaedia of Crystal, Gem and Metal Magic*, Llewellyn, 1988. Magical properties of most gemstones available today.

Scott Cunningham, *The Complete Book of Oils, Incenses and Brews*, Llewellyn, 1989. Magical preparation and use of oils, incenses and other mixtures.

Janet and Stewart Farrar, *The Witches' Goddess*, Hale, 1987. Examination of some of the more common Goddesses.

Janet and Stewart Farrar, *The Witches' God*, Hale, 1989. Examination of some of the more common Gods.

Marian Green, *A Calendar of Festivals*, Element Books, 1991. Descriptions of festivals, not just Pagan or Wiccan, around the year with practical things to do, make and cook.

Mrs M Grieve, *A Modern Herbal*, Jonathan Cape, 1931; reissued Tiger, 1992. A detailed reference for the serious herbalist; identification, preparation and use of herbs, ancient and modern. Also available on the Internet at http://www.botanical.com/botanical/mgmh/mgmh.html.

Paul Katzeff, *Moon Madness*, Citadel, 1981. A study of the effects of the Moon and many of the legends and mythology associated with it. Not an easy read, but well worth the effort.

Kate Marks (compiler), *Circle of Song; Songs, Chants and Dances for Ritual and Celebration*, First Circle Press, 1999. As it says, songs, dances and chants from many different belief systems, many of which can be used to enhance your Rituals. Comes with a CD so you can actually hear what they should sound like!

Patricia Monaghan, *The Book of Goddesses and Heroines*, Llewellyn, 1981. A definitive guide to major and minor Goddesses from around the world.

Jeffrey B Russell, *A History of Witchcraft*, Thames & Hudson, 1983. A factual history of the Craft.

Egerton Sykes, *Who's Who Non-Classical Mythology*, Oxford University Press, 1993. A dictionary of Gods and Goddesses.

Tybol, *Tybol Astrological Almanac*. Annual Publication. Diary containing detailed astrological information, Goddess and God festivals of different pantheons and from many belief systems, Magical terms and much more.

Bill Whitcomb, *The Magician's Companion*, Llewellyn, 1993. Possibly the 'ultimate' reference work for correspondences and symbols.

OTHER PUBLICATIONS WHICH
MAY BE OF INTEREST

Children of Artemis, *Witchcraft and Wicca*, top quality bi-annual magazine written by Witches for Witches. Articles, poetry, Rituals, spells, art, crafts and events, and much more.

Clarissa Pinkola Estes, *Women who Run With the Wolves*, Rider, 1993. This is not a book on the Craft. However, it discusses the hidden meanings behind many tales and fables, and as such it opens the mind to the interpretation of stories which may have suffered through time and translation. Whilst this 'self-help' book is written for women it does have relevance for both genders.

Terry Pratchett, *Witches Abroad, Wyrd Sisters, Masquerade, Lords and Ladies, etc.* Corgi Books. I recommend these books for their powers of relaxation and the regeneration of a sense of humour after a hard day. They are pure fiction and give a humorous perspective on the world of fictitious (?) Witches!

POINTS OF CONTACT

The following organizations facilitate contact, or provide information on Witchcraft and Paganism. Please always enclose a stamped addressed envelope, and remember that some of these organizations may not allow membership to people under the age of 18. For further information on getting in touch safely with other Witches or Groups please read the advice in *The Real Witches' Handbook*.

The Children of Artemis
Initiated Witches who seek to find reputable training Covens for genuine seekers. Their magazine *Witchcraft and Wicca* is almost certainly the best on the Craft today and their website is outstanding. BM Box Artemis, London WC1N 3XX. http://www.witchcraft.org <contact@witchcraft.org>

ASLaN

Information on the care and preservation of Sacred Sites all over Britain.
http://www.symbolstone.org/archaeology/aslan. <andy.norfolk@connectfree.co.uk>

The Hearth of Hecate

The website of the author's group of Covens. Direct contact is best made by writing care of The Children of Artemis, or through the publishers.
http://www.pyewacket.demon.co.uk

The Witches' Voice

One of the best American sources of information about the Craft. PO Box 4924, Clearwater, Florida 33758-4924, USA. http://www.witchvox.com

Inform

Totally independent and not aligned to any religious organization or group. Their primary aim is to help people by providing them with accurate, objective and up-to-date information on new religious movements, alternative religions, unfamiliar belief systems and 'cults'. Houghton Street, London WC2A 2AE. 020 7955 7654

INDEX